JAPAN'S MODERN THEATRE
A CENTURY OF CHANGE AND CONTINUITY

Japan's Modern Theatre
A century of change and continuity

Brian Powell
University of Oxford

Taylor & Francis Group
LONDON AND NEW YORK

JAPAN'S MODERN THEATRE
A CENTURY OF CHANGE AND CONTINUITY

First published 2002 by
Japan Library

Japan Library Routledge Curzon
11 New Fetter Lane, London EC4P 4EE

Transferred to Digital Printing 2004

RoutledgeCurzon is an imprint of the Taylor & Francis Group

© Brian Powell 2002

All rights reserved. No part of this publication
may be reproduced, stored in a retrieval system, or
transmitted in any form or by any means,
without prior permission from the Publishers in writing,
except for the use of short extracts in criticism.

British Library Cataloguing in Publication Data
A CIP catalogue entry for this book is
available from the British Library

ISBN 1-873410-30-1

Typeset in Plantin 10½ on 11pt by Bookman, Hayes, Middlesex
Printed and bound in England by Biddles Ltd., King's Lynn, Norfolk

Contents

Preface		*ix*
Acknowledgements		*xv*
Introduction: The Setting		*xvii*
Chapter 1	*Kabuki* and the Challenges of a Changing Theatre World	1
Chapter 2	New Acting, New Production, Some New Playwriting	24
Chapter 3	Artists, Ideologues and Ideological Artists	55
Chapter 4	Diversity in Adversity	83
Chapter 5	Theatre Mobilised	114
Chapter 6	Consolidation	135
Chapter 7	One Tradition Promoted, One Challenged and One Created	162
Notes		*198*
Bibliography		*201*
Index		*207*

To my many friends in Japanese theatre
(several now, alas, deceased)
who have helped and inspired me
over the past forty years.

Preface

Some excellent work in introducing and assessing certain aspects of modern Japanese theatre has been done by the small number of Western scholars working in the field. Over the past forty years or so students of modern Japanese theatre who read English and other European languages have been well served by a number of specialist works. J. Thomas Rimer's introduction of important playwrights such as Kishida Kunio, David Goodman's work on the little theatre movement of the 1960s, and Jean-Jacques Tschudin's studies of *kabuki* since 1868 and proletarian theatre are three examples (roughly in chronological order) of how areas of this largely unknown territory have been mapped in the recent past. (Rimer 1974; Goodman 1986 and 1988; Tschudin 1989 and 1995) Donald Keene brought modern Japanese plays within the purview of students of literature by giving substantial space to drama in *Dawn to the West*. (Keene 1984) The availability of doctoral dissertations through University Microfilms has brought more knowledge to students fortunate enough to study at a university where the libraries have the will and resources to buy them. In this context one can mention Eric Gangloff's pioneering study of Kinoshita Junji, Carol Sorgenfrei on Terayama Shūji, David Goodman on Satoh Makoto, and many more. The *Asian Theatre Journal*, with its frequent articles on modern Japanese theatre and its translations of modern plays, has played a pivotal role in encouraging scholarly work in this field, and from time to time theatre journals of more general scope have included work on Japan. The main journals of Japanese studies have also occasionally included articles on this subject.

General surveys and outline histories of modern theatre are few, however, and so far have been confined to the concluding chapters of books which give most attention to the abundant classical heritage. (Kawatake and Kubota 1963, Ortolani 1990) This book accords well-deserved priority to the also abundant theatre of modern Japan. It is an attempt to pull some of the strands together and give them a brief historical context. It focuses on theatre in Japan which has encouraged new playwriting and developed new dramaturgy. Thus, the rise and progress of new genres such as *shimpa* and *shingeki* have been described, together with the classical genre *kabuki*, for which the volume of new playwriting in the twentieth century was remarkable. The relatively few plays assessed here were chosen mainly for their importance to Japanese theatre history as performed drama.

The narrative starts in 1868 at the time of the Meiji Restoration, but it by no means claims to encompass all theatrical activities in the hundred years after that. Such has been the variety of theatre during the modern period (generally defined here as from 1868 to the present day) and so huge has been the number of people involved in it and the number of plays written for it that a short book would rapidly become a list of names. One senses occasionally in secondary Japanese sources the dilemma that the writer has had to face in selecting what is significant to describe. There are often simply too many facts that must be mentioned and while the resulting lists of, for example, new plays or interesting productions are useful for the theatre historian, they would seriously interrupt the narrative of a brief book such as this.

Secondly, it has been necessary to restrict the focus of the narrative mainly to Tokyo. In the world of *kabuki* there has always been some movement between Edo/Tokyo and the Kansai region (the area in the west of Japan which includes the theatre centres of Osaka and Kyoto). Sometimes these have taken the form of the triumphant progress of an actor who has conquered one area's theatre proceeding to the other; alternatively an actor who has fallen on hard times in one place has gone to the other in the hope of reviving his fortunes. Both have happened in modern genres too. As we shall see, in 1917 an actor called Sawada Shōjirō, who was trying to establish a new form of theatre, went to Osaka when his first venture failed in Tokyo. Having achieved great popularity in Osaka Sawada returned to similar acclaim in Tokyo.

While this and a few other such cases have left their mark on the development of theatre in both Kansai and Tokyo, on the whole in the modern period Tokyo has been in the forefront of theatrical development and has enjoyed the resources and cultural ethos to sustain new forms. Books on pre-modern Japanese theatre have to pay close attention to what happened historically in Osaka and Kyoto. The new theatre or *shingeki* movement of the modern period, however, was almost entirely a product of metropolitan culture, and the theatre history of post-1868 Japan was to some extent shaped by the interaction between *shingeki* and *kabuki*. Thus for a number of reasons the focus here will inevitably be on Tokyo.

It is also inevitable that there will be many omissions in a narrative that is as compressed as the one presented here. Such omissions may also reflect the author's background in Japanese theatre, both as a spectator and a researcher, and I might here beg the indulgence of the reader as I explain what my own background is. It is practically impossible in Japan to acquire a recognised expertise over the whole range of theatre, as there is simply too much of it. It requires great dedication to become a specialist just in one of the main classical genres and only a few Japanese critics in the last half century have been able to review across genres with equal authority. While I have watched and read about all the types of theatre that I mention in this book, I have not devoted enough time to any one of them to be able to claim status as a specialist.

My earliest work was on modern left-wing drama of the 1920s. (Powell 1971) This was an extreme example of a modern genre which had arisen from a clash with classical theatre and seemed then to have acquired a momentum of its own. It was a source of some surprise to me how rapidly new types of theatre (in this case, first modern theatre – *shingeki* – and then 'proletarian drama') acquired their own conventions and committed themselves to them. I began to look at people and organisations that stood apart or at least left a definite mark on the environment within which they had begun to operate. An early actress and a maverick *kabuki* company came into that category. (Powell 1975b and 2001) Latterly, I have concentrated on two playwrights who both conformed to and reacted against the theatrical conventions within which they led their creative lives. One worked in *kabuki* and is best known for plays which presented a severe challenge to the actors. (Powell 1990) The other worked in modern theatre and found that his highest cultural expression needed the combined talents of actors from both the modern and the traditional theatres. (Kinoshita 2000)

I started my career being much biased against *kabuki*, which I regarded as unable to adjust to the rapidly changing society that I observed in Japan during regular visits from the mid-1960s onwards. The reader of this book will see that my opinion of *kabuki*, and specifically *kabuki* actors, has changed radically. In general what has impressed me about all the various forms of Japanese theatre that I have watched over the past forty years has been the manifest dedication of all the artists involved in them and I hope that this will be apparent in the narrative that follows.

Any survey of such a rich theatre history will contain a large number of names and to readers without prior knowledge of modern Japanese theatre these names will be unfamiliar. In general

I have given essential information about the holders of these names (dates of birth and death, etc) only at their first occurrence; subsequent reference back via the Index should always be possible. A few figures, however, will appear only infrequently and over a long span of time, and I have occasionally repeated the information. It is usual still in books written in English about Japan to warn the reader of how names of people are to be presented. Family names precede personal/given names in Japan and an author of a book in English about Japan may choose to preserve the Japanese order or not as he or she wishes. I have chosen to preserve the Japanese order.

In theatre history, however, things are not quite as simple as this. The multiplicity of names used to refer to a single person can be bewildering to specialist and newcomer alike. A *kabuki* actor, for example, has a name by which his birth is registered, but there is not a single one of these in this book. All *kabuki* actors, and some actors in other genres, use stage names, and these are the ones quoted here.

After the first reference to the full name just one name is frequently used. In the case of most playwrights, theatre personalities, critics and theatre scholars this will be the family name, as would be the norm in the West. Thus Osanai Kaoru will appear as Osanai. In Japan he would never be referred to as Kaoru, his given name. Some eminent writers, however, become known by the pen-name that corresponds to their given name, and I have ocasionally adopted that convention. For example, the great pioneer of modern theatre in Japan and translator of Shakespeare, Tsubouchi Shōyō, was commonly referred to as Shōyō. The situation becomes more complicated with *kabuki* actors. Such stage names as, for example Ichikawa Danjūrō VII, had three elements: a family name, a name specific to the individual holding it and specially presented to him by his seniors, and a generation number indicating how many previous holders of the name there had been. Commentators and critics in Japan are accustomed to referring only to the given name, in this case 'Danjūrō', and this convention will be followed here after the first reference. The generation number will be given where clarity requires it. Because *kabuki* actors' names also indicated their status in the profession, some names having more prestige than others, most leading actors had several names during their careers.

Readers familiar with Japanese will find an apparent inconsistency in the use of either 'n' or 'm' before 'b' or 'p' in Romanised words. This will be most noticeable where the text refers to a new genre of theatre that developed in the 1890s. This genre is ubiquitously referred to (including on the official website) as '*shimpa*', although general practice now and the British Standard for Romanised Japanese, which is followed in this book, requires '*shinpa*'. One of the theatres most associated with '*shimpa*', the Romanisation which I will observe here but only for this word, is the Shinbashi Enbujō. Shinbashi is an area of Tokyo often Romanised 'Shimbashi'. I hope any possible confusion will be lessened by the Index, where I have given both possible Romanisations.

Japan's Modern Theatre is a servant of two masters: the reader who knows Japanese and may even work on Japanese theatre, and the reader who does not know Japanese but is interested in Japanese theatre. It is clear to me from working with doctoral students that no-one doing research on a particular aspect of modern Japanese theatre will gain anything from my treatment of that same aspect here. On the other hand I have kept such readers in mind by reference to the main Japanese sources that I have used and, as the entries in the Bibliography cover a greater span of time than would usually form the subject of MA or PhD work these days, perhaps a few of these references will be useful. I have, however, been principally concerned that through this book readers with no knowledge of the Japanese language can be introduced to the main trends in modern Japanese theatre and then guided to English work on more specialist aspects of the subject. Sometimes the endnotes have been used to point the way, but on the whole I have preferred references to whole books in the Bibliography in the hope that any reader frustrated by my sketchy introduction to some seemingly important episode may pursue the matter further. This book has been written by someone who has never ceased marvelling at the sheer abundance of theatre in modern Japan and it will have succeeded if some of its readers come to share that admiration and wonder.

Acknowledgements

I would like to express my gratitude to the two readers of my manuscript, one at the beginning of an academic career and one with a distinguished academic career already behind him. Rachel Payne, a recent graduate student working on Meiji *kabuki*, read every chapter meticulously and was then able to reverse the relationship of teacher and pupil that she had laboured under for three years. Pat O'Neill, one of my earliest mentors, graciously interrupted his retirement to check carefully the manuscript that came through his letterbox somewhat unexpectedly one day. Needless to say, any mistakes that remain are mine.

I would also like to express belated apologies to my long suffering family. I should also mention my long suffering editor, Paul Norbury, who believed me when I confidently predicted that an outline history of theatre in modern Japan could be written in a short time. Even I was surprised at the riches I discovered just scratching at the surface.

Introduction: The Setting

One of the principal themes of this book is that the *kabuki* theatre, often now described as one of Japan's classical theatre genres, has by no means operated in an exclusively classical way in the modern period. At several points in modern Japanese theatre history *kabuki* has encouraged new playwriting and *kabuki* actors have transcended their genre by appearing in theatrical forms that did not exist during *kabuki*'s development into the consummate art that we know today. *Kabuki*'s presence has been pervasive throughout the modern period. The actors who pioneered new modern genres were forced to define themselves against it. At a later stage actors in the Western-based *shingeki* theatre felt they had to reject *kabuki*. Later still *kabuki* gave employment to former left-wing (and hence *a priori* anti-*kabuki*) directors and playwrights, thus implicitly recognising that there were common goals which could be shared across genre boundaries.

While *kabuki* has thus interacted extensively with genres of theatre that have appeared in the modern period, the same cannot be said of *nō* and *bunraku*, the other two main classical forms. *Nō* matured as theatre around the end of the fourteenth century. Over the previous two centuries a number of entertainment forms based on some combination of the elements of singing, dancing and mime had evolved into playlets, in which the often simple plot was expressed variously in speech and song. During the second half of the fourteenth century two actors, father and son, who benefited from powerful patronage, organised and systematised this rough and ready performance genre into the symbolic and intensely spiritual form that the West knows as '*nō* drama' or '*noh* drama' today. (O'Neill 1958; Keene 1990; Hare 1986)

The son's name was Zeami (1363-1443) and the name of the acting family that he led was Kanze. The Kanze house still exists today, as one of five active *nō* families or schools. Zeami, like his father Kan'ami (1333-1384), was a superb actor and an accomplished playwright. Early in his career he acquired the patronage of the young shogun and he utilised to the full the advantages that access to the court gave him. Never forgetting the practical side of acting, he wrote a number of treatises on all aspects of *nō* performance that range through rigorous and lengthy physical and spiritual training for the actor, play composition, audience–actor rapport, and much else. Zeami defined the ideal mood to be created by a *nō* play in performance as one of *yūgen*, or elegant depth and peace. (Rimer and Yamazaki 1984)

In the fourteenth and fifteenth centuries *nō* groups had been largely dependent on powerful shrines and temples, where they gave regular performances as part of special observances, but they came to compete more and more for the patronage of the military lords who between them ruled the country. While private performances given for these lords were deliberately paced, it is known that the many public outdoor performances were at least twice as fast in tempo. Progressively, however, as *nō* became more closely associated with Japan's military rulers, it was the private performances that dictated its overall character. Over the next century the military class began to exert a monopoly over *nō* actors and *nō* lost contact with the popular audiences that had earlier sustained it. This is symbolised most clearly in 1571 when the Kanze troupe left Kyoto to join their main patron Tokugawa Ieyasu in Hamamatsu in the east of Japan. Ieyasu was to become the first in a line of fifteen shoguns who ruled Japan from 1600 to 1868. He was formally given the title 'shogun' by the emperor in 1603 and he celebrated this appointment with special performances of *nō*. To emphasise further the identification of *nō* with the military class the government granted *nō* actors official stipends in 1619, thereby building them into the apparatus of the feudal state. (Komiya 1969: 76)

While regular patronage and regular salaries ensured *nō*'s survival in the face of the development of new popular theatre genres during the seventeenth century, its very existence was challenged fundamentally when the government system that had supported it was discredited and dismantled after 1868. At a stroke *nō* actors lost their stipends and although intermittent programmes of *nō* were organised for special occasions (for instance, entertaining foreign dignitaries), morale among the main *nō* acting families sank very low during the last decades of the nineteenth century.

Nō revived, and even thrived, through the fortuitous combination of a number of circumstances. During the early Meiji period it had an energetic practitioner in Umewaka Minoru (1827-1909) who almost singlehandedly organised performances and maintained interest in *nō* as an important theatrical heritage. The West's interest in *nō* was marked in the 1910s and 1920s, when both Arthur Waley, who published a selection of *nō* plays in translation in 1921, and the playwright W B Yeats, who wrote plays of his own in *nō* style, gave this classical Japanese theatre genre considerable publicity. Within Japan scholarly interest in *nō* was aroused with the discovery and subsequent publication of Zeami's treatises on *nō*. After World War II *nō* began a period of regular activity sustained by large numbers of amateur practitioners and an established reputation as an important contributor to world theatre.

At certain points in its history *nō* has in a limited way interacted with other theatre genres. Many *nō* plays have been adapted for *kabuki* and Kawatake Mokuami (1816-1893), the foremost *kabuki* playwright of the second half of the nineteenth century, created many such adaptations. The most famous *matsubame-mono*, as they were called from the pine (*matsu*) painted on boards (*h/bame*) at the back of the *nō* stage, was *Kanjinchō* (*The Subscription List*), adapted for the *kabuki* actor Ichikawa Danjūrō VII in 1840. Danjūrō was rebuffed when he tried to obtain advice from a *nō* actor for *Kanjinchō*, perhaps hardly surprising given the wide difference in social status between *nō* actors with their official stipends and *kabuki* actors who were treated as outcasts. *Nō* actors showed more willingness to help in Mokuami's time, but aloofness was difficult to maintain in the 1870s when *nō* was struggling to survive.

The story of *nō* in the twentieth century was one of maintenance of standards, preservation of tradition and some cautious experimentation. The bulk of the repertory of the five schools of *nō* has consisted of the two hundred or so plays that have survived since the fifteenth century, but a few new plays have been performed. One that attracted some attention in the 1990s treated the issue of organ transplants. *Nō* has always accepted ghosts as characters and they regularly appear both in their own time and later. Thus someone whose heart was taken for transplant before death was absolutely certain, could return later to bewail the fact.

For almost all the modern period *nō* actors have kept to themselves and the great actors of the twentieth century are in the main only known in *nō* circles. *Nō* requires such lengthy training (over thirty years to reach one's prime) and, probably because of its centuries of seclusion within the households of feudal lords, has evolved a performance style so different from other classical forms as almost to exclude meaningful interaction with actors from different traditions in the modern period. The main exceptions to this have been two members of the Kanze house, Kanze Hisao (1925-1978) and Kanze Hideo (1927–). These two brothers actively sought to participate in Japanese theatre in the wider sense.

Kanze Hideo was even associated with the radical movement in the 1960s which took modern theatre beyond the realism that had been its preoccupation for half a century. In 1978 he also joined actors from a wide variety of different traditions in a ground-breaking play that aimed to establish a completely new dramaturgy.[1]

Nō's comic counterpart, *kyōgen*, has experienced the modern period in much the same way.[2] Zeami had made *kyōgen* subordinate to *nō*, but he had included prescriptions for its acting and performance in his treatises and it had been performed alongside *nō* throughout its history. *Kyōgen* actors had been integrated into their respective *nō* troupes until the competing patronage of the military lords had resulted in in the break-up of these comprehensive groupings. Unlike *nō*, however, *kyōgen* uses a non-poetic stage language that is near to the vernacular of Zeami's time. Ghosts do not appear in *kyōgen* and time is generally linear. This gave *kyōgen* more liberty to explore topical subjects and the repertory includes many plays which contain references to contemporary fashions or concerns. For example, *Niwatori Muko*, which probably dates from Zeami's time, treats both a timeless human problem and a topical fad. As the word *muko* (son-in-law) in the title indicates, it is one of a group of plays describing a son-in-law's first visit to his in-laws after his marriage to their daughter, an occasion fraught with nervous tension on both sides. *Niwatori*, however, means a 'cockerel' and refers to a contemporary craze for cock-fighting. In the play a son-in-law is tricked by a friend into crowing like a cock in front of his father-in-law, who then copies him out of anxiety that he will be thought uncouth if he does not reciprocate.

This ability of *kyōgen* to be topical, its engagement with the concerns of everyday life and its approachability in presentation should have allowed it to participate in moves towards realism in modern Japanese theatre. Up until World War II this did not happen, possibly because *kyōgen* was still much under the shadow of *nō*. After the war, however, with the surge in interest among intellectuals in Japan's folklore heritage, *kyōgen* was able to take up new plays based on folk tales but not specifically written for *kyōgen* actors.[3] Its capacity for presenting human foibles within a stylised but flexible format encouraged other experiments and in the late 1980s Takahashi Yasunari, a professor of English literature at Tokyo University, created a successful *kyōgen* version of Shakespeare's *The Merry Wives of Windsor*. This was followed in 2001 by his adaptation of *The Comedy of Errors* entitled *The Kyōgen of Errors*, which was performed in Shakespeare's Globe Theatre in London.

In the latter part of the twentieth century *kyōgen* also had its innovators in the persons of Nomura Mansaku (1931–) and his son, Nomura Mansai (1966–). Both travelled abroad extensively holding *kyōgen* workshops and observing the reaction to *kyōgen* of people from other cultures. Both maintained regular activity in *kyōgen* performance within Japan but also made contact with with actors and directors in other genres and sometimes participated in their productions. Both appeared in *The Kyōgen of Errors*.

In the case of both *nō* and *kyōgen* this process of preserving the classical art while seeking a wider application for its technique accelerated in the 1980s and 1990s. This accompanied a realisation throughout the Western world that the hitherto linear development of its own mainstream theatrical tradition could benefit from traditions which at a certain point in time had chosen to preserve and maintain rather than develop and change. This only happened, however, in the case of those genres of Japanese classical theatre which used live actors as the principal medium for conveying to the audience the significance of the performance. The Japanese puppet theatre – now referred to generally as *bunraku* – has not had the same impact on other theatre traditions.[4]

Japanese theatre itself would today be immeasurably poorer without *bunraku*. By a strange quirk of fate Chikamatsu Monzaemon (1653-1724), universally acknowledged as Japan's greatest playwright, wrote almost all his many masterpieces for the puppet theatre. The plays he wrote between 1703 and 1724 provided artistic sustenance not only to the puppet theatre for which he had written them but also for the actor-based *kabuki* theatre that was developing at the same time. It is also the case that the three most famous post-Chikamatsu plays in Japanese theatre history were written for puppets, all within the decade of the 1740s. One of these three – *Kanadehon Chūshingura* (*The Treasury of Loyal Retainers*, 1748) – provided the first extended treatment of a story that afterwards was dramatised more than two hundred times and in the twentieth century was widely adapted for new media such as film and television. Even in a culture like Japan's, where audiences have long welcomed either the straight repetition of a favourite play or the frequent reworking of a favourite theme, *Chūshingura* has been something of an exceptional phenomenon. (Parker 2002)

The rise to prominence of the *bunraku* puppet theatre took place in the seventeenth century, although the name *bunraku* itself only dates from the nineteenth. A far-sighted combination of a musical instrument (the three-string *shamisen*), puppets and a very popular chanted narrative concerning a Princess Jōruri created essentially the *bunraku* puppet theatre that we know today. (Keene 1990) *Ningyō* (puppet) *Jōruri* is an alternative name for the genre and is chronologically more correct for puppet theatre up to the nineteenth century. What developed in the latter half of the seventeenth century was a theatre of one-man puppets which acted out a story narrated by a chanter who was accompanied by a *shamisen* player. As time went by, the puppets became more complicated until by the end of the 1730s they were one metre high with movable fingers, eyes, eyebrows and mouths, and they were worked by three puppeteers. In the West we have been used to puppeteers who are not seen, and it was the same in Japan until 1703. In that year, as a daring experiment, the single puppeteer operated his puppets in full view of the audience. In modern times the main puppeteer has been unmasked and recognised as a main performer in his own right. Originally the chanter, who spoke the lines of all characters, was also invisible to the audience, but this too changed and from 1705 all the main human participants in a puppet performance could be watched by the audience. This is the situation today: the chanter and *shamisen* player sit on a dais to the right (facing) of the stage and it is not uncommon for members of the audience to be looking at them rather than the puppets. (Adachi 1985)

Thus what we know as Japanese puppet theatre developed rapidly during the late seventeenth and early eighteenth centuries. *Kabuki* was developing at the same time, and the competition between it and the puppets was intense. One of the principal keys to success during this period seemed to lie with particular playwrights. *Bunraku* was fortunate in that it was able to monopolise Chikamatsu for the first two decades of the eighteenth century and it was Chikamatsu who established the canons of *bunraku* much as Zeami had done for *nō* three centuries earlier.

Zeami's father had created pieces for performance before socially mixed audiences, but Zeami himself, who had certainly experienced the necessity of pleasing large numbers of spectators, had refined the genre so that it was more suitable to performance before a few cultured connoisseurs. *Bunraku* and *kabuki*, on the other hand, started as popular forms during the first century of the Tokugawa period (1600-1868) and remained firmly based among what was defined by the government as the lowest class in society, which included those who worked with their hands, in the service sector, in trade and in manufacturing – the working class and the new bourgeoisie. (Ernst 1974; Brandon, Malm and Shively 1987) The range of cultural background in Chikamatsu's audiences, therefore, was similar to that Shakespeare experienced at the London theatres in which his plays were performed. In Japan Chikamatsu is often referred to as the Japanese Shakespeare and in the reception by the audience of the playwright's language there may be a comparison to be made. Chikamatsu's language combines contemporary vernacular and bawdy with flights of sophistication that needed a subtle mind for their full appreciation. Many of his characters seem to come straight from the streets along which the audience would have walked to the theatre, and the banter between prostitute and potential customer on the stage would have been very familiar to audiences of the time. At certain points in the plays, however, the language would be heightened into passages where there are as many as four layers of meaning. Such passages now need extensive annotation to be fully understood. (Shively 1991)

Chikamatsu's corpus of plays for the puppet theatre numbers about 150 and these have been sub-divided in various ways. The major classification, still used today, has been into *sewa-mono* (contemporary piece; *mono* means 'piece' or 'play') and *jidai-mono* (period piece). No great playwright's work could be meaningfully divided into just two categories and recent work on Chikamatsu has emphasised both the diversity within each group and the overlapping that often occurred between the two. (Gerstle 1986) However, the terms *sewa-mono* and *jidai-mono* were still being used freely and generally in theatrical circles during the Meiji period (1868-1912) and are in common use in the *bunraku* and *kabuki* worlds today.

The *sewa-mono* could be thought of as a type of tragedy in that the two leading characters, usually a pair of lovers, die at the end of the play, but they die in the hope of rebirth in the Buddhist paradise, and the journey of life, symbolised by the highly poetic passage that describes the lovers' route to the place where they will die (*michiyuki*), is only a way station towards ultimate salvation. What makes it necessary for them to die is not a fatal flaw of character on a heroic scale. They are always ordinary people, the man typically at the beginning of a career in trade and the woman a low-ranking prostitute. Their mistake has been to fall in love, as any two of their fellow citizens might have. The problem is that they are young and are subject to a number of binding norms both within the context of their work and in the society as a whole. Their love inevitably offends against one or more of these norms and the only way they can be together is in death. The interplay between the different forces that affect the main characters varies from drama to drama, but in essence the *sewa-mono* dramatised for its audiences a familiar situation that could only be resolved at the cost of considerable sacrifice in this world.

Chikamatsu's *jidai-mono*, by contrast, showed their audiences a world with which they were not familiar at all. In the middle of the seventeenth century the Tokugawa shogunate, concerned to enforce and maintain social stability, had instituted a fixed class system with the samurai at the top, farmers next, followed by artisans – swordsmiths, workers in silver etc – and at the bottom merchants, who with their families and their various employees formed the bulk of *bunraku*'s (and *kabuki*'s) audiences. *Jidai-mono* related historical incidents in the samurai world, far removed in time and social class from the audiences which thronged the puppet theatres. The plots of these plays often included sacrifices, for honour or a great cause, but in the end the hero usually won through.

One feature of *jidai-mono* has particular relevance to this book. Even an event of recent history would be set in an earlier era, sometimes several centuries earlier. There were thus both plays on real historical subjects and plays supposedly dramatising an event of the distant past but actually referring to something recent. Both types were set in the past, but there was no attempt at historical accuracy. *Jidai-mono* were 'period pieces' (*jidai* means 'period' or 'epoch') with no pretence of accurately representing the period in question. European playwrights, Shakespeare in particular, were often prone to interpret history freely according to the needs of their age. (Lindenberger 1975) In the case of Japanese historical plays of the early eighteenth century the objective seems mainly to have been to create good theatre – to incorporate models, male and female, of bravery, dutifulness and self-sacrifice. This was what the audiences wanted.

Bunraku's urban audiences were not averse to seeing transgressions of social norms punished by death in the *sewa-mono*, because the continuation of their relatively advantageous social conditions depended on this as long as they themselves were politically weak. The authorities, too, were well pleased if plays in the theatre reinforced the Confucian norms that kept society stable. They were also content for commoner audiences to be shown the grandly heroic behaviour of which only the samurai class was capable. Chikamatsu wrote many more *jidai-mono* than *sewa-mono* and this must have been because his audiences enjoyed what was to them largely escapist drama.

This acceptable face of theatre, however, did not in any way allay the deep suspicion in which the government and especially its Confucian advisers held the popular theatre in general. To ensure order among the lower ranks of society (which furnished the audiences for theatre) the assiduously cultivated myth of serene stability at the top had to be preserved at all costs. Only a century had passed since a bitter and protracted civil war, and old animosities among the feudal lords lingered on. Some incidents involving the families of powerful lords were excellent theatre material, but straight dramatisations of subjects such as these were forbidden. Hence the convention throughout the Tokugawa period that any such contemporary events had to be dramatised as if they had happened in the remote past. This probably deceived no-one, but it usefully maintained the fiction of a well-ordered society. It also had the effect of freeing historical dramas from their historical context so that, if it served the drama, historical facts could be lightly changed and conventions of staging which had no relevance to the events portrayed could be established.

The most spectacular instance of this concerned a series of events that took place between the spring of 1701 and February of 1703. Two lords quarrelled in the shogun's palace in Edo. This resulted in one of the two being ordered to commit *seppuku* (*harakiri*) and some of his retainers eventually taking vengeance on the other party. Chikamatsu dramatised this within a few years but set the play in the fourteenth century. In 1748, however, a version was written for the puppet theatre that became the defining classic for both *bunraku* and *kabuki*. This was *Kanadehon Chūshingura*. (Brandon 1982)

For a number of reasons the story of this revenge caught the imagination of the theatre-going public in Japan. The principal historical figures were Asano, the lord of a medium-sized domain in the west of Japan around modern Okayama, his adversary Kira, the head of a house that was hereditarily charged with organising and overseeing ceremonies in the shogun's palace, and Ōishi Kuranosuke, chief retainer of Asano, who was in his lord's castle five hundred kilometres away from Edo when the incident happened. Asano, by rotation, was due to be master of ceremonies for the entertainment of imperial envoys and for this he needed instruction from Kira. For reasons unknown (but speculated on actively in most dramatisations) there was bad blood between Asano and Kira. Just before the ceremonial greeting of the imperial envoys Asano drew the only weapon he was allowed to wear in the palace, his defensive short sword (*wakizashi*), and struck Kira on the forehead and shoulder. Kira was only superficially wounded. A hastily convened court of government ministers judged Asano guilty of a capital offence. As a feudal lord, Asano had the privilege of an honourable death and he disembowelled himself himself a few hours later at the residence of another lord.

Most of Asano's retainers were in his domain. His staff in his Edo residence sent messengers who arrived at the castle several days after Asano's death. After much discussion, led by Ōishi Kuranosuke, the law-abiding option was taken. The 350-odd retainers dispersed and the castle and domain lands were handed over peacefully to government representatives. Feelings had run high, however, and there could well have been resistance to the hand-over, because the circumstances of Asano's trial and death led many of his retainers to believe that he had been grievously wronged. In the event forty-seven of them decided to avenge their lord by conspiring to kill Kira. Unemployed samurai, as they now were, were referred to as *rōnin* (wave men), and the vendetta became known as the revenge of the forty-seven *rōnin*.

To attack a well-guarded residential compound in the centre of Edo with nearly fifty armed men and then to identify (not one of the *rōnin* had ever set eyes on Kira) and kill an enemy who was well aware of the possibility of a revenge attack was a complicated military operation that required meticulous but secret planning. Kuranosuke's feigned dissolution in a pleasure district near Kyoto is the best known of several methods used to allay Kira's suspicions. Finally in December 1712, after twenty-one months of preparation, the attack took place and Kira was killed. The *rōnin* took his head and presented it before the tomb of Asano in Sengakuji temple. They then gave themselves up to the authorities. The government debated for some time what to do with the *rōnin*, who had been split into four groups and placed under house arrest with four lords. The sentence passed on the *rōnin*, who were self-confessed murderers, was an honourable one and they were allowed to commit *seppuku*, which they all did on 4 February 1703. The historical sequence of events surrounding this incident stopped there.

Popular interest in the story did not stop, however, because it included several themes of enduring concern to generations of Japanese. Firstly, loyalty: not the blind loyalty promoted by the militarist leaders of the country in the 1930s (and incidentally imputed wrongly by them to *Chūshingura*) but the loyalty of followers who have good reason to believe their lord had been provoked into the deed for which he had died. Secondly an anti-authoritarianism which opposed high-handed behaviour on the part of representatives of authority. Thirdly, and most problematical, a justification of manly modes of conduct which solved problems outside the framework of law. The times in which the incident occurred were exactly right to bring out the full dramatic force of these themes. 1701-3 was towards the end of what is referred to as the Genroku Period. Formally lasting from 1688-1704 this period is usually regarded as taking in the first two decades of the eighteenth century. It was an extraordinary time of cultural development when many new forms and new possibilities of cultural expression were being developed. While the Neo-Confucian orthodoxy fostered by the government was emphasising a rational approach to politics, the law and social organisation, playwrights, fiction writers and pictorial artists were revealing how varied and unpredictable human beings could be. Furthermore, in the 1690s memories were still kept alive of a period, only a century before, in which instinctive bravery in battle could change a family's fortunes in a few hours. Samurai whose great-grandfathers had lived by the sword were now expected to be full-time bureaucrats. Many of them chafed at this, and to many members of the lower classes in Edo society a proud sword-bearing samurai seemed something of an anomaly in the peaceful civil society that was fast developing.

The dramatisation of the vendetta which has dominated Japanese theatre for two and a half centuries is *Kanadehon Chūshingura*. The word *kanadehon* in the title refers to a model writing exercise which a calligrapher prepared for his pupils to copy. The text of this model was the forty-seven graphs (*kana*) which made up the main Japanese phonetic syllabary. In the play each of the forty-seven *rōnin* is identified by one of the *kana*, and they are of course models to be followed. The play, in ten acts, was written by a trio of playwrights and this had become the norm by the 1740s.[5] The senior playwright would write the central scenes and the rest was the responsibility of his subordinate colleagues. *Kanadehon Chūshingura* was a play for puppets and it was therefore composed of narrative sections interspersed with dialogue. Even though a version for *kabuki* was soon produced which dispensed with the narrator, live actors still sometimes preferred to perform the original *bunraku* text, so that a chanter and *shamisen* player would sit to the side (stage left) of the *kabuki* stage narrating the actions and the live actors would speak the dialogue passages.

Kanadehon Chūshingura dramatised an event of nearly fifty years earlier, but this did not allow it to be set in its own time. It was clear from the title that the revenge of the forty-seven was the subject of the play, but to enable it to pass the censors its setting was pushed back four hundred years to the twelfth century.

A list of historical inaccuracies in *Kanadehon Chūshingura* would be very long and would serve no purpose here. It is generally assumed that historical drama will reflect the political and theatrical circumstances of the age in which it is written and in any case the writers of *Kanadehon Chūshingura* would not have had access to many of the materials that historians use today. *Chūshingura* was written for an exuberant popular theatre which for more than half a century had portrayed great heroes succeeding in their ventures and great lovers dying for their love. The audiences for plays in the 1740s were also less receptive to the subtleties of language that Chikamatsu had employed. Historians do not know the cause of the quarrel between Kira and Asano, but *Kanadehon Chūshingura* spends its first and third acts showing how villainous Kira is. Historically the revenge was plotted by Asano's retainers several days' journey away from Edo, but in *Kanadehon Chūshingura* Kuranosuke arrives just as Asano is about to expire and is ordered by his dying lord to take vengeance. In this way a set of stereotypes was created which have become part of Japanese popular mythology. The discrepancy between the heroes and the villains of this myth on the one hand and the historical record on the other has itself allowed for many reinterpretations in the modern period.

Kanadehon Chūshingura was one of three plays written by the same trio of playwrights in the 1740s. All three are similarly grand in scale, emotional tension and characterisation, and all three have become classics of both *bunraku* and *kabuki*. The theatre for which they were written was confident in its own artistic achievement and enthusiastic about giving its audiences a memorable theatrical experience. *Kanadehon Chūshingura* was quickly adapted for *kabuki*, which had borrowed many successful *bunraku* plays during its early history. While for much of the eighteenth century these two theatre forms were vigorous rivals, *kabuki* came to the fore in the 1780s and from that time on dominated the theatre world, especially in Edo.

Whereas a *bunraku* audience of the 1760s would have been

interested in watching the chanter as well as the puppets, the *kabuki* audience came to see the actors. The design of the theatres, with the *hanamichi* raised walkway running through the auditorium at one side (sometimes both sides) and the thrust stage, ensured that actors and fans were physically close to each other. The fans participated in the performance by appreciative cries (*kakegoe*) directed towards their favourite actor and timed perfectly to draw even more attention to the dramatic pose he would be striking.

Kabuki had developed at about the same time as *bunraku*, in the second half of the seventeenth century.[6] The spectators' attention was focused on the performers from the first, partly as artists and partly as possible sexual partners. It was the linking of dancing and acting in simple dramatic sketches with first female and then male prostitution that led the authorities to ban performers of *kabuki* – or *risqué* turns, as the term originally meant – who might be thought attractive to those wanting to pay for sexual services. Thus from the early 1650s onwards *kabuki* was performed only by male actors over the age of seventeen. Liaisons between handsome young actors and fans did not cease by any means, but this and other government regulations helped to ensure that the primary object of a *kabuki* performance was not prostitution but a display of acting talent.

Out of this grew an institution that is still regarded as central to *kabuki*: that of the *onnagata* or the (male) actor who specialises in female roles. Some of the greatest stars of *kabuki* have been *onnagata* and this still holds true today. Far from being restricted by government regulations *kabuki* developed the art of portraying symbolic femininity to a high degree. As in Britain at the time, cross dressing did not conflict with theatrical effect. Theatre audiences in Japan had historically been accustomed to seeing actors of one gender playing characters of the other. In *nō* and *kyōgen* all parts had always been played by men. Okuni, the shrine dancer credited with initiating the process that resulted in *kabuki* in the seventeenth century, had herself appeared dressed as a man. Overwhelmingly, however, the cross dressing has been by men posing as women and women were generally excluded from active participation in theatre throughout the Tokugawa period. Playwrights over more than two centuries wrote female parts in the knowledge that they would be played by men. One effect of this has been that *kabuki* audiences have long been conditioned to expect that femininity will be portrayed in *kabuki* plays in a certain way, and actresses have not been welcomed by audiences and critics on the few occasions in the modern period when they have appeared on the *kabuki* stage. The effort that the *onnagata* has to make to become a woman before even beginning to interpret his role appears to enhance his performance when compared to that of an actress, who starts from the relaxed attitude of knowing that her movements are naturally feminine.

The historical legacy has presented a great challenge to modern *onnagata*, as extremely high standards were set at an early stage of *kabuki*'s development. *Kabuki*, like *nō* and *bunraku*, benefited from the appearance of individuals who established criteria of a high order for their art. In *kabuki*'s case these individuals were three actors of whom one was an *onnagata*. Yoshizawa Ayame (1673-1729) worked his way up the theatre hierarchy by dint of great attention to detail and unsparing endeavour until he became the leading *onnagata* of the Genroku period. Rejecting the limited ambitions of most of his predecessors simply to reproduce the erotic mien of courtesans and insisting on studying character motivation minutely, Yoshizawa Ayame laid an obligation on all future *onnagata* to combine impersonation with interpretive acting. So conscious was he of the need to minimise the disadvantage of being male in his chosen profession that he behaved, and expected others like him to behave, as far as possible like a woman in his life outside the theatre. Apart from dressing as a woman in public, which other *onnagata* were already doing, he tried to avoid talking about his wife and children, he ate the sort of food that women would choose and he ate it in a demure way, he was deferential towards others as a woman would be, and in many other ways endeavoured to create a base of naturalism on which to build his stylised stage movements. (Kominz 1997; Dunn and Torigoe 1969)

The allure of the *onnagata* was matched by the players of martial heroes. Whereas *bunraku* was principally based in Osaka, *kabuki* developed in both the Kansai area and Edo, and in somewhat different ways. The *kabuki* actors of the shogun's capital specialised in a style of acting that was referred to as *aragoto* (roughness). These actors required their playwrights to fashion roles for them which would require aggressive confrontational gestures, stage fights and elaborate costumes and make-up. The range of plays available to *kabuki* audiences in Edo was not markedly different from that in Kyoto or Osaka and Edo *kabuki* had its *onnagata* too, but at about the same time as Ayame was active in Osaka, Edo was the venue for the remarkable career of Ichikawa Danjūrō I (1660-1704). Although his career went through several vicissitudes, Danjūrō's place in *kabuki* history is that of someone who dominated the Edo stage (and the Kyoto stage as well for a while) over a long period and established *aragoto* acting as one of the three main acting styles in *kabuki*. He founded an acting dynasty which lasted unbroken until the death of Danjūrō IX in 1903. The seventh Danjūrō (1791-1859) drew up a list of eighteen *aragoto* plays which had been performed by Danjūrō I and II and these were known as the Kabuki Jūhachiban (*jūhachiban* can be translated 'eighteen plays'; this collection is variously referred to in English: Eighteen Grand Plays of Kabuki, Eighteen Kabuki

Favourites, etc). Seven of these have been firm favourites of *kabuki* audiences ever since. Danjūrō VII has a greater claim to fame for having created the first *kabuki* drama to be based on a play from the *nō* repertory. This was *Kanjinchō* (*The Subscription List*), first performed in 1840 and the most popular of all *aragoto* plays since that time.[7]

Kanjinchō is important in Japanese theatre history for many reasons apart from its great popularity. Its plot involves an intense and complex view of loyalty, as the warrior monk Benkei can only save his master Yoshitsune by being so disloyal as to beat him in front of others. The theme of this play is part of a popular tradition of sympathy for those who have fallen on hard times and *Kanjinchō* is the most impassioned representation of this. (Morris 1976: 67-105) Perhaps its primary importance is as the best known of the many borrowings between genres in Japanese theatre. We have seen above how *Kanadehon Chūshingura* began life as a play for puppets and was subsequently adapted for *kabuki* actors, and this is just one of many plays that moved from *bunraku* to *kabuki*. The present *kabuki* repertory of about three hundred items consists of roughly equal numbers of plays written specially for *kabuki*, plays borrowed from *bunraku* and dance pieces (*shosagoto*) which are desigend to show off the actors' skill at dramatic dancing. With *Kanjinchō* this process of borrowing was taken one step further and later in the second half of the nineteenth century many other *nō* plays were taken over into *kabuki*. Borrowing between genres is not uncommon in Western theatre, but the scale on which this happened in Japan far exceeds anything known in the West. It seems to be a product of a theatre culture that places some importance on themes being familiar to audiences, as borrowings often provided the impetus for further adaptations within the same genre. In the modern period many such themes have made their way into film and television, *Kanjinchō* itself having been adapted for both. *Kanjinchō* has thus not only been performed so many times that even a casual *kabuki*-goer will have seen it, but its existence is felt by anyone wishing to write a variation on its plot. Many new plays in the *kabuki* repertory have conscious echoes of previous versions of the same story.

The trio of basic *kabuki* acting styles is completed by *wagoto*, which stands in direct contrast to *aragoto* and was originally associated with the Kansai region, especially Kyoto. The prostitutes played by the *onnagata* of the *kabuki* stage were prone to fall in love with pale, indecisive, weak young men who seem hardly to be equipped for life in the competitive world of seventeenth and eighteenth-century tradesmen. *Wagoto* was the style of acting that was designed to express the essential qualities of such stage lovers, who are redeemed only by the depth of their love and their willingness to die for it. The actor who gave this style its defining characteristics was Sakata Tōjūrō (1647-1709). Tōjūrō was a supremely dedicated actor who devoted much effort to perfecting the acting techniques necessary to bring his lovelorn characters to life. He also seems to belie the image of the *kabuki* star as an actor mainly absorbed in drawing attention to himself, as Tōjūrō spent much of his time carefully instructing the *onnagata* who played with him. All in all the historical record reveals a consummate man of the theatre who expected very high standards from himself and those who played with him.

It would be strange in Western theatre history to identify just three main acting styles and it is partly due to the commanding presence of these three actors – Danjūrō, Ayame and Tōjūrō – that the styles they epitomised have come to represent *kabuki* acting. It is characteristic of *kabuki* and other classical entertainment forms in Japan to categorise and formalise certain aspects of performance, but no play could be performed as *aragoto* from beginning to end. Like actors anywhere the *kabuki* actor adjusted and adjusts his performance to the situation being enacted on the stage. The names of *kabuki* acting styles are usually associated with specific characters and it is an accident of history that the style associated with Ōboshi Yuranosuke, the hero of *Kanadehon Chūshingura*, is not as well known as *wagoto* and *aragoto*. The actor who plays Yuranosuke acts in a *jitsugoto* style, indicating a greater emphasis on the restrained expression of inner emotion in tense situations. It so happened that Tōjūrō's great rival in Kyoto in the 1690s was a *jitsugoto* actor and Tōjūrō's decisive victory over him has resulted in Kyoto *kabuki* being defined by *wagoto* rather than *jitsugoto*.

The vocabulary of *kabuki* contains many more such acting styles and their frequent association with particular characters attests to a formalised approach to the presentation of a scene on the stage. While the literal and metaphorical foregrounding of the star performers would not have been unusual in eighteenth and nineteenth-century Western theatre, it would rarely have been so thoroughgoing as in the *kabuki* theatre. A leading actor would, and still does, expect his colleagues in major parts to remain motionless while he delivers his lines. If those lines contained something which was likely to provoke a strong reaction from the other actors, they would hold their reaction back until the end of the speech. Thus nothing detracted from the concentration of attention on the star actor when he was delivering his lines. Even the physical positioning of star actors on the stage could reflect more their status relative to the other actors than any requirements of the text. The playwrights would usually arrange that minor characters, who would be played by minor actors, would deliver their lines at the beginning of scenes before the audience had settled down. This did not apply to scenes involving a fight or other sequence of movements requiring more than one actor, but there was a static quality to episodes which relied primarily on dialogue. Moving during dialogue was something *kabuki* actors had to adjust to when faced with the different expectations of modern playwrights in the twentieth century.

A theatre of categories and conventions and endless revivals of earlier plays such as *kabuki* was in the eighteenth century might suggest that after only a century of history the adjective 'classical' might not be inappropriate. Although *kabuki* only came to be regularly so described in the second half of the twentieth century, many of the factors that would stamp it as 'classical' already existed at the end of the eighteenth. These characteristics continued into the nineteenth century and beyond, but they were overlaid by new trends that furnished an episode of uncertain significance in the history of *kabuki*. One can see in much twentieth-century playwriting for *kabuki* the basic types of plays, characters and moral dilemmas that were established for the genre in the first fifty years of its existence. The plays written for *kabuki* in the first half of the nineteenth century, however, seem to exist in a kind of vacuum. They unwittingly fulfilled the function of providing something against which *kabuki*'s modernisers could unhesitatingly react, but little drama seeking its inspiration in them has appeared in modern times.

The plays of Tsuruya Nanboku IV (1755-1829) are usually taken to typify the trends in *kabuki* during the early part of the nineteenth century. In the history of Japanese drama Nanboku takes his place beside Chikamatsu Monzaemon and Kawatake Mokuami as a playwright of great stature. He achieved recognition from the *kabuki* theatre as a playwright in 1801 after a great revival of *kabuki*, long in the shadow of the puppet theatre, in the last two decades of the eighteenth century. The first use of the full revolving stage in 1858, enabling a complete set of scenery to be transformed into another before the spectators' eyes, and the employment of numerous trap-doors and stage lifts had all increased the possibilities for spectacle and *kabuki*, particularly Edo *kabuki*, eagerly embraced them. The *kabuki* theatre in the nineteenth century was dominated by Edo and it was there that Nanboku built his career.

The distinguished historian of Edo culture, Nishiyama Matsunosuke, characterises *kabuki*'s main achievement in the early decades of the nineteenth century as the development of an 'aesthetic of evil'. (Nishiyama 1997: 223–5) Nanboku played a major part in this with a series of leading characters who plumb the depths of the evil of which human beings are capable. Iemon, the hero of his best-known play *Yotsuya Kaidan* (*The Ghosts of Yotsuya*, 1825), is a totally unregenerate figure, who fascinates through his apparent ability to plan evil actions that exceed the audience's imagination.[8] Iemon has no redeeming features and his haunting and ghastly murder by his principal victim (his wife) awake no sympathy. The sheer energy of this and other plays by Nanboku has led Nishiyama to describe them in terms of protest against the stultifying official Confucian moral system imposed by the shogun's government. Nanboku was the first major exponent of a new category of *kabuki* play, the *kizewa-mono*. The original meaning of this term was probably 'pure' *sewa-mono*, plays that delved more deeply than ever before into the personalities of ordinary people. Nanboku varied this by giving historical subjects, such as that of *Yotsuya Kaidan*, the immediacy of a *sewa-mono* domestic drama. Other playwrights of *kizewa-mono* returned to contemporary themes but pursued increasingly radical expressions of evil among people at the bottom of society, whose environment was most likely to foster crime. Edo citizens delighted in plays portraying villains and eagerly supported the theatres that provided them.

Scenes of grotesque violence became commonplace in Edo's *kabuki* theatres and the government, for two centuries anxious about the theatre's effect on the morals of the urban populace at large, brought in a series of edicts in 1841 to restrain what it perceived as the excesses of *kabuki* at the time. The so-called Tenpō Reforms required the centrally situated three large theatres of Edo to relocate to an outlying area to the north of the city. Strict regulations were issued concerning the construction of these theatres in an attempt to lessen the fire risk. Not only the large theatres suffered. Edo was dotted with small *yose* theatres, which provided popular variety shows on a daily basis. Before the reforms there were approximately 150 such theatres; afterwards the number was a mere fifteen.

At the same time restrictions were announced on the professional and personal lives of actors. They were strictly forbidden to tour to the provinces with productions of plays. Their low social status below the four officially established social classes was reemphasised by prohibiting association with anyone from those classes. Actors lost the freedom to live where they wanted to and were required to live in one designated quarter near the new remote theatre district. All other employees were forced to live there too. If actors ventured into the city, they had to cover their faces by wearing a large sedge hat, and many were fined when caught not doing so. (Engeki Hakubutsukan 1962: vol 4, 102–3)

The minister who had been the prime mover in these measures, Mizuno Tadakuni, fell from power only two years later and by the mid 1850s *kabuki* had largely returned to its pre-reform conditions. Kawatake Mokuami emerged to assume Tsuruya Nanboku's mantle as a writer of plays about villains of all kinds committing innumerable acts of violence, sometimes imaginative in the extreme. Mokuami's *kizewa-mono*, however, were distinguished by the musical background, which he adopted from the *bunraku* theatre, and the regular prosody and poetic quality of his scripts. Like all playwrights before him he wrote parts for specific actors and many of his plays from this time were styled to suit the acting talents of Ichikawa Kodanji IV (1812-1866), an actor who although he was a disciple of the great Danjūrō VII found domestic dramas more to his liking than the *aragoto* of his teacher. Kodanji excelled at portraying Edo low life and became the leading actor in Edo.

Thus, apart from a certain uniformity of subject matter in new plays, *kabuki* after the Tenpō reforms retained many of the characteristics that marked it in its periods of greatest popularity. Costumes had gradually regained the magnificence that they had temporarily lost as a result of Tenpō restrictions; elaborate sets moved on the revolve and delighted the spectators. Above all high-quality actors drew large audiences to the theatre quarter in spite of the distance and inconvenience of the new location.

In general *kabuki* in the first half of the nineteenth century was well served by its actors. There was no let-up in the rigour with which aspiring actors were trained, especially if, like Kodanji IV, one started with the disadvantage of not having been born into one of the leading acting families. Training within a family began at an early age – four or five – and the importance given traditionally to family lineages encouraged actor fathers to devote much effort to bringing on their sons as actors. As in the case of the *nō* acting families and Japanese society in general, however, adoption was not uncommon, if one's sons were obviously not suited to the stage. An outsider, as Kodanji originally was, could beg a senior actor to accept him as a disciple. Whatever the route one chose, or had chosen for one, trainee actors spent most of their waking hours in the theatres seeing to the needs of established actors and observing their art. In time – earlier if a career was being pursued from within an acting family; rather later in most cases if from without – an actor would be granted a name recognised as part of the *kabuki* actor hierarchy.

Although, as we shall see, *kabuki* in the early years after the Meiji Restoration of 1868 attracted much criticism for its vulgarity and decadence, it had little to be ashamed of as it progressed into the modern period. It had a superb playwright in Kawatake Mokuami and it had benefited from the careers of a number of talented actors. In terms of acting resources *kabuki* was better equipped to meet the challenges of a period of change than it had been a century earlier. The first half of the nineteenth century had had its complement of actors, such as Danjūrō VII, who specialised in classic styles of acting.[9] It also had those who, like Kodanji, specialised in new styles that had developed during the century. In addition this period saw the emergence of *kabuki* stars who were versatile and could take advantage of the blurring of the boundaries between the basic play types. Onoe Kikugorō III (1784-1849) and Nakamura Utaemon IV

(1798-1852) were noted actors who astonished their audiences by assuming more than one role and even gender in a single play. (Gunji 1990) In spite of the appearance of two celebrated playwrights within the space of a few decades, late Tokugawa *kabuki* was still centred on its actors. They had proved themselves able to adapt to the changes in *kabuki* that the early nineteenth century brought; the following chapters will examine how they faced the greater challenges that were to come.

1
Kabuki and the Challenges of a Changing Theatre World

Going to the theatre in Tokyo in 1869 was not at all different from going to the theatre in 1867, in spite of the fact that a momentous historical event called the Meiji Restoration had taken place in 1868. Historians have been at pains to point out the many continuities that mark the transition from the institutionally feudal Japan of pre-1868 years to the modern nation state of the Meiji period (1868–1912). In the immediate post-Restoration years much theatre continued as before, except that the fall of the military regime that had patronised the *nō* theatre meant a sharp drop in the fortunes of *nō* and *kyōgen* actors.

The dominant theatre genre during the Meiji period was *kabuki* and *kabuki* is still being performed today. Many other elements of pre-Meiji culture also flourish today, notably poetry, the tea ceremony and the martial arts. Most visitors to Japan seeing *kabuki* for the first time and being told a little of its ruling conventions would conclude that it had changed little since the days when samurai walked the streets of Japanese cities and geisha ruled the entertainment districts. *Kabuki* has changed considerably, however, and it has been joined by a host of competitors over the past hundred or so years. Theatre-going in 1889 was significantly different from theatre-going in 1869; ten years later it was different again, and by the end of the Meiji period in 1912 was beginning to be unrecognisable to anyone old enough to remember the theatres of Edo.

This chapter will look at the first forty years of Japanese theatre after the Meiji Restoration.[1] During this period we will see some parts of the *kabuki* world consciously adapting to the new age. We will also see pressure to change being applied to *kabuki* from outside. Official interference was something that historically *kabuki* was well used to, but the aim of this new pressure was quite different. In addition, as Western drama became known in Japan, intellectuals also took an interest in theatre, again in a rather different way from the censorious Confucianists of earlier time. Finally, the male *kabuki* actors' monopoly of cast lists came to an end as others felt the pull of the footlights (also, incidentally, introduced during the Meiji period).

PLAYGOING IN EARLY MEIJI

1868 started badly for the citizens of Edo. As the city which had been the location of government and place of residence for many thousands of samurai bureaucrats and their families, its livelihood depended on the demand for goods and services from this national ruling class. In January the shogun was defeated in a battle near Kyoto by the forces of those anxious to overthrow him and he fled to Edo. It could only be a matter of time before his enemies, who were also the enemies of his government, would be at the gates of Edo. The city could well be sacked and fired; there was turmoil, and the theatres closed.

In the event, they only closed for the one month of January. In February regular productions started up again, and by the end of the year it was as easy to see *kabuki* as it had been during the previous twenty years. Audience numbers were certainly down, not surprising in the conditions of recession following the fall of the government. The hand-over of political power in April, however, was bloodless, and the Edo citizen, renowned for his happy-go-lucky spirit, got on with life much as before. Barrels of saké, a gracious gift from the emperor, were distributed throughout the city in October. There was much rejoicing, and *kabuki* actors were among the many loyal subjects who paid their respects in front of the palace.

A citizen of Tokyo (as it now was) who wished to watch theatre in October 1868 would have had a reasonable choice before him. Of the three main traditional genres, the *bunraku* puppet theatre and *kabuki* were available to him. *Bunraku* had not been as popular in Edo as in Osaka in recent years, but there were two theatres operating in central Tokyo in 1868. At the Tokyo citizens' disposal, too, were numerous temporary theatres that would appear in temple or shrine grounds or in the main retailing areas of the city. Theatre was good for raising money for religious purposes and for attracting customers to your wares. *Nō* would not have been available to him, but then urban dwellers had had few opportunities to see *nō* for more than two centuries. *Nō* had been one of the privileges of the ruling samurai families and had now lost its patronage. The circumstances now existed for *nō* to take its place among other public theatre forms, but instead most of the leading families were completely demoralised and bankrupt and, at least in Tokyo, the tradition was in danger of dying out.

To the vast majority of Tokyoites, however, a trip to the theatre would mean going to see *kabuki*. And it was a trip. The three theatres that were all the previous government had allowed were situated well to the north of the city, next to the Yoshiwara pleasure quarter, and performances only took place in daylight. Theatre-going in 1860s Tokyo, therefore, was a neat reversal of what has become the norm in countries with metropolitan cultures. Instead of travelling into the city from your suburban home and staying up late at night, you awoke at the crack of dawn in your city-centre home and travelled out, maybe partly by boat, to the somewhat remote area where the theatres were situated.

Your shoes, probably mired from the long walk, would be left at the entrance, and unless you had money enough for a box, you made your way to the stalls. These consisted of mat-floored squares created by a grid of low wooden partitions just wide enough for one person to walk on. The squares were meant to seat six or seven people in close proximity to each other. This was the space in which you and your friends or relatives lived for that day. Food and drink would be brought to you by attendants balancing on the partitions or you could do simple cooking for yourselves. You would need to leave the theatre from time to time, along the grid, to go to the toilet or to the neighbouring tea-house. All this went on during the performance, as long intervals were rare; the atmosphere was lively and noisy. Western visitors to Japan at the time have left records expressing their horror at the ill manners of the *kabuki* audiences, but there are many now, in Japan and the West, who regret that watching *kabuki* soon came to resemble the Western theatre experiences to which those visitors were comparing 1860s *kabuki*.

The performances watched by the *kabuki* audiences in October 1868 would have been very similar to those they had seen many times before. All three theatres during this month were performing plays with similar plots. Two were performing exactly the same plays, as they were economising on expenses by using the same actors but performing in alternate ten-day periods. The third was competing with something similar. In October there was no choice but to watch *Chūshingura*, the vendetta story that had so captured the interest of the Japanese theatre for nearly two centuries.[2]

The main attraction for the spectators, as always in *kabuki*, would be the actors.[3] Two in particular dominated *kabuki* at this time, but with the changes that were about to come their names were soon to be forgotten. Had the audiences for *Chūshingura* in October 1868 but known it, the three theatres already had in their companies the manager, actors and playwright who were in turn to dominate the world of *kabuki* as it came to terms with its new environment in the following decades. These are names that will recur frequently in this chapter. The manager was Morita Kan'ya XII (1846–1897), who was 23 at the time. The actors were three in number: Ichikawa Danjūrō IX (1838–1903), Onoe Kikugorō V (1844–1904) and Ichikawa Sadanji I (1842–1904). They were all young – 31, 25 and 27 – and not particularly well-known. The names as given here are all famous ones in the *kabuki* acting hierarchy; two of the three acquired them later, being listed under other names at this time. Only Sadanji retained his name for the rest of his life, which was unusual. The playwright changed his name soon to Kawatake Mokuami (1816–1893). At 53 Mokuami was at least ten years younger than his two rivals in the other two theatres, but he was about to take over from them as leading playwright of the era.

THE STATE AND THEATRE

The next fifteen years were a time of bewildering social and political change. *Kabuki* as an art did not change very much, but the environment in which that art was practised acquired some fundamentally new elements. So much changed that exact motives for some of the reforms are hard to determine. Why exactly did the government in the autumn of 1868 encourage the three *kabuki* theatres to move from their existing sites, when they had been placed there by government command in 1841? How did it come about that Danjūrō and Kikugorō suddenly found themselves the chief actors at their theatres in the spring of 1869? Many questions remain unanswered from this period, but one gets a strong impression of accumulation. Each change eventually fits into a line of development that becomes clearer as the years go by.

No theatres moved in 1868, but the possibility of moving, something they had not known for nearly thirty years, had been presented to them. While the new ability to move could be regarded as a freedom, it may not have been viewed as such by the government. They seem to have had a specific role in mind for the theatre. Events of 1872 indicated that actors were now regarded as popular educators and thus expected to reinforce the Neo-Confucian ideology of the Tokugawa period by performing plays that ostensibly promoted the rewarding of virtue and punishing of vice. At least the theatre had been given a modicum of recognition and some actors, officially outcasts before, were delighted at being required to pay taxes for the first time. They still, however, needed a licence to act.

Positive interaction between the government and the *kabuki* theatre had been unknown before, and Morita Kan'ya was very quick to seize the opportunity offered. He did this in two ways. Firstly he moved his theatre – the Morita-za (*za* means 'theatre') into central Tokyo. He acquired a site in a former entertainment district known as Shintomi-chō in the modern Kyōbashi area, and in October 1872 the downtown Morita-za opened. Kan'ya not only moved physically nearer the centre of power. Through a connection he had gained an introduction to the then Minister of Finance, and when the minister left by ship for the United States and Europe as a member of a fact-finding mission, Kan'ya went to see him off. Such ritual send-offs have always been taken seriously in Japan, and there Kan'ya met other members of this mission. Two in particular were destined to become powerful in the world of politics and finance and great friends of the theatre (although not all theatre-goers saw it this way). They were Itō Hirobumi (1841–1909), who served four terms as Prime Minister between 1885 and 1901, and Fukuchi Ōchi (1841–1906), a prominent journalist and politician.

The move of the Morita-za had symbolic significance, but the changes in management practice introduced by Kan'ya for this new theatre were more than symbolic. Theatre management had previously been a nightmare, primarily because the theatre building and its administration were not autonomous. Theatres were locked into a web of financial arrangements that did not always work to their advantage. Kan'ya in the new Morita-za made a start on claiming independence for himself as manager. All spectators were to go into the theatre past the box-office, not, as many did, through the backstage area, which was a world unto itself. Toilets were provided inside the theatre for the first time; no longer was it necessary to repair to a nearby tea-house, where the spectator would spend money that could otherwise have been used for services within the theatre. Thus in a small but significant way Kan'ya began breaking down some of the long-standing conventions that, as he saw it, could hinder the proper work of the theatre.

Whether Kan'ya was aware that theatres in the West were independent or whether he just wanted to do his job in his own way can only be guessed at. Right at the beginning of a consideration of Meiji theatre we come up against the problem of how much reforms originated in a propensity to copy the West and how likely it was that such reforms would have occurred anyway. The Westernisation/modernisation debate engaged much of the energy of historians and social scientists in the 1960s. While theatre was never subjected to the scrutiny that other areas of Japanese culture underwent during that debate, there seems little point in pursuing the question here. Japan's experience in having been isolated internationally during two centuries of economic and social change elsewhere is an unusual one, but all societies have had to adapt to increased international contact over the last century and if anything Japan has proved itself overall quite selective in adopting ideas from other cultures. To the relief of many theatre scholars Japan has retained large parts of its traditional theatre, while enthusiastically experimenting with many new forms. The result is a richness that transcends the issue of the exact extent of the Western impact.

That having been said, the Meiji government's interest in theatre in the 1870s was clearly neither wholly nor even principally, an artistic one. The mission (known as the Iwakura Mission from the name of its leader) in which Itō and Fukuchi took part soon discovered how differently the theatre was regarded in the West. To their surprise, and initially horror too, some of the official entertainment of their group took place at the theatre, something that could not be contemplated in early Meiji Japan. It is true that some official visitors to Japan at the time were entertained at private performances of *nō*, which were much appreciated, but the Meiji government wanted for political reasons to impress the Westerners on their own terms. In Japan too the theatre would have to become a place where the élite gathered for entertainment. Japanese theatre had to become respectable.

Morita Kan'ya was already initiating reforms in theatre management that were bringing the unruly atmosphere of the auditorium under control and he responded with alacrity to the government's concerns. He reconstructed his theatre, renamed the Shintomi-za in 1875, with the government's objectives very much in mind. The opening ceremony in June 1878 was a glittering affair. Ministers and ambassadors were greeted by *kabuki* actors in frock-coats, while music for the event was provided by Japanese military bands playing Western marches. It is easy to be amused by this, but the whole occasion was taken very seriously at the time. The atmosphere was laden with symbols of many kinds. Fukuchi, journalist and politician now turning his attention to the stage, wrote the speech that Danjūrō read to the assembled company on Kan'ya's behalf. Government and theatre (or at least this one theatre) were pursuing the same goals, and the theatre seemed to be succeeding brilliantly.

The rather sedate atmosphere of modern *kabuki* theatres derives ultimately from Kan'ya's reforms in 1878, and many *kabuki* fans regret the passing of the more robust audience participation that characterised the earlier Edo theatre-going experience. Kan'ya, however, introduced other reforms in the Shintomi-za that were to have far-reaching effects on Japanese theatre-going from then on. Gas lighting was installed, thus making evening performances (the first at the Shintomi-za was held in August 1878) possible. Such innovations had been tried elsewhere (in Yokohama), but Kan'ya was the first to institute them on a regular basis in a major Tokyo theatre. The concept of going to see a play after a day's work was thereby established, as opposed to arranging a whole day's holiday. More important in the eyes of one leading Japanese theatre historian was the fact that Kan'ya's stage did not project beyond the curtain. The traditional thrust stage that had allowed the actors in first *nō* then *kabuki* to act in the midst of their fans was apparently not necessary for *kabuki* performances in the Shintomi-za. Some later theatres even dispensed with the *hanamichi* walkway, and drama that had been created with this stage configuration in mind began to seem classical and remote.[4] (Kawatake 1959:1145-6)

NEW PLAYS

The main item on the programme of the first season of the new Shintomi-za was acted by a company headed by Danjūrō and written by Kawatake Mokuami. During the 1870s Danjūrō had been causing some disquiet among his fans. He had been tinkering with the familiarity that had been an important element of the enjoyment of watching *kabuki*. He had tried acting without the use of clappers to emphasise moments of high tension. Not only that, he had noticeably restricted some of the histrionic gestures that his fans were always waiting for. The latter was particularly worrying, because *kabuki* shorn of its stylised movement would to them no longer be *kabuki*. The period plays (*jidai-mono*) in which Danjūrō specialised had never pretended to the slightest historical verisimilitude, but Danjūrō was beginning to show an interest in the actual lives of the historical characters in the plays. His passion for collecting antiques has been cited as a contributory factor, but whatever his motivation Danjūrō was beginning to make his roles appear a little more real. (Toita 1956: 6) These experiments gathered pace until finally with his October 1878 performance for Kan'ya at the Shintomi-za a popular writer coined a new term for plays which paid attention to historical fact. They were henceforth to be known as *katsureki-geki* or 'plays where history is brought to life'. Danjūrō was to be their great exponent and Mokuami was to write them for him.

It was still the norm for playwrights to write *for* actors, and indeed this is still the case today. For half of his career Mokuami was an Edo playwright and he does have the distinction of leaving his name to posterity as such (along with Chikamatsu and Tsuruya Nanboku IV). In the early years of Meiji, however, he was still writing 'to give life to' (in a direct translation of the Japanese term often used) the particular acting art of individual actors. He wrote for both Kikugorō V and Danjūrō IX during this time, suiting the plays to their different acting talents.

Kikugorō was stronger on *sewa-mono* domestic plays, while Danjūrō specialised in *jidai-mono*. Contemporary society, especially the pleasure quarters, had long furnished the subject matter for *sewa-mono*, and it is perhaps not surprising that Mokuami used contemporary Japan for the plays he wrote for Kikugorō. As on the streets of Tokyo, male characters in these plays began to appear sporting Western dress and minus the elaborate top-knot hairstyles of pre-Meiji Japan. These plays were classified as *zangiri-mono* or 'plays where the hair was cut and let down' (as opposed to being tied up). Superficially the novelties of early Meiji Japan – brick buildings, the telegraph, etc. – were very evident in these plays, but, not surprisingly as you do not have to change your ideology to operate a telegraph machine, interpersonal relations between characters and the motivations for their actions remained firmly rooted in pre-Meiji Japan. It is conventional to describe *zangiri-mono* as a genre which quickly died out, but from time to time throughout the past century *kabuki* has been performing plays set in post-Meiji Japan. Kikugorō's performances of *zangiri-mono* in the 1870s demonstrated that there was no inherent contradiction in *kabuki* actors using their traditional and highly polished acting skills to portray contemporary life. Their technique was never realistic and therefore never identified with a specific period in time. The *kabuki* actors who performed *zangiri-mono* in the 1870s indicated to generations of actors after them that *kabuki* acting technique was sufficiently flexible to cope with the new demands that would be made on it.

The *katsureki-geki* living-history plays have both a similar and a different significance in the development of modern Japanese theatre. With their increased approximation of stage and real-life actions they too demonstrated the potential of *kabuki* acting technique. Perhaps more important than that, however, they took a hesitant step towards realism in playwriting. This has implications not only for later *kabuki* but for the Western-based *shingeki* movement that was to develop in the early twentieth century. One of the plays performed in the first season of the Shintomi-za was a *katsureki-geki* by Mokuami. The play concerned incidents in the life of Ieyasu, founder of the Tokugawa dynasty and unifier of Japan in the early years of the seventeenth century. Two scholars were involved in providing historically accurate material for the play, thus becoming the first outsiders to contribute to a work for the theatre. The precedent set by them had important consequences for the later development of playwriting as an art independent of specific theatrical circumstances.

Throughout the 1870s in small ways the boundaries of the *kabuki* world were being pushed back. Those whose opinions could be brushed aside before as ill-informed might now have to be respected by the *kabuki* establishment. Commentators were looking at Japanese culture as a whole, and they were not prepared to spend half their lives in theatres in order to become knowledgeable about drama. They had other things to see and hear. If such people were in or near government, they had to be listened to. Increasingly, however, *kabuki* came under a different kind of scrutiny, as those who wrote on *kabuki* shifted their focus. Debate began on how *kabuki* should be evaluated. Information on *kabuki* became more widely available. In 1879 there appeared the first issue of a monthly journal that was dedicated to spreading knowledge of *kabuki*. (Matsumoto 1974: 24252) In *Kabuki Shinpō* (*Kabuki News*) for the first time there appeared texts of plays, previously not allowed beyond the small circle of performers. The play was symbolically being detached from the performance and from the particular theatre company. It no longer belonged solely to the actors, often even a single family of actors; it was now entering the public domain.

REFORM OF *KABUKI*

We can only guess how *kabuki* would have developed as a stage art if it had been left simply with the problem of attracting enough patrons to support its activities. In fact *kabuki* had a part in the grand plan of the Meiji government firstly to prevent Japan suffering from the interference of the Western imperialist nations, as China had, and secondly to establish Japan as a strong and prosperous nation state in its own right, able to stand beside those imperialist nations. One important element in this was Western recognition of Japan as a civilised country. Christianity was essential to the Western view of civilisation at the time and Japan would not go as far as adopting Christianity as a state religion. Civilisation, however, also meant a high culture – regular gatherings of a not very large social, financial and political lite whose members entertained each other by polite conversation, dancing, etc., or were entertained by musicians, singers, actors or thoroughbred racehorses. Here was where *kabuki* fitted into the picture.

Kan'ya had ingratiated himself with some of Japan's new leaders by seeing them off at Yokohama and constructing a theatre to which they and their foreign guests were invited. In October 1872 the Lord Mayor of London had taken them twice to the theatre, an experience that was repeated many times during their visit to the West. If Japan was to influence those nations that held all the power, it would have to have its own respectable theatre. Kan'ya had shown that with special effort it could be done. In the eyes of several influential people in or near the government, now was the time to reform Japanese theatre culture as a whole so that it could fulfil a similar social function to theatre in the West. In 1878 Danjūrō, Kikugorō and Kan'ya were invited to a meeting at which Itō Hirobumi recounted his experiences in Europe and invited them to contemplate a high-class culture where actors were recognised as artists and held in high esteem. (Ishizawa 1964: 14)

Reform was in the air, and during the 1880s reform was publicly advocated for many areas of Japanese life and culture. (Kornicki 1982) 'Reform societies' of every kind sprang up, one of the most prominent being the Engeki Kairyō-kai (Theatre Reform Society) founded in 1886. The list of signatories to the manifesto, published in *Kabuki Shinpō*, that accompanied its foundation attests to the public interest in theatre reform. The Foreign Minister and Education Minister both signed, as did Fukuchi Ōchi, now editor of a major newspaper, and many others prominent in social and cultural life.

The Society was founded by Suematsu Norizumi (1855–1920).[5] This is a name quoted in all histories of theatre in modern Japan, but Suematsu's theatrical achievements in a strict sense were non-existent. By 1879, when he left for study in Britain, he was a well-connected, highly energetic young journalist, who soon after his return became Itō Hirobumi's son-in-law. (Itō was Prime Minister at the time.) Seven years in the West convinced Suematsu of the need for theatre reform and the manifesto of the Society embodied his ideas on the subject. It advanced three aims:

'1. To reform the evil conventions of hitherto existing theatre and cause the realisation of good theatre.
2. To cause the writing of plays for the theatre to be an honourable profession.
3. To build a properly constructed auditorium which will be used for theatre performances, music concerts, song recitals, etc.' (Matsumoto 1974: 295)

From what Suematsu and others wrote at the time it is clear that social acceptability was uppermost in their minds. 'Good theatre' was theatre which could be watched by upper-class ladies and gentlemen who perceived it necessary to be shielded from obvious manifestations of sex or violence. Playwriting was to be honourable, but this seems to have meant being accepted by the proposed new audiences rather than having one's function as an independent artist within the theatre confirmed. All this had to take place in a new theatre building, which was probably envisaged as like a European opera house. (Matsumoto 1974: 296)

As if to crown the efforts of Suematsu and his high-placed fellow campaigners the emperor and empress and members of their courts watched *kabuki* for the first time in April 1887. Theatrically the event did not have much significance. Socially it changed Japanese theatre irrevocably. In spite of attempts by court officials to pretend that it was something of a coincidence that the emperor should have chanced upon *kabuki* while on a visit to Foreign Minister Inoue Kaoru's residence, no member of the Meiji élite could henceforth have scruples about going to the theatre and indeed many would now positively want to do so. It was reported that the emperor and especially the empress had enjoyed the performance.

Suematsu, who had been the main organiser, Kan'ya, the backstage manager, and the three actors Danjūrō, Kikugorō and Sadanji had scored a triumph. Their traditional fans had been rather surprised to turn up to watch them perform in the usual place only to find the theatre closed and dark. With the imperial performance *kabuki* moved several steps closer to becoming a classic, even a national theatre. As a classic theatre, it might not change very much over the following years; if it became a national theatre, it might be the focus for aspiring playwrights and actors nationwide. In the event both happened. *Kabuki* today is a classic theatre which all tourists are taken to see, but it also performs many plays written by playwrights more widely engaged in Japanese culture as a whole. It must be said, however, that still very few actors come from outside the traditional *kabuki* acting families.

A student of Western theatre and drama might well ask why this chapter has travelled two decades into the Meiji period without describing or assessing any plays. The answer is connected with the lack of autonomy of dramatic texts. As was usual in the Tokugawa period, in most cases new plays did not exist outside the run in which they, along with others, were performed. Until the 1890s it was still rare for plays to be published in any form. It was not the practice even to give actors full scripts of the plays in which they were appearing. Most actors were given, and would only have required, the text of their own parts. Relatively few plays have survived from this period. As playwrights were still writing for, and often at the request of, the leading actors, if these actors were espousing change this would naturally be reflected in the plays that were written for them and this happened most clearly in the *zangiri-mono* and *katsureki-geki*. During this time, however, one leading actor, Danjūrō, and one influential manager, Kan'ya, were considerably in advance of their regular audiences. The tension between their ambitions and their audiences' desire to be entertained in a familiar way coloured much of the playwriting of the time.

BEGINNINGS OF DIVERSITY

By the end of the 1880s the theatre world of Meiji Japan was set to enter a period of unprecedented diversity. The *kabuki* mould had been broken and conservative *kabuki* fans, if they wanted to continue their theatre-going, were forced to make choices that extended beyond their favourite actors, who might be performing in a play or a theatre of which they disapproved. New hybrid forms appeared, as outsiders impinged more and more on the development of theatre. Important for the first time among the latter were those concerned with the burgeoning new world of literary theory and modern literary practice.

SHIMPA

Drama reform had been supported and encouraged by the

government and drama was obliged to reflect its wishes. The 1880s, however, were characterised by a great intensity of political debate. In 1881 the emperor promised the establishment of a constitution and parliamentary assembly, and during the next decade it was to be decided what practical form of political system the new Japan should adopt. The distinction between political opposition and treason, however, had yet to be precisely formulated and repressive measures were taken to stifle any unwanted criticism. This resulted in supporters of opposition political groups having to find indirect ways of spreading their political beliefs. 'Freedom and popular rights' was the catchphrase for this period and out of the movement associated with it several new cultural phenomena appeared. The 'political novel' is the best known of these and many were published at this time. Political themes made their way into a number of popular entertainment forms, including songs, music hall and a type of narrative recitation called *kōdan*. Drama was not excluded.

The theatre that developed out of the political atmosphere of the day showed a number of variant forms during the next thirty years or so, and each new manifestation was given a new name. Depending on one's point of view, these variations were either significant enough to warrant different treatment or similar enough to each other to allow of generalisation. The view taken here tends toward the latter, and it will be convenient to use a generic term, even though some of the later practitioners in the 1900s specifically rejected the term commonly used. The word *shimpa*, which in fact only came into currency around the turn of the century, aptly indicates the relationship of this new theatre with *kabuki*, as it literally means 'new school' where *kabuki* was referred to as 'old school'. Confusingly, in Japan at the beginning of the twenty-first century *shimpa* denotes historically a genre and to the contemporary theatregoer a single company. The form flourished in the 1900s and 1910s, but its popularity has gradually waned since the Second World War and by the 1990s *shimpa* referred to one company that gave rather few performances.

Two main strands developed in *shimpa* between the late 1880s and the early 1900s. Some scholars believe that one had strong implications for the *shingeki* movement that was about to start up in earnest, while the other may have helped *kabuki* to adapt to the modern age. However modern *shimpa* may have seemed in the 1880s and 1890s, it is worth repeating that still the only yardstick by which audiences and critics could judge theatre was *kabuki* itself. New types of theatre were still defining themselves against *kabuki* four decades later in the 1920s.

The political drama that was performed by political activists (*sōshi*) in Osaka in 1887 is conventionally regarded as the start of *shimpa*. The company was led by Sudō Sadanori (1867–1907), an ex-policeman and a journalist on one of the first anti-government newspapers. Sudō's brand of theatre was very similar to what others had been experimenting with before him, but this production was the first in the new style to attract attention and hence Sudō's elevation, challenged more than once since, as the founder of *shimpa*. Sudō, like his largely forgotten counterparts, had noticed the tendency towards limited realism in *kabuki* and the incipient participation by outsiders in its previously closed activities, and had decided to exploit these for his own purposes. He and the actor/ dramatist Kawakami Otojirō (1864–1911), who quickly followed his lead, were taking a stage further the work started by the scholars, politicians and businessmen involved in the Drama Reform movement. Coincidentally, the Drama Reform Society disbanded itself in the same year that Sudō began his theatrical venture.

Sudō and Kawakami's motives seem to have been both political and commercial. The plays performed in the early years of *shimpa* were mainly adaptations of the so-called political novels that were popular at the time. The word 'political' when applied to these novels seemed to refer mainly to the idea of the individual making a success of his life in the new Japan in spite of the hurdles of low birth or misfortune. This was a kind of political issue in a country where status had long been determined mainly by birth. *Shimpa* also provided dramatic narratives in the re-enacting of political events, such as the attempted assassination of the opposition politician Itagaki Taisuke in 1882.

These were subjects which had never been seen on the stage before, but we must be careful how we define 'stage'. In the early years *shimpa* was performed only in the Kansai region, whereas theatre was dominated by Tokyo. *Shimpa* could only be said to be seriously introducing something new to Japanese theatre if it drew audiences to watch plays on these new subjects in Tokyo itself. This soon happened. Kawakami's company performed in Tokyo in June 1891 with great success. His Osaka fame had gone before him, and even Danjūrō and Kikugorō attended his first Tokyo venture. The melée on stage as actors playing student activists grappled with the man who had attacked Itagaki Taisuke (the play was entitled *Itagaki-kun Sōnan Jikki, Disaster Strikes Itagaki – the True Account*) differed considerably from the set-piece fights on the *kabuki* stage. What stole the show, however, was an interlude piece that Kawakami performed in front of the curtain. With the nonsense title *Oppekepe*, it was vulgar, satirical and topical and it created a merchandising boom. (Engeki Hakubutsukan 1962: vol. 1, 450) From then on through the rest of the 1890s Tokyo theatregoers had frequent opportunities to watch *shimpa*. *Shimpa* enjoyed great commercial success during this time, and *kabuki* had to take note of the threat it posed.

ACTRESSES

The plays *shimpa* performed were unshapely and the acting was amateur. But 'professional' still referred exclusively to *kabuki* actors who had been through many years of rigorous training. Sudō even requested help from a well-known *kabuki* actor and the latter sent one of his assistants to give Sudō's actors some instruction. It was not too difficult to mimic some of the grand set gestures of *kabuki*, beloved and regarded as essential by all theatregoers, and the *shimpa* actors interspersed their more realistic style with such movements copied from *kabuki*. *Shimpa* also exploited one considerable advantage which it had over the senior genre; it was able very quickly to take advantage of the relaxing in 1888 of the government prohibition on actresses. During the 1890s *shimpa* acquired its own *onnagata*, partly because its popularity attracted low status but talented actors away from *kabuki*, but it also mounted the first large-scale production performed by a mixed cast in November of 1891. That the *shimpa onnagata* survived alongside the actresses, indeed even flourished in the early 1900s, is a testament to the tenacity of the convention of female impersonation in Japanese theatre. This led to the often criticised anomaly in *shimpa* theatre, where a scene between two female characters would often be played by actors of different genders. This seems not to have jarred with Japanese audiences, and the gradual professionalisation, and therefore stylisation, of *shimpa* acting meant that such confrontations lost much of the inevitable initial contrast in acting styles.

Shimpa presents a very confused picture in the 1890s. It seems as though almost everyone acted with almost everyone else, as the commercial success of these novel productions ensured that backers were usually available. It is possible, however, to discern two main trends, one created singlehandedly by Kawakami Otojirō, who well outlasted Sudō as a force in Japanese theatre. The other trend was followed by all other *shimpa* companies (although some actors would act for both camps), and so sharp was the distinction between them in Kawakami's eyes that in the early 1900s he gave his brand of theatre a special name.

TWO TYPES OF *SHIMPA*

Kawakami's theatre retained its political and topical content, although the politics changed. His productions in Tokyo had attracted the notice of top politicians, and two of them paid for him to travel to France in 1893 to observe theatre there. In early 1894 he dramatised a political scandal with such success that two sequels followed, also sell-outs. (Komiya 1969: 268) The outbreak of the Sino-Japanese War on 1 August that year gave him a new idea; he crossed to the mainland, took in the battlefields and by the end of the month was performing a dramatised version of what he had seen to ecstatic audiences. This was no anti-war protest. Kawakami rode on the crest of a wave of tremendous public enthusiasm for Japan's first war for several centuries and it took him in May of 1895 to the theatre which was regarded as the home of *kabuki* – the Kabuki-za, a magnificent theatre opened in 1889. For whatever reason – the topicality, the uninhibited acting, the sentimentalism, the novelty – Kawakami made a great impact on the theatre in the 1890s and he even received the compliment of *kabuki* productions that tried to copy his style.

Meanwhile, the type of *shimpa* that essentially exists today began to develop its special characteristics. Initially led by an actor named Ii Yōhō (1871–1932), it had a powerful backer in the person of Yoda Gakkai (1833–1909), an extraordinary figure who capped nearly twenty years of high government service with practical involvement in the reform of theatre. It was Ii and Yoda who had promoted the first high-profile mixed production in November 1891, and thereby began a process of emphasising *shimpa*'s artistic potential. In spite of the participation of actresses, the style drew closer to *kabuki* as the performers acquired professional expertise. The plays were generally not political in content, but portrayed the lives, loves and sorrows of the new middle class. The clash between the power of money and the pull of love, a variation on the *sewamono* themes of the Edo period, frequently provided the dramatic tension.

Maintaining an adequate supply of plays for the rapidly increasing number of *shimpa* productions was something of a problem for the new genre. Outsiders had only recently been granted a role in theatre and playwrights were still few. *Shimpa* solved this problem by tapping into a new development in popular culture that had begun in the 1880s. This was the newspaper novel, serialised over a long period and often the cause of a boost in circulation for the newspaper concerned. *Shimpa* began dramatising these in the 1890s and such productions became wildly popular. In 1898 a *shimpa* company performed an adaptation of *Konjiki Yasha* (*The Gold Demon*) by Ozaki Kōyō (1867–1903), one of the most widely read serial novels of the Meiji period. Ozaki had only begun publishing it the previous year, and it was still unfinished when he died in 1903. *Shimpa* was therefore adapting a portion of a long novel still in its early stages. The initial situation, however, was already established. The story of a young man, deeply in love, apparently being jilted in favour of a fat banker, and then turning obsessively to usury as his career, seemed to catch the public imagination, and further adaptations for *shimpa* followed in 1902 and 1905. The great popular success of *shimpa* in the 1890s and also in the 1900s, when it almost eclipsed *kabuki*, can be attributed to its dramatisations of newspaper novels.

Kawakami Otojirō, on the other hand, did not think this was the way the new drama should be developing. Uniquely among theatre people active in the 1890s he had seen theatre in the West, having been sponsored to go to France in 1893. Later he had taken a company of nineteen actors and actresses, including his ex-geisha wife Sadayakko (1872–1946), on a long tour to the United States, Britain and France between 1899 and 1901.[6] Performing in Buckingham Palace was only one of several extraordinary events that occurred during this trip, as 'kabuki' was suddenly discovered by leading Western cultural figures.

Ironically, these trips abroad strengthened Kawakami in his conviction that the hallmarks of *kabuki* – especially the continuous background music and the use of *onnagata* – had no place in *shimpa*, and on his return he initiated what he called a movement to establish 'correct drama' (*seigeki*). There was no background music; coloured gels were used in the lights; the *hanamichi* was ignored. The plays were mainly adaptations of Shakespeare (*Othello* and *The Merchant of Venice*). (Ōzasa 1985: 51ff) In commercial terms, however, Kawakami's attempts ended in failure, and his productions in the 1900s enjoyed none of the success of what was now regarded as mainstream *shimpa*. His health deteriorated and he died in 1911.

DRAMA AS ART

From the second half of the 1880s, while the practitioners of theatre were feeling their way into the new age, writing about theatre and especially written drama – dramatic literature – began attracting attention for the first time. It was astonishing how much was achieved in this area in only the next decade, as the baseline was salacious comments on the physical attractions of the actors, on a par with similar assessments of prostitutes. There was considerable surprise in polite circles when Tsubouchi Shōyō published an essay on fiction and drama in 1885, for he was a graduate of (what was later called) Tokyo University and a lecturer at a well-known private institution of higher education (later Waseda University). What had the intellectual élite to do with literature and theatre? By 1900, however, the idea that well-respected people could engage in serious discussion about theatre was well-established, and much of the credit for that goes to Tsubouchi and his friend and intellectual opponent Mori Ōgai (1862–1922).

Stimulated by the introduction into Japan from about 1877 of much Western dramatic literature, especially Shakespeare, and no doubt partly stung by his own inability to discuss the character of Gertrude in *Hamlet* to the satisfaction of his American teacher, Tsubouchi began defining what he regarded as the essential features of literature and drama. His 1885 essay, *Shōsetsu Shinzui*

(*The Essence of the Novel*), was primarily concerned with fiction, which he considered to have wider scope than drama, and he followed this up with a major statement on drama, *Wagakuni no Shigeki* (*Japan's Historical Drama*) in 1893-4. Arguing that creative writing existed as art in its own right, he tried to shake off the didacticism that had been forced on it by the Neo-Confucianism of the Tokugawa period. For both fiction and drama he urged attention to characterisation and dialogue, in the hope that greater care in this area would lead to a better balanced two-way relationship between character and situation.

Mori Ōgai thought Tsubouchi had gone too far towards letting plays be driven by realism. There developed between the two of them the first public debate on literature to involve drama, indeed the first significant such debate in Japanese literary history. Like most of its successors, it ended inconclusively, with Tsubouchi implicitly acknowledging Mori Ōgai's superior grasp of the latest European literary theory. (Keene 1984: 508-12; Matsumoto 1980: 206-28) They were writing at cross purposes, Tsubouchi anxious that a consciously targeted Confucian ideal of goodness be eliminated from drama, and Mori Ōgai certain that a universal ideal had to inform any work of literature. The direct effect on drama in general at the time was probably negligible, but some important principles had been stated in print by two scholars in positions of some intellectual influence.

Mori Ōgai is usually credited with confirming for drama the right to be considered part of Japan's literature. Literary criticism developed apace through the rest of the Meiji period. The 1890s were dominated by Romanticism, as through Western writers such as Byron and Goethe young Japanese writers, particularly poets, discovered the liberating pleasure of unashamed exultation of human emotions. There was something of a vogue for 'dramatic poetry' (*gekishi*) and several poets tried their hands at poetic dramas. Notable among these was Kitamura Tōkoku (1868-1894), who was convinced he could only express himself adequately in poetic plays. He wrote several, and one, *Hōraikyoku* (*Ballad of Mount Hōrai*,1891) regularly appears in anthologies of drama, but none were performed. From this time on literary men regularly turned to drama alongside their fictional writing as a means of coping with the complicated reality they were trying to reflect. It was some decades, however, before their efforts and the practical theatre came together.

Tsubouchi Shōyō, on the other hand, was more conscious of the need to stay close to those who would perform the new plays. He wrote his own historical dramas, trying to observe his own prescriptions for the genre. To see them performed now, one wonders how any other mode of production apart from *kabuki* could have been contemplated for them, but the professional stage ignored them at the time. They were historically accurate, there was some attempt at believable characterisation and the plot structures were noticeably tighter, but to *kabuki* fans they were not *kabuki*; they were a pale reflection of it that was less attractive than Kawakami-type abandon.

THEATRE AFTER THE TURN OF THE CENTURY

In the fourth decade since the Meiji Restoration the Japanese theatre scene was far less settled than it had been in 1868. In general *kabuki* was still preeminent, and there were more productions of *kabuki* than of any other form of theatre. But it now had to contend with strong competition from two types of *shimpa*. Its own attempts to reform itself, mainly under the leadership of Danjūrō IX, had not been welcomed by its fans. The strength of *kabuki* was still in traditional productions of classic favorites performed with Danjūrō or Kikugorō V in the lead parts. Sadanji I, regarded by now as almost on a par with these two, had successfully branched out at his own theatre, the Meiji-za, built with the help of a huge loan in 1893. Here he had experimented with new *kabuki* plays that had proved quite popular with his fans.

Soon after the turn of the century, however, the Tokyo *kabuki* world was thrown into confusion by the deaths in succession of Kikugorō (February 1903), Danjūrō (September the same year) and Sadanji (August 1904). The deaths of Kikugorō and Danjūrō particularly affected the Kabuki-za, the most influential *kabuki* theatre in Japan at the time and very expensive to run. The productions put on by their successors failed to please and audiences fell off rapidly. There was considerable friction between the management and the actors, and highly publicised defections to other theatres took place. In the meantime the Meiji-za did well, but Sadanji had no obvious successor and his death was a disaster for the theatre. The outbreak of the Russo-Japanese War in February 1904 seemed to present an opportunity to profit from war plays again, but this time the response from the fans was muted. *Kabuki* entered a period of depression.

Shimpa by contrast went from strength to strength. Apart from Kawakami and Sadayakko, four actors dominated *shimpa* at this time. Ii Yōhō led his own company at the Masago-za in central Tokyo, where he had attracted much attention over the previous three years with his text-conscious productions of Chikamatsu Monzaemon. Takada Minoru (1899–1977) returned to Tokyo from a highly successful few years in Osaka and took over the Hongō-za theatre also in central Tokyo. Under his leadership the next three years are known in *shimpa* history as the 'Hongō-za period'. Kawai Takeo (1877–1942) had developed, much to his father's disgust, into *shimpa*'s first popular *onnagata*. His good looks and beautiful voice ensured him an enthusiastic following and he was a powerful draw for Ii's Chikamatsu productions after joining him at the Masago-za in 1901. He also played occasionally for Takada after 1904. Finally Kitamura Rokurō (1871–1961) returned to Tokyo slightly later (in 1906) after a successful career as an *onnagata* in Osaka and joined the Hongō-za company.

Shimpa is often dismissed as a purveyor of repetitious melodrama, but apart from the question of whether even that was undesirable in Japanese theatre at the time, the range of plays performed by *shimpa* in Tokyo during these few years is remarkable. Dramatisations of newspaper serials were still the staple, reflecting commercial considerations, the lack of original plays to perform, and also a certain pressure from the newspaper companies themselves, who foresaw a rise in circulation if a popular actor portrayed a character in one of their serials. But newspapers already had a lot of money and considerable influence and they were able to sign up the best writers of the time. Some adaptations for *shimpa*, for example those of novels by Izumi Kyōka (1873–1939), combined an exquisite evocation of the age with depiction of feelings accessible to their Meiji audiences but deeply redolent of the Tokugawa period.[7]

Several other types of play attract attention in the repertory lists of *shimpa* from these years. Beginning in November 1904 there was a succession of plays with characters from the social class that was referred to as 'new commoners' (*shin-heimin*) at the time. 'New commoner' was a Meiji euphemism for the well-known minority that had suffered discrimination for centuries before the Meiji Restoration. The subject was taboo, and it may not be surprising that critics at the time did not give any prominence to these productions. The plays depicted socially unreal expectations in these characters and in this way may themselves have been discriminatory, but putting them on the stage at all shows some awareness of the range of contemporary social problems.

One also finds a sprinkling of plays adapted from Western literary works. Shakespeare, Daudet and Goethe were introduced to *shimpa* audiences at this time. *Shingeki* is usually credited with introducing Western drama into Japan, and in terms of quantity and general coverage that was certainly so. Several years before the first *shingeki* companies appeared, however, *shimpa* felt confident enough in its standards of performance to take on the challenge of foreign plays. This is one of the factors which has caused recent theatre historians, notably Ōzasa Yoshio, to cite *shimpa* as a forerunner of modern theatre in Japan rather than as a hybrid offshoot of *kabuki*.

COMEDY

The first decade of the twentieth century also witnessed the rise of comedy as a force in modern Japanese theatre. As mentioned in the previous chapter, comedy in the form of *kyōgen* has a long history in Japan. During the Edo period *kyōgen* had, along with *nō*, become part of a somewhat refined theatrical culture with a limited audience. As comedy, however, it had a popular counterpart in the *niwaka*, small groups of comic players who performed extempore skits often in the streets. (*Niwaka* means 'on the spot' and is itself an abbreviation of the full name *niwaka-kyōgen*). *Niwaka* reached a peak of popularity in Osaka in the 1830s with pieces that parodied the grand dramas of *kabuki*. Parody was still its staple fare in the early Meiji period, when it seemed almost anything could be given a comic twist. *Kabuki niwaka* was epitomised by the most famous *niwaka* performer of the era, Tsuruya Danjūrō (1845–1909), whose stage name was itself borrowed from two prominent *kabuki* actors of the day. Otherwise there were *sōshi niwaka*, parodying early *shimpa*, *shinbun niwaka*, which specialised in making fun of grave newspaper (*shinbun*) articles, and many more. Like *shimpa*, *niwaka* tried its fortunes in the capital after achieving fame in the Osaka/Kyoto area, and at its first appearance there in 1898 it drew capacity audiences. However, *kabuki* actors in Tokyo were not as indulgent towards parody as their Osaka counterparts and the main Ichikawa house was so deeply offended at Tsuruya Danjūrō's comic version of *Kanjinchō* that he changed the title in mid-run.[8] (Ōzasa 1985: 118)

It was *niwaka* which inspired one of two brothers who dominated the Japanese comedy stage for the first two decades of the twentieth century. Convinced after seeing Tsuruya Danjūrō in 1903 that the future lay in comedy, the man known to Japanese theatre history as Soganoya Gorō (the name is also a *kabuki* parody) persuaded his brother Soganoya Jūrō to join him in a new theatrical venture, which they termed *shin-kigeki* (new comedy). *Kigeki* as the Japanese translation of 'comedy' was a word that had only been coined in 1901 by Tsubouchi Shōyō in connection with Shakespeare translation. It had gained more currency in 1902 when Ozaki Kōyō had prefixed it to his translation of Molière's *L'Avare*. The Soganoya brothers adopted it with the prefix '*shin*' ('new') to indicate that they were moving on from previous Japanese stage humour, which had mainly presented single topics in a short format. For about a decade from 1897 there was something of a boom in Molière with many translations and several productions. Although much of their early material resembled *niwaka*, the Soganoya brothers set themselves to explore comic themes in an extended way that allowed for more complicated plots and structure. As this type of playwriting was not yet established in

Japan, they wrote their own plays.

The Soganoya brothers took on the challenge of the Tokyo theatre world only a year after first forming their company. Initially they were not very successful and for three years they experienced the humiliation of being forced to move into progressively smaller and less desirable theatres as they continued to draw only modest audiences. So dispirited were they that they decided on a (somewhat oxymoronic) second Tokyo debut in 1906, when a programme including a play with an English title, a claim to be a French comedy and a plot apparently based on a well-known *kyōgen* was very successful. After this Soganoya comedy never looked back, playing regularly in large theatres both in Tokyo and in the Kansai. With their capacity audiences increasingly attracting members of the new intelligentsia, the Soganoya brothers gradually built up their subsequent reputation as the fathers of modern comedy in Japan. (Ōzasa 1985: 12732)

BIG BUSINESS IN JAPANESE ENTERTAINMENT

Not only did the various *shimpa* companies of the early years of the twentieth century make a lot of money for themselves, one of them contributed directly to the growth of one of the world's greatest entertainments conglomerates. In Kyoto in the 1880s two male twins, born in December 1877, were passing their formative years in and around a theatre. Their father ran an in-house shop and while helping him with it they were able to watch the *kabuki* plays being put on at the theatre. At some point they both decided to become theatre managers and they independently tried their hands at theatre management when they became old enough.

Their break came in 1902 when they jointly sponsored a young *shimpa* player named Shizuma Kojirō (1868–1938). Shizuma had broken away from Kawakami and formed his own company in 1899. The two brothers recognised both his and *shimpa*'s potential and together rebuilt the theatre in Kyoto in which Shizuma had enjoyed phenomenal success for a year before it had burnt down. The theatre was renamed Meiji-za and the brothers took one Chinese character from each of their names to form a company name. Each Chinese character can have several readings in Japanese and the joint name that resulted has been pronounced in two different ways, but the reading by which it has become a legend in the Japanese entertainment world is Shōchiku.[9] Shizuma and the Meiji-za enjoyed record-breaking success for more than ten years, allowing Shōchiku to acquire more theatres and put more actors under contract in the Kansai region until by the mid-1910s, when the company carried out a successful theatre-buying policy in Tokyo, it was by far the biggest single entrepreneurial force in Japanese entertainment.

THE THEATRE-GOER IN 1906

While Shōchiku and other entertainment companies were to bring a great range of theatrical presentations within the means of the ordinary citizens of Tokyo, already by the middle of the first decade of the twentieth century an open-minded theatre buff would have had considerable choice. If he or she had been old enough to have attended the theatre about forty years earlier around the time of the Meiji Restoration, he would have marvelled at the array of plays now available to him.

Let us say that he is deliberately sampling as much as possible of the stage entertainment being performed in February 1906. As in 1869, there is *kabuki* in abundance. Three theatres, including the prestigious Kabuki-za, are between them putting on no less than twenty-one *kabuki* plays (including the usual excerpts and dance pieces). Not only that, but if our theatre-goer had happened to be a prominent businessman, he would also have been able to take in a special programme at the Kabuki-za mounted in honour of Prince Connaught, brother of the British monarch and in Japan on a state visit. On the other hand, so many foreign dignitaries had watched *kabuki* since the opening of the Shintomi-za that our friend would probably not have been surprised that *kabuki* was yet again being used as part of the Japanese diplomatic effort.

Shimpa he would also find without much difficulty. Within walking distance from the Kabuki-za was the Masago-za, well-established by now as a *shimpa* theatre and featuring two of *shimpa*'s greatest stars during February. The main play on the programme was a new one by a playwright known for his skilful portrayal of lovers balked by social circumstances beyond their control. Our friend might enter into the spirit of the play and shed a tear or two, like the middle-aged ladies sitting aound him; he might also shiver with them at the paper snow falling heavily on the stage. Or he might feel that this was too sentimental for him; he could accept sentimentalism expressed in the formalised gestures of *kabuki* but not when at least some of the acting was clearly aiming at a kind of realism. In which case he would want to try something quite different.

At the Meiji-za, about thirty minutes rickshaw ride east towards the River Sumida from central Tokyo, he might (if he had not by this time become rather blasé about the vigour and vitality of the culture round him) be surprised to see billboards announcing the production of a European play that would still have been fresh in the minds of Paris or London theatre-goers. Maurice Maeterlinck's *Monna Vanna*, a play on a historical subject but written in the Symbolist style that had made the playwright a leader of this literary movement, was being performed with Kawakami Otojirō and Sadayakko in the lead parts.

A theatre-goer who had penetrated this far into the Meiji theatre world might well have had Japanese academic friends who could tell him of other recent developments. They might not have been much interested in *kabuki* or *shimpa*, but the *Monna Vanna* might have caught their attention as an opportunity to discover what sort of play it was. Well into the 1920s some intellectuals were still going to the theatre simply to learn about the Western plays being performed. In February 1906 intellectuals interested in the arts would have taken note of press reports on the founding meeting of a new arts association based at Waseda University. Given the name Bungei Kyōkai (Literary Arts Association), its drama section promised to quicken the pace of change in Japanese theatre. Some detected in Tsubouchi Shōyō's speech as head of the new organisation an intention to bring more foreign plays in translation onto the Japanese stage. There was in fact little evidence of this in the various short dramatic pieces performed by the association's members on this occasion, but critics noticed a clarity and beauty of diction that was new. These amateurs moved and gestured clumsily, but they were superior to professional actors when it came to the speaking of lines.

Attention to the words of the text – the words written by the playwright – and a concern to speak them meaningfully were to become one of the hallmarks of the next stage in modern Japanese theatre history. The first forty years of the Meiji period had seen some of the old, fixed conventions broken down with the involvement of outsiders and the interest of high society. Japanese society was still changing fast as the Meiji period came to a close, and as yet it could not be predicted what type of theatre would prove most congenial to theatre-goers even a few years in the future.

2

New Acting, New Production, Some New Playwriting

Commercially the early part of the Meiji period had been good for *kabuki*. Latterly its main derivative, for it is difficult not to refer to *shimpa* like this, also enjoyed commercial success. As the Shōchiku twins realised, there was much money to be made out of the theatre, if the theatre was responsive to the requirements of its audiences. Meiji society was a vibrant mix of conservative values, eager curiosity, patriotism and sentimentality, and at various times and in various shapes the theatre took advantage of each of them.

At the end of Meiji *kabuki* existed much as it had before. It had been joined by *shimpa*, and at the end of the Taishō (1912-26) period both were still being performed in their familiar way and they too had been joined by other theatre genres. The difference during this coming period was that new forms appeared that did not make money. Whereas *kabuki* and *shimpa* had mainly followed what they perceived to be popular taste in theatre, the next generation of theatre groups moved ahead of their audiences. *Kabuki* had tried to do this with the *katsureki-geki*, but it had not persisted when its audiences manifested their disapproval. The Taishō period, by contrast, saw the emergence of groups that were sufficiently sure of their principles to see educating their audiences as part of their duty.

Audiences did pay to be educated in the theatres but not as much or in such numbers as they were prepared to do when they were paying for pure entertainment. Kawakami had provided Western plays, but his shows were highly entertaining, as some of his critics pointed out. A new stage had been reached in modern Japanese theatre history once companies decided there were plays that they wanted to perform and ways of performing that they wanted to try to develop, whether their efforts were commercially viable or not. From now on theatre companies were subject to new tensions, as they attempted to persuade their audiences to try something different and then stay with it. New ways of financing productions were experimented with, and when they failed or were thought inappropriate, compromises had to be made with audiences' own tastes.

The history of Taishō period theatre is one of inevitable mismatches. Plays were beyond the actors available or simply beyond acting altogether. Experienced critics found themselves with no useful experience by which to assess some of the new experiments. Playwrights wrote new plays for performance in theatres which were manifestly unsuitable. The society depicted on the stage and the society watching the stage could be so different as to be mutually unintelligible. Once the settled and superbly developed *kabuki* lost its position at the centre of an enviably integrated entertainment milieu, there was bound to be a hiatus before anything comparable emerged either to take its place or exist alongside it.

Much of Taishō theatre history is therefore concerned with what were at the time minor groups, in the sense that, considering the whole spectrum of theatre, they did not change the general image of theatre in the larger society. Their importance is historical, in that with hindsight they can be judged to have laid the foundations for major developments later, but their contemporary importance should not be underestimated. They may have engaged the attention of relatively few people, but the intellectual élite of the evolving new Japan was concentrated in Tokyo, where these groups operated, and in their audiences the presence of leading intellectuals and writers was often recorded.

Two such groups have dominated historians' attention, Bungei Kyōkai (Literary Arts Society), mentioned at the end of the previous chapter, and Jiyū Gekijō (Free Theatre). Most of the leadership and initiative in the founding and administration of Bungei Kyōkai came from two men, Tsubouchi Shōyō and a pupil of his named Shimamura Hōgetsu (1871–1918).

BUNGEI KYŌKAI

Soon after the appearance of Tsubouchi's essay on historical drama in 1893 a department of literature was established at Waseda and Tsubouchi held meetings devoted to readings and discussion of drama for the students of this department. Most of the texts studied were his own historical plays. From 1896, however, Tsubouchi was heavily involved in pre-university education, so much so that he has an assured place in any history of elementary education in Meiji

Japan, and the students that he had inspired with enthusiasm for drama found themselves with less leadership than they had hoped. Events in the traditional and commercial drama world of the early years of the twentieth century encouraged them to think that they should plan actual performances and they prevailed upon an unwilling Tsubouchi to found a society in 1905 which would give performances as well as readings.[1]

In spite of his reservations about attempting what he believed was beyond the powers of his actors, Tsubouchi grasped the opportunity to return to theatre work and give practical realisation to his developing artistic ideas. His abiding concern was the problem of creating a new drama which would retain the most valuable elements of the classical forms. He was also by this time increasingly preoccupied with the development of a new dance drama in Japan, as Western opera and ballet had excited his interest. (Akiba (1986): vol 1, 86) He had published the text of a dance drama in 1904, which aroused much interest at the time.[2] For this new society's first studio performance Tsubouchi chose a scene from a popular *kabuki* classic rewritten in courtly Japanese from the Nara (eighth century) period, thus attempting, at the urging of his students, to distance this new stage in Japan's theatrical development from the more familiar *kabuki* cadences that Tsubouchi loved so much. The performance aroused much favourable comment, partly at least because of the acting of Doi Shunsho (1869–1915) and Tōgi Tetteki (1869–1925), who were to remain Tsubouchi's lead actors for the next nine years. All the other actors were also students, and none of them had been trained in traditional acting methods. The success of this first venture was such that the society's members urged the establishment of a larger more permanent organization. Tsubouchi was again hesitant, preferring to wait and ask the advice of Shimamura, who was at this time studying in Europe.

Shimamura was a recently appointed young lecturer at Waseda and had established his position in the literary world just before departing for Europe in 1902 by the publication of a work on aesthetics referred to as 'epoch-making'. (Fujimura 19501: vol. 3, 440) He had been favoured by Tsubouchi's friendship while a student and although influenced greatly by him, had inclined more towards the ideas of Tsubouchi's rival in literary theory, Mori Ōgai. (Kawazoe 1953: 5) By this time, however, Shimamura was in the process of transferring his intellectual support from Romanticism to Naturalism and he was soon to become one of the main theorists of the latter literary school.

On his return to Japan Shimamura enthusiastically joined the cause of those who wished to expand the new society into a more ambitious undertaking. After discussions between members of the society and sympathetic literary men from the university plans were put forward for a large-scale cultural organization, to be called Bungei Kyōkai, which was to concern itself with a wide range of activities. Tsubouchi was asked to be president, but refused for reasons of health and lack of time and because he was convinced that their preparations were inadequate.

In spite of this Tsubouchi did involve himself in a production of *Hamlet* that Bungei Kyōkai mounted in the Hongō-za, usually the home of professional theatre, in November 1907. The production aroused much interest in intellectual circles. Something of its importance in influencing ideas on theatre may be gauged by the presence in the audience of Ōkuma Shigenobu, President of Waseda University, who had not been to the theatre for some years previously, and Ichikawa Sadanji II, the rather unpromising son of the great Sadanji I, who was to be the leading exponent of new *kabuki* plays three decades later. The story of *Hamlet* was well-known in Japan by this time and there had been performances of adaptations, notably by Kawakami Otojirō. The Bungei Kyōkai production was different in the importance given to Shakespeare's text (for instance, by including all soliloquies, which had not happened before) and thereby emphasizing that a work of literature could be successful as a play in performance.

As Tsubouchi had rightly feared, Bungei Kyōkai's activities were rather desultory and the *Hamlet* production, in spite of full houses, left the company with large debts to the theatre. A new start was needed and in 1909 Shimamura appealed to Tsubouchi on behalf of the managing committee to help them realise their long-standing plans for a purpose-built drama study centre. Tsubouchi responded by making available a site on the plot of land on which his own house stood and then paying all the building costs. The centre was completed by September that year and consisted of a lecture room, rehearsal room, an office and common rooms.

Thus in 1909 Bungei Kyōkai started a new life as a drama study centre. Initially the student body numbered twenty-two. The fact that they were students is significant. Bungei Kyōkai was now an educational establishment. It had both male and female students and was one of the first such institutions in Japan to be mixed. It drew its male students mainly from the English literature department of Waseda University. The female students were also mainly from institutions of higher education, including the Peers' Women's School. Bungei Kyōkai was now dedicated to the practical fostering of modern drama in Japan and Tsubouchi considered that this aim could best be furthered by using people who had had no regular, active contact with existing theatre. He intended to train amateurs to be the future professional actors of modern drama in Japan.

Classes were held only in the evenings, to allow those still pursuing full-time education and those with employment to continue with these during the day. Three hours of classes were normally given each evening. Overall artistic direction was firmly in the hands of Tsubouchi, who now saw his opportunity to exploit comprehensively the declamatory style of delivery that he had been developing since his own university days. Perhaps influenced by American teachers of English who, following a contemporary fashion for elocution and oratory, had emphasised the reading of texts aloud, Tsubouchi had devoted much of his time, on his own and with students, to experimenting with differing methods of voice projection. By the time of the drama study centre Tsubouchi's *rōdoku*, as it was called, was a declamatory acting style with full body gestures which retained many features of *kabuki* acting technique, notably the sound quality. Through his experience and theoretical conviction Tsubouchi was far superior in *rōdoku* technique to all his students and assistant teachers, and everyone felt obliged to copy Tsubouchi as exactly as he or she could. The style of acting that resulted from this training was soon referred to in a rather unkindly fashion as the 'Bungei Kyōkai mannerism'. Its employment as a basic technical requirement for Bungei Kyōkai students reflected Tsubouchi's continuing determination to preserve elements of an older tradition.

The new Bungei Kyōkai mounted its first full-scale production in May 1911 and its last in June 1913. The organisation split up soon after the last production. In the two years of its active existence it mounted six full-scale and two smaller productions in Tokyo and took four productions on tour to Osaka.

Bungei Kyōkai's first production was of *Hamlet*, a greatly improved repeat of its earlier attempt, with the same Hamlet but all female parts played by actresses and in particular Ophelia played by the woman who is probably the best known actress in Japanese theatre history, Matsui Sumako (1886–1919). (Kano 2001) The play was translated and directed by Tsubouchi. This was followed, in September of the same year (1911), by a studio production of Ibsen's *A Doll's House*, directed by Shimamura and with Nora played by Matsui Sumako. This was accompanied on the same programme by a new dance drama created and directed by Tsubouchi. These two plays then formed the first two parts of the next full-scale programme, whose third part was the trial scene from *The Merchant of Venice*. In May of 1912 the third full-scale production was of Hermann Sudermann's *Die Heimat*, with Matsui Sumako playing Magda, directed by Shimamura. This general pattern continued. Tsubouchi directed his new dance dramas and Shakespeare, whom he valued more highly that the European Naturalists whose works had flooded into Japan after the death of Ibsen in 1906. Shimamura directed Ibsen, Sudermann, Shaw and Meyer-Forster.

Noticeably absent are dialogue-based plays by Japanese playwrights. It is not that Japan had no such plays at the time. Plays on historical subjects were turned out by the month for *kabuki*, and large numbers of plays on contemporary subjects – often adaptations of novels serialised in newspapers – were being produced for the *shimpa* stage. In general these genres were heavily influenced by commercial considerations and most of the new plays written for them have disappeared from view. What was felt to be lacking in the early 1910s were plays that could reflect the kinds of concerns already being explored by Japan's novelists. The Japanese Naturalist novelists had by now investigated and exposed human feelings that would have remained hidden before, and Natsume Sōseki was already probing guilt as an individual rather than a collective phenomenon. Some obviously derivative Naturalist and Symbolist plays had been written by Japanese playwrights, but Shimamura was disinclined to select them for performance in view of the increasing availability of Japanese translations of the very plays that were exciting the West.

Here perhaps is the first of the mis-matches referred to earlier. Foreign plays, in a country with a long playwriting tradition, on subjects that had little general relevance to the Japanese society of the time, were performed by actors and actresses trained in a semi-classical acting style. Intellectuals were ecstatic about the plays they watched Bungei Kyōkai perform, but their cerebral modernity was far ahead of general social thinking and one of the productions provoked the first serious collision between new theatre and the established authorities. The slam of the door behind Nora at the end of *A Doll's House* had reverberated round Tokyo society, stimulating debate among the few intellectual members of the incipient feminist movement but occasioning much condemnation elsewhere. Sudermann's *Die Heimat* caused more serious problems, because in this play the heroine Magda defies her father to the end and the play finishes with the father dying of a stroke brought on by his daughter's behaviour. The censors, who saw playscripts before they were performed, warned that the play would be banned if it did not present a moral system that was appropriate to Japanese society. The guidelines issued to would-be directors by the Tokyo Metropolitan Police Department still began with the requirement that plays should reward virtue and punish vice, and even when permission had been given for a performance, any policeman could close it down on his own initiative. (Rubin 1984: 239) As a result Shimamura was forced to rewrite the final scene and in 1912 Japan Sudermann's defiant heroine was shown in a more dutiful light. (Imai 1971: 110–1)

MATSUI SUMAKO

Matsui Sumako was the actress in the middle of this controversy.

Ophelia, Nora and Magda brought fame to her and most commentators agreed that she had set new standards for acting by women; as one put it: 'she will long be remembered as having solved for the first time Japan's actress problem . . .' (Toita 1963: 845) She had come to Bungei Kyōkai with a fierce determination to succeed and an utter devotion to acting. Her former life had been unhappy and she suggests in her autobiography that the stage offered her the chance to express her pent-up emotions freely. Her acting was indeed passionate and emotionally uninhibited and she worked harder than anyone else at rehearsals. She was a woman in what was still predominantly a man's world and she impinged seriously on the self-assurance of the more experienced male members of Bungei Kyōkai. Shimamura fell in love with her and she with him. Tsubouchi had been a strict guardian of his students' morals and had expelled thirty of them for, in some cases minor, infringements of his puritan rules on male/female socialising; he was more indulgent towards his love-lorn disciple, Shimamura, but the scandal (Shimamura was married with children) grew to such proportions that he could delay no longer. Matsui Sumako was expelled from Bungei Kyōkai in May 1913 and mainly because of this the Society was disbanded two months later.

Bungei Kyōkai is often credited with pioneering *shingeki* in Japan and it may be appropriate here to consider briefly what the word *shingeki* meant at this time. As a word it had been in currency for several decades; it dates back to the drama reform movement and was variously applied to some *kabuki* productions and plays, much of *shimpa* and to some amateur theatre. (Ishizawa 1964: 57) The two characters simply mean 'new' 'drama/theatre' and thus could loosely be used to describe anything even slightly experimental. With Bungei Kyōkai, however, it begins to take on the meaning most commonly ascribed to it in Japanese theatre history. This includes a conscious acknowledgement that modern Western drama in certain fundamental ways – partly to do with realism, but also including respect for the text, artistic cohesion of all aspects of performance, etc – had much to offer Japanese modern theatre. The word *shingeki* was also from this time associated with a rejection of the energetic commercialisation of theatre under the Shōchiku company.

The break-up of Bungei Kyōkai temporarily dissipated the concentration of effort that it had put into developing *shingeki*. Tsubouchi henceforth busied himself with his translation of Shakespeare, not being active again in actual performances until his brief interest in pageants in the early 1920s. The other members of Bungei Kyōkai participated in the founding of three *shingeki* groups, of which one, led by Shimamura Hōgetsu, achieved instant prominence. The other two continued largely the work of Bungei Kyōkai by putting on well-rehearsed productions of Western plays that mostly drew critical approbation but were not financially self-sustaining. Shimamura, however, had a superb actress in his company and he began in the knowledge that Matsui Sumako's notoriety, for her (and his) personal life and the roles she had played, would attract attention to his own enterprise.

GEIJUTSU-ZA AND ITS TWIN-TRACK POLICY

His theatre company was given the name Geijutsu-za (Art Theatre). Its activities were surrounded in controversy in that it made money, and the contemporary anxiety about this shows how quickly the idea of anti-commercialism had taken hold in the *shingeki* world. It seems that Shimamura had been concerned about the financial side of *shingeki* from the start of Bungei Kyōkai and by early 1914 he was convinced that a shake-out of *shingeki* groups was imminent. (Ōzasa 1985: 149) This conflicts with the usual picture of him as languid and out of touch with reality, but he did have a dream of founding a university of the arts and he was well aware of the scale of funds that this would require.

There was considerable bad blood between Matsui Sumako and the leading male actors of the Geijutsu-za in the weeks before its first production, but in the event the company survived these troubles and gained a great success. The plays chosen for this first programme were both by Maurice Maeterlinck: *L'Interieure* and *Monna Vanna*, and it was not lost on some at the time that in Europe Vanna had been played by Maeterlinck's mistress who later supplanted his wife. The ten-day run was completely sold out weeks before the premiere, but in spite of that Geijutsu-za was left with a very large debt. The second production, of plays by Ibsen and Chekhov, attracted minimal audiences and Geijutsu-za came close to collapse.

Then came the production of *Resurrection* and everything changed. Tolstoyan humanism was much in vogue in intellectual circles at the time, in particular being championed by an influential group of writers and artists known as the Shirakaba-ha (White Birch School). Several dramatizations of *Resurrection* had been performed in the Europe and were known about in Japan. Geijutsu-za's *Resurrection* was performed in the Imperial Theatre (Teikoku Gekijō), which in the two years since its construction had become the fashionable theatrical venue for the new middle class, and it included a song. Katusha's song, sung by Matsui Sumako, ensured the commercial success of this production, both in Tokyo and later on tour throughout Japan and abroad (to Taiwan and Manchuria). It is sometimes forgotten that it was a good song, with affecting lyrics by a noted writer (Sōma Gyofū) and a plaintive tune by Nakayama Shinpei (1887–1952), who became famous later for the quality of his popular music. Everyone who saw the show talked about the song and whistled or sang it.

With the success of *Resurrection*, and the corresponding eclipse of the Japanese play by a rapidly maturing playwright (Nakamura Kichizō, 1877–1941) on the same programme, merchandising occurred that was unprecedented in Japanese theatre. The record of the song was Japan's first pop hit; Katusha combs and hair ornaments were bought everywhere. (Ōzasa 1985: 149)

What had happened was that Shimamura's attempt to find money to support his serious projects had run away with him. He soon had the financial resources to construct an arts centre, which was named Geijutsu Kurabu (Arts Club), in 1914. It contained a rehearsal room, a small auditorium for studio productions and accommodation for Shimamura and Matsui Sumako. In the process, however, the character of Geijutsu-za had irrevocably changed. Shimamura did try to convince the outside world of the seriousness of his twin-track approach: popular shows to make money, serious studio productions to push forward the development of *shingeki*, but it was Sumako who made the money and the tensions that developed as she first became the star of Geijutsu-za and then, by all accounts, behaved like one, meant constant friction between the main actor members of the company. Apart from the fact that she was a woman succeeding above her male colleagues, *shingeki* already had a strong *esprit de corps* and instinctively distrusted the exaggerated star system of *kabuki*.

Not that Geijutsu-za did not have critical success with some of its serious productions. In 1916 a production of Tolstoy's *The Power of Darkness* earned unanimous praise from the critics and was described as the most significant *shingeki* production to date. So good was it, commented one, that what came at the audience from the stage was Tolstoy, not Matsui Sumako or Sawada Shōjirō, the lead male actor. (Ōyama 1969: vol 2, 29) In 1917, as part of a programme billed as a 'Production to encourage the Spread of Shingeki,' *Kamisori* (*Razor*) by Nakamura Kichizō attracted similar praise. /fn14/3 (Tanaka 1964: 122)

Perhaps to reconfirm how much Geijutsu-za depended on its two leading personalities, the company collapsed in 1919 once they were no longer there. In the summer of 1918 it had signed a contract with Shōchiku which ensured financial stability for the future but only further exasperated those who resented its previous compromises with commercialism. But in November that year Shimamura fell victim to the influenza pandemic that was sweeping the world and in January of 1919 Matsui Sumako followed him in death by hanging herself.

Bungei Kyōkai and Geijutsu-za both directly, in the ways outlined above, and indirectly laid the foundations for the modern theatre movement in Japan. Almost all those who led or sustained this vigorous movement over the next decades had had some contact with one or both of these groups. Most chose to follow the ethos set by Bungei Kyōkai and continued by Geijutsu-za in its studio productions – to search for a new drama that would satisfy what they thought audiences ought to need rather than what they actually wanted, and this somewhat idealistic anti-commercialism was still much in evidence fifty years later. Secondly, by their judgement that modern Western plays satisfied that need rather than new Japanese drama, they caused *shingeki* to be seen as foreign-dominated theatre where part of the 'fun' of theatre-going was to be instructed about the West. This too was still in evidence in the 1960s.

JIYŪ GEKIJŌ

A different route towards the establishment of a new Japanese drama was taken by Jiyū Gekijō (founded in 1909) and in addition by small, ephemeral groups formed by leading *kabuki* actors. Like the new Bungei Kyōkai, Jiyū Gekijō was also under the direction of two men, Osanai Kaoru (1881–1928) and Ichikawa Sadanji II (1880–1940). Osanai and Sadanji, however, were very different from Tsubouchi and Shimamura, both in background and in their approach to the group that they led. Both were young men – about 30 – when the group was formed, whereas Tsubouchi had been over 50. Osanai had only graduated (from the English Literature Department of the Tokyo Imperial University) three years before. During his time at university he had taken part in many extra-curricular literary activities. He wrote novels and published a poetry magazine together with six friends. In drama he was attracted by Naturalism and after graduation joined the Ibsen Society, among whose members were distinguished Japanese Naturalists such as the novelist Shimazaki Tōson.

Osanai wished to make the theatre his profession, but he was not in Tsubouchi's circle and *shimpa* was the only branch of theatre open to him at the time. Through a connection with another major novelist and playwright, Mori Ōgai, Osanai was invited to work backstage at a *shimpa* company, for which he prepared adaptations of, among other things, a Shimazaki Tōson novel and *Romeo and Juliet*. Osanai soon became disillusioned with *shimpa*, however, and retired to his study. There he devoted himself to literature, in particular to a literary journal intended to introduce Western literature, especially the works of Ibsen to Japan. For the next two years he was prolific in publishing essays and translations that informed literary people of the time and intellectuals in general about the latest developments on the European literary scene. He was attracted strongly by the ideas of Edward Gordon Craig, in superficial ways the very antithesis of the *kabuki* theatrical tradition, and eagerly discussed these with Ichikawa Sadanji II, a *kabuki* actor who had travelled extensively in the West observing theatre in 1907.

Sadanji II was the son of Ichikawa Sadanji I, one of the three great *kabuki* actors who had sustained *kabuki* theatre during the last two decades of the nineteenth century. He did not have natural talent as a classical *kabuki* actor and was derided during his father's lifetime for his lack of ability at dancing. In addition he was to be burdened early with heavy responsibilities. His father had died when he was only in his early twenties and Sadanji II inherited responsibility for his father's *kabuki* company and the Meiji-za theatre, together with enormous accumulated debts. Sadanji soon proved that he could be very successful in the world of *kabuki*, and the production at the Meiji-za at which he took the name of Sadanji II, much to the disgust of the critics, made enough profit for him to be able to undertake an eight-month fact-finding trip to Europe.

Sadanji was a man of great passion and enthusiasm, and there are many testimonies to this. Stimulated by performances in Japan of Western opera, he applied himself enthusiastically to the task of creating a modern Japanese drama. Although a trained *kabuki* actor himself, he was convinced that this new drama could never come from *kabuki* or *shimpa* but rather depended on a thorough absorption of Western ideas and life. To this end he even entertained hopes (frustrated finally) of finding a Western bride on his travels. Maybe he did not have time. His schedule in Europe was packed with visits to the theatre, not to mention several weeks receiving tuition from teachers of voice production and expressive technique in London. (Saeki and Kano1981: 351) His trip confirmed him in his beliefs about Western culture and he returned to Japan determined to put them into practice.

This was a courageous thing to do, for he aroused the hostility of many of his associates. His attempt to use the Meiji-za company of *kabuki* actors to create his new drama resulted in failure, as did a separate enterprise in partnership with Kawakami Otojirō. Finally Sadanji even parted with his friend and mentor the playwright Matsui Shōyō (1870–1933), who had greatly helped him in the running of the Meiji-za and had accompanied him to Europe. The reason for this parting seems to have been Sadanji's decision to join Osanai Kaoru in a completely new venture.

This was the Jiyū Gekijō, which gave its opening performance, of Ibsen's *John Gabriel Borkman*, in November 1909. Jiyū Gekijō was modelled on the English Stage Society, one of a number of theatre clubs in Europe which fostered new drama and had much impressed Sadanji (Osanai had not yet been abroad at this time). Jiyū Gekijō thus generally took its inspiration from the European little theatre movement. Its original promise was of two productions per year and this was fulfilled in 1910, 1911 and 1912. During 1913 and 1914, however, only one production was mounted in each year, and from then until just before the formal break-up of the company in 1919 there were none at all. The active period of Jiyū Gekijō therefore corresponds roughly to that of Bungei Kyōkai. The Western plays chosen for the first three productions echoed the interest that Bungei Kyōkai was showing in Naturalism and realism, being by playwrights such as Ibsen, Wedekind, Chekhov and Gorki. In common with Shimamura's Geijutsu-za, however, Jiyū Gekijō also showed an interest in Maeterlinck and Andreiev, and in the eyes of many young intellectuals this showed that Jiyū Gekijō was more in touch with current literary trends than Bungei Kyōkai.

As men of the theatre, both Sadanji and Osanai were disillusioned with established drama and determined to build a new drama based on Western importations. Both were modernists in wishing to be 'new' Japanese, free from traditional restrictions. The word 'new' (*atarashii*) was much in vogue at the time; plays written by Japanese playwrights aware of literary currents in the West began to be termed 'new plays;' Matsui Sumako, or at least her roles, became the prototype 'new woman'.

Jiyū Gekijō did not have a building which could provide a focus for its activities, as did Bungei Kyōkai. Sadanji was unwilling to let the Meiji-za serve this purpose, as he was well aware of the problems of mixing *kabuki* and *shingeki*. A membership system, on the European model, was planned in order to give a corporate identity to the venture and to provide financial support. Membership was open to anyone over eighteen, and everyone who participated in Jiyū Gekijō's productions, including the actors, had to join. The leaders of the company hoped to maintain membership numbers at 1500, but this target was never reached, and in spite of a succession of full houses Jiyū Gekijō was beset by financial difficulties throughout its existence. During its period of greatest activity the spirit and enthusiasm of its leaders, actors, technicians, its closest advisers (mainly young literati) and its supporters ensured that these difficulties had no serious effect. It was only later when this enthusiasm waned, the leaders in particular taking on other interests, that financial problems were effective in preventing regular activity.

The fundamental difference between Bungei Kyōkai and Jiyū Gekijō came in their approach to their actors. Bungei Kyōkai actors were students, mostly without previous connection with established theatre. Jiyū Gekijō by contrast used the *kabuki* actors belonging to Sadanji's company and this had important consequences for its productions.

It was obvious to these actors that the training they had received and the technique they had acquired were not suitable for productions of plays such as *John Gabriel Borkman*. Their main occupation was still *kabuki* and it was *kabuki* that provided their livelihood. During the third production (of Gorki's *The Lower*

Depths) the actor playing Klestch was appearing in *kabuki* during the same month. This situation meant that not only did the actors have insufficient free time for Jiyū Gekijō rehearsals, but they also had a vested interest in not working hard to acquire a technique that could well interfere with their careers in *kabuki*. Osanai's dictum to his Jiyū Gekijō actors: 'Become amateurs!' seems unreasonable in the circumstances of the time. Osanai's *kabuki* actors had none of the advantages of their modern counterparts, who have demonstrated how versatile a classically trained *kabuki* actor can be. Most of them had had no opportunity of seeing Western acting practice in the flesh and the Western films being shown in Japan would not yet have indicated the range of this type of acting.

In addition to this, the performance of Western plays presented many technical problems to the *kabuki* actors. Naturalist plays required realistic movement and diction. It was, moreover, quite a new experience for Sadanji to have to speak his lines while moving about the stage – lines in *kabuki* are usually delivered from a stationary position – and he frequently 'dried' in mid-speech. Then there was the difficulty of the dialogue itself. It is inevitable that translations into modern Japanese are longer than the originals and Mori Ōgai's version of *John Gabriel Borkman* was no exception to this. Osanai, who directed this first production, singled out the particular problem of long passages which had to be delivered without a pause for breath. (Akiba 1971: vol 2, 155) Furthermore *kabuki* actors were used to extemporising if they could not remember their lines correctly. While this was easy for them in *kabuki* plays, it was almost impossible in an unfamiliar Western play and every line had to be learnt perfectly.

Another consequence of using *kabuki* actors was that *onnagata* played the female parts. *John Gabriel Borkman* begins with a long dialogue between two female characters that takes approximately thirty minutes in English. While Japanese theatregoers at the time would still have been unsurprised at men playing women's parts, actresses had begun to make their mark on Japanese theatre and it was incongruous for a company like Jiyū Gekijō, whose non-acting members prided themselves on their modernity, to continue with single-sex productions. They did so, however, using actresses only when a suitable *onnagata* was unavailable.[4]

For the first two and a half years of Jiyū Gekijō's existence Sadanji was the only actor in the company who had watched theatre in the West. Osanai as a director felt this disadvantage keenly and his solution to this problem may be symptomatic of his general approach to modern Japanese theatre at the time. For *John Gabriel Borkman* he found out as much as he could about actual performances of the play in the West and then tried to reproduce them in his own production. In this case he relied on letters and sketches provided by a friend staying in Vienna, but in 1912 he was himself to travel to Europe and while there he took meticulous notes on every gesture and move he saw in stage productions. While every *kabuki* actor had at his disposal gestures, not all of them extravagant, to express the various emotions, Osanai tried to impose a new set of codes on them.

It was perhaps not surprising that there was little enthusiasm among these actors to pursue the aims of Jiyū Gekijō once the two leaders found other interests. The achievements of Jiyū Gekijō were, however, substantial. While Bungei Kyōkai produced actors and actresses who carried forward the *shingeki* movement for the next two decades, Jiyū Gekijō seems to have inspired playwrights and directors in a more general way. In its first two years of activity Jiyū Gekijō performed five plays by Japanese playwrights to one (and even that was by Tsubouchi himself) performed by Bungei Kyōkai. There was much more intellectual interest in Jiyū Gekijō and mentions of visits to its performances often appear in autobiographical writings. The inadequacies of the acting – if indeed it was perceived as such by spectators only accustomed to *kabuki* and its derivatives – could not detract from the satisfaction of learning about Western drama by seeing it on the stage and watching new Japanese playwriting develop.

It was the former – the chance of a first acquaintance with Western plays – that dominated intellectual horizons in the 1910s and it was probably this that encouraged the dichotomy of repertory that is a feature of this period. Some groups, most of whose actors were unknown in the theatrical world, concentrated on Western drama. Others, usually led by well-known *kabuki* or *shimpa* actors, chose more plays by contemporary Japanese playwrights. This was probably reasonable in the circumstances. The former could be sure of audiences of intellectuals drawn by the plays, and the surge of theatrical activity in the West in the decades around the turn of the century meant that there was a wealth of plays to choose from. In addition the pressures of Japan's translation culture, which emphasised speed of publication, were adding to the number of available plays by the day. On the other hand, groups led by known theatrical personalities could attract audiences with the names of the leading actors and, if they wished to perform a new play, were more likely to choose one that was at least set in a Japanese environment. The consequences were that the new actors were learning on plays that seemed to have only remote relevance to Japan, and the new playwrights were writing plays reflecting the changing Japanese society around them which were performed by classically trained actors more used to playing medieval heroes or eighteenth-century commoners.

ENTERTAINMENT AT TOKYO'S PREMIER LARGE THEATRES

If intellectuals were talking and writing about Bungei Kyōkai, Geijutsu-za and Jiyū Gekijō, it is clear from the annual reports on theatre in the main theatre magazine of the day that most theatregoers in the early 1910s were drawn towards the high-profile productions at the Kabuki-za and the Imperial Theatre . There was some overlap, as the Imperial Theatre was the venue for Bungei Kyōkai's *Hamlet* in 1911 and Geijutsu-za *Resurrection* in 1914, but in such cases the runs were usually of only a few days, the theatre being rented out for short periods when its main activities allowed.

TEIKOKU GEKIJŌ (IMPERIAL THEATRE)

The opening of the Imperial Theatre in 1911 had finally realised the dream of the drama reformers of the 1880s to provide Tokyo with a large Western-style theatre. On a smaller scale the Yūraku-za, built in 1908, had pioneered Western-type theatregoing and was throughout this period an important venue for *shingeki* productions; the Imperial Theatre was its counterpart in the world of high-spending commercial theatre and its sheer magnificence captured the imagination of the media and the public. It symbolized the middle-class cultural attitudes and life-styles that were developing in the 1910s and took its place in people's minds alongside new private housing estates and department stores. '*Kyō wa* Teigeki, *asu wa* Mitsukoshi' ('Today the Imperial Theatre, tomorrow the Mitsukoshi Department Store') was the catch-phrase of these years.

In its architectural design, both outside and inside, the Imperial Theatre was entirely Western: the exterior was in what was described as a French Renaissance style, and the interior was as ornate as any large nineteenth-century European theatre. The proscenium arch was a baroque extravaganza of moulded and painted plasterwork, featuring a flock of alabaster doves suspended from the ceiling on one side. Perhaps reflecting the social mood of the general theatregoing public more accurately than Bungei Kyōkai, the Imperial Theatre trained its own company of actresses, but it did not cast them in plays such as *A Doll's House* or *Die Heimat*. Much of the Imperial Theatre programming was of *kabuki* classics, using its own *kabuki* actors often aided by guest appearances of famous actors from other companies. Sometimes it mixed actors and actresses in these productions and as such may claim a pioneering role in trying to integrate male and female acting in *kabuki*.

Perhaps of equal importance to its significance in modern Japanese theatre was the Imperial Theatre's fostering of the other staples of European middle-class and aristocratic entertainment, opera and ballet. For a while the Imperial Theatre had its own opera company, under the leadership of an Italian named Giovanni Vittorio Rosi (1867–?). Curiously opera was not popular as genteel entertainment and Rosi went off to the entertainment district of Asakusa, where the extraordinary phenomenon of 'Asakusa opera' brought the most famous classical operas to ordinary people and errand boys were whistling arias on their bicycles as they made their deliveries. The Imperial Theatre also invited foreign theatre, opera and ballet companies. Anna Pavlova danced there in 1922 and greatly stimulated moves to reform *kabuki* dance. Adding to all this its concerts of European classical music and showings of the latest American films, the Imperial Theatre provided a cosmopolitan cultural atmosphere that could not be found elsewhere in Tokyo.

This was probably due partly to the management style of the Imperial Theatre. For the first time in Japanese theatre history, management was in the hands of a team that came primarily from the world of business. The whole enterprise was organised and administered along business lines. Actors and actresses had seventeen-month guaranteed contracts – unknown in theatre up to this time – thus making it an attractive place to work. The various backstage and front-of-house positions of responsibility were given new names and their duties rationalised. (Toita 1956: 1368)

KABUKI-ZA

In popular perception the Imperial Theatre's main rival was the Kabuki-za, which since the deaths of the three leading *kabuki* actors in 1903–4 had been struggling to re-establish *kabuki* as Japan's main theatre genre. By a quirk of fate the actors thought of as the natural successors to the deceased Danjūrō, Kikugorō and Sadanji had all been young and it had taken them a few years to secure their credibility with their traditional fans. By the 1910s they had largely been successful and *kabuki*, principally at the Kabuki-za and the Ichimura-za, entered a period of stability which seems to have allowed many of its actors to think beyond performances of the classical repertory.

Their very successes in the classical favourites confirmed *kabuki* as a tradition worth keeping and as a good investment. Shōchiku, which already owned the Imperial Theatre, gained control of the Kabuki-za in 1913. At the Kabuki-za Utaemon V (1865–1940) and Uzaemon XV (1874–1945) had large followings. Utaemon, an extraordinarily graceful *onnagata*, was regarded as the senior actor in *kabuki* from this time. The Ichimura-za had two superb actors in Kikugorō VI (1885–1949) and Kichiemon II (1886–1954) and its manager was so successful in exploiting their talents that the mid-1910s were referred to as the Kiku-Kichi Epoch. From 1912 Shōchiku was also able to benefit from the work of Sadanji II, as he signed a contract with them in that year. This was also significant for the vitality of *kabuki* in this decade. Sadanji had attracted the attention of Ōtani Takejirō, one of the two brothers who owned Shōchiku, and for the rest of his career he enjoyed an enviable patronage. This not only meant the opportunity, which because of his limited classical talents he might not have had, to appear with such consummate artists as Utaemon and Uzaemon, but also an assurance that his drive to be a progressive force in *kabuki* would be supported. Ōtani teamed Sadanji up with a playwright named Okamoto Kidō (1872–1939) and between them they mounted some highly successful productions of new plays. Independently and in competition with all these heavyweights Kan'ya XIII (1885–1932), a skilled actor of romantic parts, drew attention with his productions of classical and new plays. Yet another *kabuki* actor to have an impact on the period, in this case primarily with his new dance movement, was Ichikawa Ennosuke II (1888–1963) and a number of his productions of new plays are also remembered.

NEW PLAYWRITING FOR *KABUKI*

Reports of performances of classical *kabuki* did not differ markedly during this decade from what had gone before. Each actor had his own special strengths, and most of them had at least one spectacular success during the period. What distinguishes the leading actors of the Taishō period from their predecessors was the proportion of them actively willing to push forward their art by performing original plays written by playwrights with varied literary and dramatic outlooks. Perhaps Jiyū Gekijō had encouraged *kabuki* actors to have confidence that their acting technique was sufficiently flexible to encompass plays that might well be informed by a modern consciousness. Whatever the motivation behind the Taishō experiments, Japanese playwriting has reason to thank these progressive actors from the *kabuki* world. The plays they fostered are known a *shin-kabuki* (new *kabuki*), a general term for works written for *kabuki* actors in the modern period.

Singular successes by *kabuki* actors in new plays mark the beginning and the end of the decade of the 1910s. The first of the two plays in question had been written by a playwright with a particular actor in mind for the lead part and the second was the work of a member of a literary group and published in the group's journal. They thus illustrate the two main strands of playwriting in the Taishō period: that written for a specific actor and often commissioned and that written by a literary person with an interest in expressing himself creatively through the medium of theatre.

Okamoto Kidō's *Shuzenji Monogatari* (*The Tale of the Shuzen Temple*) was given its premiere by Sadanji in 1911 and soon became an established favourite with *kabuki* audiences. Okamoto had been on the fringes of the theatre world, writing and publishing plays as a hobby when his work as a journalist allowed. From 1908 he began writing specifically for Sadanji and several of his plays were performed by Sadanji's company over the next few years. With the very successful production of *Shuzenji Monogatari* in 1911 the relationship between *kabuki* actor and playwright was cemented and Okamoto Kidō saw many of his plays performed by Sadanji over the next two decades.

To someone unfamiliar with *kabuki* watching *Shuzenji Monogatari* today (and there are many opportunities to do this) the difference between this play and classical *kabuki* may appear slight, but in 1911 its success may have depended on Sadanji's audiences being prepared for something new. Its traditional features include a heavy dependence on situation, a histrionic focus on the actor playing the lead part and a tolerance in performance of extreme variations in tempo. Unlike classical *kabuki*, however, its dialogue is delivered without background music (although in other plays Okamoto, in common with many new writers for *kabuki*, indicated background sound effects wherever possible), and the concentration on the dialogue that this allowed the audience would have emphasised the changing ideas of interpersonal relations that were now being expressed on the stage.

Shuzenji Monogatari concerns a carver of wooden masks named Yashaō (played by Sadanji) who has been commissioned by the shogun Yoriie (1182–1204) to carve a mask in his likeness. Whatever mask emerges from his work, however, has a cast of death about it. Yashaō has two daughters and the elder of these chafes at the thought of being a craftsman's wife. When the shogun appears to claim his overdue mask, she gets her chance, as he falls in love with her. Yashaō's instinctive fear concerning the mask is proved right when the shogun is indeed killed by his enemies – but so is Yashaō's daughter, because she has tried to protect her new lover by wearing the mask. The audience's acceptance of the tender way in which Yoriie addresses someone who will after all just become another of his women has been cited as a significant achievement in the depiction of emotion on the *kabuki* stage. (Ōyama 1969: vol. 1, 62)

At the other end of the decade Kikuchi Kan's *Chichi Kaeru* (*Father Returns*), given its premiere in 1920, similarly established itself as a modern classic after a rapturous reception by its audiences. After graduating from university in 1916, Kikuchi (1888–1948) took time to establish himself as a short-story writer and playwright while working as a journalist, but in the 1920s he was one of the most powerful figures in the literary establishment. It was due to him that Japan's two most prestigious literary prizes were instituted. Kikuchi was active in the literary world as soon as he left university, helping to republish a temporarily defunct literary journal, *Shinshichō* (*New Tide in Thought*) with some of his school contemporaries. It was in this journal that Kikuchi published *Chichi Kaeru* in 1917, one of several plays and short stories of his that appeared in its pages. *Kabuki* actors like Ennosuke II, who were eager to perform new plays, kept themselves informed of what was being published in theatrical and literary journals and Ennosuke chose *Chichi Kaeru* to be on the first programme of a new experimental group that he had founded.

The father who returns in *Chichi Kaeru* has been away for twenty years after abandoning his wife and young family to run away with his girlfriend. The elder son, on whose shoulders the responsibility for supporting the family has fallen most heavily, cannot accept his father, now a broken man, back into the home. The conflict between his reasonable resentment and the fundamental love that the others still feel for the father is an intense one and finally, after the father has been sent away, the elder son relents and sends after him.

This was a play without great subtlety but treating a problem that everyone in the audience could understand. It was real enough for it to become a frequent choice for amateur drama groups after the Pacific War, but it did not strain credulity when ranged alongside plays from the classical repertory in a *kabuki* programme. For Ennosuke it was an experiment and it was played after a wordy play by the novelist Tanizaki Jun'ichirō (1886–1965), also a considerable dramatist, concerning Buddhist statues made in the likeness of lovers of certain of the characters.[5] In contrast with Tanizaki's play, *Chichi Kaeru* was stark in its portrayal of emotions. Nothing happened in it as startling as the cutting down of two characters in Tanizaki's play, but it did not need action to achieve its effect.

Both *Shuzenji Monogatari* and *Chichi Kaeru* have been judged artistic as well as commercial successes by theatre historians. Both have had more impact on Japanese theatre history in the modern period than any other plays of the time and both were introduced to the theatregoing public by *kabuki* actors.

The list of new playwrights supported and encouraged by these experimental *kabuki* groups is impressive. They span all the main literary groupings at a time of intense interest among writers in the possibilities offered by new types of writing introduced from the West. Kikugorō with his group gave opportunities to two young symbolist poets who were both active as playwrights thereafter. Ennosuke initially tended towards Naturalist drama with his group, performing an acclaimed *Wild Duck* in 1913 and introducing the work of Nagata Hideo (1885–1949). The playwright often bracketed with Nagata, Nakamura Kichizō, also at this time a Naturalist, had been introduced by Geijutsu-za but was also taken up by Kan'ya's company. Kan'ya was the most energetic in championing drama by new playwrights and his list includes, apart from Nakamura, Kikuchi Kan, the Tolstoyan humanist Mushanokōji Saneatsu (1885–1976), Yamamoto Yūzō (1887–1974) and Ikeda Daigo (1885–1942). Ennosuke added Kurata Hyakuzō (1891–1943), whose most famous play is driven by his strongly held Buddhist beliefs, in addition to Osanai Kaoru himself, who included playwriting among his many theatrical activities, and Kume Masao (1891–1952). Sadanji's company too had a varied repertory of contemporary plays.

It is difficult to imagine what it was like to be an aspiring playwright in Taishō Japan at a time when translations of the latest Western plays were easily available and most intellectuals so inclined could have either first-hand or at least vicarious experience of Western theatre. It might be extreme to suggest that their feelings could have been similar to ones Ibsen himself might have had if there had only been opera singers available to perform his social dramas (even conventional actors had some problems with his plays), but their sense of insecurity must have been acute. While a novelist could use the printed word to mediate his view of the new age directly, the playwright's creative works, if they were to be performed (and many were written only to be read), depended on actors who had neither the technique nor a family or social environment conducive to a modern outlook. In the 1920s some of these playwrights were to complain of the restrictions under which they had tried to work creatively.

Naturalism in the Japanese novel was by this time rapidly developing into the author-centred narratives known as *shi-shōetsu* (autobiographical novel). Building on the moves towards realism in fiction during the last two decades of the nineteenth century, the major novelists had not found it impossible to reproduce the descriptive objectivity professed by the European Naturalists, but their narratives increasingly became focused on the subjects that they felt most confident about describing with scientific detail – their own lives and emotions. While there are some notable plays in modern Japanese drama which are closely based on personal experience, in general the mediation of the actor seemed to close off the option of detailed personal exposure to the playwrights of the 1910s.

Nakamura Kichizō wrote a trio of plays that were popular during this period. All were first introduced by Geijutsu-za but later also performed by *kabuki* actors. Geijutsu-za, known at the time mainly for its high-profile productions of European plays, found that Nakamura's plays were better received on tour to the provinces, thus perhaps confirming the metropolitan dominance of cultural development based on imports. *Kamisori* (*The Razor*, 1914) stresses the wide difference in life opportunities that can be caused by differences in the material circumstances of the home even in the supposedly meritocratic new Japanese society. Frustration at this, aggravated by personal animosity, causes the leading character, a barber, to murder (with his razor) his undeservedly more successful school friend. Nagata Hideo's *Kikatsu* (*Starvation*, 1915) was performed first by *shimpa* actors in 1916 and then by Kikugorō in 1921. Said to represent the pinnacle of Nagata's achievement as a Naturalist, it depicts in merciless detail the agonies of a severely disabled war veteran who has to come to terms with the fact that his ailing younger brother, too sick to go to fight, has the affections of the girl he intended for himself.

Naturalism had many opponents in Japanese literary circles. That it could flourish in drama when its opponents were challenging it effectively in the novel may be due to the more complicated problems of establishing realism in the theatre. However the Naturalist tendency to emphasise the dark side of human nature did not go unchallenged in the theatre. Mushanokōji Saneatsu led the Shirakaba group of idealistic novelists and playwrights, who rejected the determinism of the Naturalist writers, and in many of their novels and plays some scope is left for their heroes' self-improvement. This is not to say that optimism and hope pervade the Shirakaba plays that have been seen as important to Taishō theatre, but somewhere there will be an intimation that life can be made to be better. One of Mushanokōji's plays, *Ningen Banzai* (*Three Cheers for Man*, written in 1922 and first performed – by Kan'ya's Bungei-za – in 1925) was an unalloyed paean to man from a self-satisfied God, but in earlier plays that attracted attention, such as *Sono Imōto* (*His Younger Sister*, published 1915 and premiered in 1919), some characters have to suffer in order for human goodness and potentiality to be glimpsed. *Shukke to sono Deshi* (*The Priest and his Disciple*, premiered by a *shingeki* group in 1919) by another Shirakaba writer, Kurata Hyakuzō, was a publishing and theatrical sensation with its deeply reverent portrayal of the thirteenth-century Buddhist leader Shinran's lifelong search for the right way in Buddhism and the almost Christian quality of forgiveness that is part of this.

It is difficult to know what to make of this explosion of playwriting energy in the 1910s. For all the plays that reached the stage there were many more than never did and were never intended to. The short story writer Akutagawa Ryūnosuke (1892–1927) wrote a number of plays but none of them were staged. There were ample opportunities to publish plays during this time, as it seemed quite within the means of small groups of writers to publish their own coterie magazines. Plays were often carried in the many such literary magazines that came into being during these years. All the individual plays mentioned here are said to have had some influence on the course that playwriting took in this early stage, but the reasons why they achieved prominence were varied and, unlike appraisals of performances of classical *kabuki*, not based on an accumulation of evolving theatrical experience. But these were undoubtedly exciting times for both spectators and writers, with perhaps more choices for both than would be available again for several decades.

SHIMPA IN THE 1910S

If *shingeki* and *kabuki* have been emphasised here, this is because *shimpa* was somewhat in decline during the first half of the 1910s. The actors that had become stars were still acting regularly, but their productions seem to have been lacklustre in general. Commentators had complained that their productions were too predictable and the acting of the stars too prone to rely on the gestures that had become their trademarks. While this would hardly have been a criticism when applied to *kabuki* actors, the expectations that people placed in *shimpa* reflected more their vision of it as a new drama than the reality of a genre greatly beholden to *kabuki* for much of its style. No greater insult could have been levelled at Geijutsu-za's *Resurrection* than that the popularisation of Tolstoy's novel had brought *shingeki* down to the level of *shimpa*. (Ōyama 1969-73: vol. 2, 26)

It is possible that the new medium of film was distracting *shimpa* actors from what had been their main task, the creation of an alternative theatrical art. *Shimpa* actors were involved in a film version of *Resurrection* only a few months after Geijutsu-za's success with it. Whereas the actress Matsui Sumako had been a sensation in the part of Katusha and some observers credited her with having established the acceptability of actresses for female parts, the film version cast a *shimpa onnagata* in the part. Both *kabuki* and *shimpa* actors were used for early Japanese films, but *shimpa* actors seemed to have been particularly successful owing perhaps to the concession to realism that they professedly made.

Films were a special attraction to Inoue Masao (1881–1950), a rising star of *shimpa* in the later 1900s. Perhaps dissatisfied with what he could achieve in *shimpa* proper (and he had done some experimental work in the early 1910s), Inoue helped bring about the boom in *rensageki* ('linked drama') in 1915. *Rensageki* was a hybrid entertainment form that linked film and live theatre. Films in Japan were never silent, as a *benshi* (commentator) would always offer his version of the story enfolding on the silent screen. While a specific film grammar was already being developed in the United States by this time, in Japan much film-making was still seen as providing a vehicle for stage actors. The audiences' expectation of a narrated accompaniment to films and this close link between films and the theatre seem to have encouraged a crude form of dubbing, with the actors standing behind or beside the screen speaking dialogue appropriate to the film being shown. A variation of this was the *rensageki*, where outside scenes, obviously unrealistic when played before stage scenery, were shown in film form, and interior scenes were played as live theatre. The actors were the same in both media, playing the live scenes in the normal way and filling in the dialogue when, at the signal of a whistle, the screen was lowered for a filmed scene.

Rensageki had already been produced for about a decade in the Asakusa entertainment area of Tokyo before Inoue began participating in them. If *Resurrection* had degraded *shingeki* to the level of *shimpa*, for a known *shimpa* actor to play in *rensageki* was degrading *shimpa* to street entertainment, as this is how *rensageki* was regarded by the acting profession because of its use of locations for the filmed sequences. Inoue was not deterred, however, even when his regular playwright resigned in protest, and *rensageki* continued to draw large audiences until it was banned in the Tokyo area as a fire risk in 1916.

Worried by frequent slighting references to *shimpa* in newspapers and magazines and under some financial pressure because of *rensageki*, the leading *shimpa* actors made a concerted effort to revive their art, and they were largely successful during the last few years of the decade. By means of a judicious mixture of the old and the new, with a measure of experimentation plus the financial security offered by Shōchiku, *shimpa* actors, if not the genre itself, created a specific identity for themselves that was recognised by the general theatre-going public.

There are some parallels between *kabuki* and *shimpa* at this time. Just as *kabuki* actors were appearing in established *kabuki* classics and sometimes including new *kabuki* plays in their programmes, by now a number of *shimpa* plays had become known as classics and these were mixed with new plays in *shimpa* programmes. Just as *kabuki* actors were actively fostering new Japanese drama by encouraging emerging playwrights, so *shimpa* actors, albeit on a smaller scale, were doing the same thing. *Kabuki* actors had prefixed the various names for these experimental productions with the word for 'new' and *shimpa* did the same. Shōchiku had teamed Sadanji up with the playwright Okamoto Kidō, thereby giving an opportunity to a new playwright to grow artistically and at the same time effectively enforcing his subordination to one actor in the time-honoured way. Both profited from the arrangement. In *shimpa*'s case too Shōchiku found a playwright who wrote for the genre and had to keep the very small number of stars in mind as he wrote.

Trading on their respective large followings and the propensity of their fans towards sentimentally expressed relations between men and women, Ii Yōhō (1871–1932) and the *shimpa onnagata* Kawai Takeo (1877–1942) started a series of 'husband and wife' dramas in which they always played the main roles. Old scripts of successful previous productions were sought out and the key scenes were rewritten to give at least an appearance of freshness. In this *shimpa* was relying on the familiarity of the subject matter appealing to its audiences and this seems to have been well calculated. A survey in the leading theatre journal of the time showed that *shimpa* audiences preferred stories that they already knew. (Ōzasa 1985: 556) All this was not much different from what had been happening in *shimpa* earlier in the decade, but the sense of crisis in 1915 and early 1916 seems to have given an edge to the performances and *shimpa* began to revive.

The experiments in which *shimpa* actors also participated at this time may have been intended to send a signal to potential audiences that theirs was still a vital art. In late 1915 a hybrid company came into being which mounted productions of Japanese plays using *shimpa* and *shingeki* actors together and another formed in late 1916. (Tanaka 1964: 158) Neither of these enterprises was of long duration and they are not more than a footnote to Taishō theatre history, but they demonstrated a determination to redefine the 'newness' of *shimpa*. In 1919 *shimpa* joined Geijutsu-za in a joint programme, performing an Anatole France play as part of its contribution. There was a *shimpa The Taming of the Shrew* in the same year at the prestigious Kabuki-za. In the early 1920s the Shingeki-za, in fact a *shimpa* company, introduced its fans to a variety of new Japanese plays by young playwrights.

It was, however, the regular programmes of recognizably *shimpa* fare that would determine whether the genre survived or not and during this period *shimpa* was dominated by one playwright, Mayama Seika (1878–1948), who is often given the credit for reestablishing *shimpa* as a serious force in Japanese theatre. Early showing great promise as a writer of Naturalist novels and plays, Mayama found himself without outlets for his work in the early 1910s because he had provoked the publishing world into boycotting him. Even so, for someone who had been recognised as having a future in the literary establishment to stoop (as that literary establishment saw it) to writing plays for *shimpa* could not have been an easy decision. Mayama was a man of extreme moods, and from his writings on the events of these years it is hard to gauge what his motives were, but he joined Shōchiku as a *shimpa* playwright at the beginning of 1914.

The position of the resident playwright (*zatsuki-sakusha*) had not changed greatly since the eighteenth century. Such playwrights drew salaries from the theatre in which they worked and were required to write plays for the specific actors who normally appeared there. There were many other jobs round the theatre for them to do – such as prompting – and even in the 1910s, by which time playwriting was being discussed at large as an accepted cultural activity, the resident playwright's position in the theatre hierarchy was not high. This was particularly the case at the start of a playwright's career. Playwriting, like acting and many other functions in the theatre, was traditionally learnt by spending most of one's waking hours in the theatre observing its various practices. This would include watching rehearsals, acquiring some idea about what was and what was not possible in the way of scene changes or lighting, being with the master playwright while he was composing and giving what help he required. He would be at the master playwright's side when the actors demanded instant rewriting of passages that did not suit them.

Many of the playwrights discussed in this chapter would have escaped these potentially degrading experiences. A distinction, though a blurred one, can be made between those playwrights who hoped for favour from actors in writing plays and those who looked to critical approval from their peers or simply wrote plays because they felt the need to. Most playwrights associated with one or other of the literary groupings of the time would have come into the latter category and Mayama was one of them. With his background, and having as he did the patronage of Ōtani Takejirō, he might have started writing scripts for *shimpa* straightaway. In the event he insisted on learning the craft of *shimpa* playwriting in the same way as the other resident playwrights. Humility was not a noticeable part of his character, as actors later discovered when they tried to persuade him to rewrite lines they did not like, but he was convinced that learning the techniques from the bottom up was the best approach.

Thus much playwriting in Taishō Japan was very particularistic. The playwrights likely to succeed would suit their plays to all the particular circumstances in which they were operating. This had implications for the life expectancy of such plays and many have disappeared without trace – literally so, in that copies of the scripts cannot now be found. Mayama Seika's unusual background meant that many of his are preserved, although performances of his *shimpa* plays are nowadays quite rare. Apparently he learnt his craft well. A leading actor paid tribute to the way his many days spent observing actors from the wings resulted in plays that took account of all their strengths, weaknesses and idiosyncracies.

At the beginning of 1917 *shimpa* began what has been called the 'era of the three leaders'. This referred to the three most prominent *shimpa* actors of the time: Ii Yōhō, Kawai Takeo and Kitamura Rokurō (1871-1961). It had been Kitamura who had first persuaded Mayama to become a *shimpa* playwright. It is probable that of the playwrights writing for *shimpa* at the time only Mayama Seika had the power to bring these three actors together. (Ōzasa 1985: 557) The first programme of this new combination of actors included an adaptation by Mayama of an Ozaki Kōyō story and later programme lists show how energetically he was writing for *shimpa* during these years. It is not an exaggeration to say that he dominated *shimpa* for nearly a decade. His output included a celebrated production of *Kanaya Koume* towards the end of 1917, which was regarded as Kawai Takeo's greatest success of his career up to that time. Koume is a wilful *geisha* who becomes involved in a number of situations with which she cannot cope. The part demanded a versatile *onnagata* and Kawai proved to his fans that he was equal to the task. Mayama's plays did not please everyone by any means, but when Shōchiku appeared to listen to his detractors and brought other playwrights to the fore, audiences declined markedly. (Ōzasa 1985: 582)

SHINKOKUGEKI

No account of Japanese theatre in the 1910s would be complete without mention of another genre for which Mayama Seika would later write. This was Shinkokugeki (New National Theatre). Strictly this is the name of a company, but what it performed was distinctive enough from all other theatre of the time to be accorded the honour of being referred to as a separate genre. Only the Shinkokugeki company ever performed *shinkokugeki*.[6]

Shinkokugeki was founded by Sawada Shōjirō (1892–1929), who is usually referred to by the affectionate sobriquet Sawashō, formed by combining the first character of each of his names. He is a colourful personality in Japanese theatre history and his career illustrates some of the problems facing young actors in the 1910s. Brought up in Tokyo, Sawada's first ambition was to join the army, but his shortsightedness prevented that. He also failed to get into the prestigious First Higher School, which would have led on to Tokyo Imperial University and membership of Tokyo's intellectual élite. Instead Sawada spent his time at the local theatre and in due course wrote a play, on which he asked Osanai Kaoru's advice. Through this connection with Osanai Sawada went to see Osanai's production of *John Gabriel Borkman* performed by Jiyū Gekijō in 1909. He now had a new ambition – to go onto the stage – and he was accepted into the English Literature Department of Waseda University. Through his Waseda connections Sawada became a student member of Bungei Kyōkai and embarked on his acting career there. (Akiba 1971: vol. 2, 4378)

Sawada was part of the second entry to Bungei Kyōkai and there seems to have been some animosity between the first year's entry and his. The first generation contained a number of actors with some experience in Bungei Kyōkai in its earlier form and they were naturally given the best parts. Matsui Sumako had come into the later Bungei Kyōkai with them, so that she had seniority of entry over Sawada, but could not claim seniority of experience. Sawada seems to have chafed at the hierarchy that was built into the organisation. Such a hierarchy would have been quite normal at the time, but perhaps Sawada expected something different from a group dedicated to the creation of a modern Japanese theatre. The well-known story of the spear-carrying Sawada wondering how things would be if he stuck his spear into the behind of the leading actor during a performance of *The Merchant of Venice* illustrates his frustration. Not only that, but he was intensely irritated by Matsui Sumako and some accounts of Bungei Kyōkai suggest it was divided into two camps, the first generation headed by Matsui Sumako and the second centred on Sawada.

After Tsubouchi Shōyō disbanded Bungei Kyōkai in 1913, Sawada and some of his contemporaries in Bungei Kyōkai joined Geijutsu-za. He became the leading male actor in the company and found himself playing opposite Matsui Sumako in almost every production. There were frequent clashes between them. Matsui Sumako is reported by many commentators to have acted in high handed way at rehearsal. It was clear from the reviews of the productions that she was the draw for the full houses that Geijutsu-za enjoyed and she was apparently not averse to reminding her fellow actors of this. Sawada also had serious doubts about the two-track policy of Geijutsu-za. He voiced his disapproval of the sentimental vulgarisation of *Resurrection*, classing it below a *shimpa* melodramatic tragedy. (Shinkokugeki 1967: 13) Sawada, together with a group of like-minded actors, a young playwright Akita Ujaku (1883–1962) and others from the literary advisers group withdrew from Geijutsu-za. It was common for theatre companies, even quite small ones, to have a number of literary advisers and this withdrawal was taken as a sign that Geijutsu-za's policy on programme schedules had deeply divided the company.

For two years Sawada took part in productions of serious plays by several different groups, but even this activity was not without its problems. A touring production to Hokkaido failed to draw good audiences and the financial sponsor insisted that *Resurrection* be performed instead of the scheduled programme of two new Japanese plays and two translated plays (*The Merchant of Venice* and Leopold Lewis' *The Bells*). However much Sawada and Akita protested that they had left Geijutsu-za precisely because of *Resurrection*, they had no alternative but to alter the programme.

Sawada organized his own company in the spring of 1917. Their first production of new Japanese plays, including one by Okamoto Kidō, was commercially a disaster, and this was compounded by a subsequent failure in Kyoto. Sawada and his company, now only eight people in all, repaired to Osaka, where with Shōchiku's help they gradually built up a following. What they were performing was a far cry from what Sawada had hoped for when he joined Bungei Kyōkai, but at least the company was acting to full houses. Sawada introduced realistic sword fights into the historical plays written for the company and these were wildly popular. *Kabuki* swordfighting was very formalised and incapable of generating much excitement. Sawada by contrast used real swords, and the actors (and of course the audiences) knew that there was a real risk of bad injury. By the middle of 1918 the Shinkokugeki company numbered about one hundred and twenty people and fans fought to get seats at its performances.

This was not without cost. Not everyone was happy with the apparent vulgarisation of the group. Its resident playwright left and returned to Tokyo. Sawada's budding reputation as a tragic actor in *shingeki* had not been forgotten by the press and he was the target for considerable criticism. In another characteristic gesture he is said to have assembled his now large company, cut out from a well-known newspaper advertisement the two Chinese characters for 'perseverance' and swallowed the cutting in front of everyone. (Ōzasa 1985: 234)

In July 1920 Sawada's perseverance bore fruit. Such was his drawing power now that he was able to persuade Shōchiku (in Osaka this meant Ōtani's brother, Shirai Matsujirō) to allow him to perform just one play per day. This was highly symbolic. One way to signal that a performance was to be of a serious play was to advertise that there would be a single programme. Small-scale popular theatre had always emphasised to its audiences that it was giving them great variety by performing multiple-play programmes that changed daily. Sawada had himself been mounting such programmes, but as a first step back to what he regarded as his true profession he could now concentrate on a single production.

The play was *Ii Tairō no Shi* (*The Death of Ii the Regent*) and it had been written by Nakamura Kichizō. After his success with *Kamisori* and other social dramas Nakamura had turned to plays of recent history, as the 'death' of the title had taken place in 1860. Nakamura brought his earlier Naturalist interest in detailed and analytical description to bear on historical events that had entered the realms of folklore. The regent Ii Naosuke had been the government official most responsible for opening Japan to the West, but, clever and intelligent politician though he was, he had not managed to avoid the implacable enmity of opponents of his policies. Hence his assassination at one of the gates to the shogun's palace on a snowy morning, a scene waiting to be dramatised. Nakamura combined the natural theatricality offered by the events themselves with a long exposition of the unfolding historical situation in a work that made few concessions to the conventions of the theatre genre – *kabuki*– that would be most likely to perform it. It was a play that could stand on its own as literature.

Sadanji was scheduled to perform this play in June 1920, but objections from the family of one of the leading characters caused

Ōtani to cancel the performance. This provoked an outcry in the newspapers and the play was rescheduled for July and duly performed. Sawada grasped the opportunity to mount a rival performance of so controversial a play and Osaka had its own production, by Shinkokugeki, of *Ii Tairō no Shi* in the same month.

The importance of this play to Shinkokugeki was not only its worth as a piece of dramatic literature, but also in the role Sawada saw for it in his future policy for his company. *Ii Tairō no Shi* was the beginning of Sawada's 'half-a-step-forward theatre' (*engekihanposhugi*). Sawada's own manifesto for this was as follows:

> Theatre's focus is its audience – the people of its time – and there can be no ideal of theatre that ignores the audience. However, pandering to the every whim of the people means there will never be any progress in the theatre and the people will never progress either. So, all you in the theatre! Always extend a kindly hand to the people, but always advance with one foot half a step ahead of the people. It must be half a step. If you advance by a full step, yours and the people's hands will part. You cannot hope for progress if you forget to advance half a step at a time. Half a step, half a step. One pace following the tastes of the people, making possible one pace towards better art. (Akiba 1971: vol 2, 443)

Sawada's frequent references to 'the people' reflect the interest shown during the 1910s in the theory of popular arts, greatly discussed among intellectuals who knew of the educational work of the Swedish feminist and social philosopher Ellen Key. The whole tone of the passage reflects the reality of Japanese theatre as Sawada, by dint of hard experience, saw it at the time. In a theatre culture so conditioned by *kabuki*, the popular theatre could still only imitate *kabuki*, and as *kabuki* depended so much on a high level of technique only acquired through years of training and a *kabuki* environment, popular drama without this could become repetitive and lacking in depth. *Shingeki* had tried to go too fast and had never attracted enough spectators to be viable commercially. *Shimpa*, though it was now changing, had courted popularity first. Sawada was trying to suggest that a middle way could be found.

FREEDOM OF EXPRESSION IN THE THEATRE

Ii Tairō no Shi was also one of many examples of management interference in play productions. The 1910s were a very uneasy period in the matter of relations between the establishment and the arts. The High Treason Incident of 1910, in which a group of anarchists was alleged to have planned an assassination attempt on the emperor, had ushered in an epoch that became known as the Winter Season (*Fuyu no Jidai*), when all anti-establishment comment was severely controlled. Apart from the usual censorship of plays, which was severe enough and had forced the rewriting of

Die Heimat, theatre management was especially nervous about offending anyone in power. Ōtani had stopped *Ii Tairō no Shi* because it had been suggested that lines in it showed disrespect to the imperial institution, apparently not noticing, or at least not being worried about, other passages of the play that attacked the inflexibility of the Tokugawa political and social set-up and by analogy possibly also the realities of Japan in the 1910s.

It was, however, a mark of the gradually improving position of playwriting as a recognised art form that the management of the Imperial Theatre was forced to back down in a similar but more trivial incident in 1922. The play in question was by Yamamoto Yūzō (1887–1974), a playwright well known in Japan for his *Eijigoroshi* (*Child Murder*), which had been a great success in 1920 with its implied criticism of a society in which some people are so poor that they lose or are driven to kill their loved ones. The play concerned here was more low key but did include the seduction of a maid by a young man of good family, who insisted on confessing to the deed. The head of the Imperial Theatre organisation watched a performance, disapproved of the suggestion that members of the élite were not paragons of virtue and the slight that the play cast, at least in his eyes, on the quality of Japan's exports and demanded a rewriting for the next night.[7]

By this time, however, playwrights were organised. A Playwrights' Association (Gekisakka Kyōkai) had been founded in 1920 and included among its members such established playwrights as Okamoto Kidō, Kikuchi Kan and Nakamura Kichizō. The Association demanded a public apology from the Imperial Theatre. The theatre management complied to the extent that an apology was issued, but they would not publish the apology in the newspapers as the Association wanted. At this point the Association declared that none of its members would allow their plays to be performed at the Imperial Theatre nor would any of them be involved in any way – for example, as directors – with future productions there. The Imperial Theatre conceded. (Ōzasa 1985: 410)

Thus, the 1910s and early 1920s can be seen as a period in Japanese theatre history where the relationships between people representing the various elements of a stage production gradually moved towards a new awareness of each others' work. Playwriting developed to the point where the value of playwrights to the enterprise of theatre was acknowledged and their status as independent artists won some acceptance. Actors were forced to examine whether their ideals for the drama of the future could be reconciled with what their audiences expected or were conditioned to expect. Management had to begin taking account of the artists they previously thought they controlled without question. If one looks solely at what was commercially successful during this period, theatre seems to have retained much of its pre-modern ethos, but fundamental changes had been initiated and theatre people in the early 1920s could look forward to the momentum being continued through the decade.

3
Artists, Ideologues and Ideological Artists

An ambitious theatre-goer in the first half of 1923 would have been able to see every kind of theatre that his or her counterpart had watched in 1906 plus at least two that had not been available then. Theatre in twentieth-century Japan showed a net increase in the variety of styles to be enjoyed, with new genres appearing and only rarely going out of existence. Such is the rapidity with which a tradition is created in Japanese theatre and such the tenacity with which tradition, once created, is defended that relevance or irrelevance to the changing society ceases to be a major arbiter of success (or at least continued existence). At the start of the twenty-first century *shimpa* is still being performed, albeit in a reduced form, and *shingeki* exists, though it is sometimes referred to by other names. *Kabuki* actors are still performing *shin-kabuki* plays. *Shinkokugeki*, by contrast, has finally expired.

In 1923, however, *shinkokugeki* was very much alive and our theatre-goers would have been able to watch the Shinkokugeki company performing in a theatre in Asakusa in any of the first eight months of the year. After that the whole company was hauled off to police headquarters on suspicion of having allowed gambling, which was illegal, to take place in the dressing room area. *Shimpa* was also available in an adaptation of a Danish film starring Inoue Masao and a young actress who was soon to be the great star of *shimpa*, Mizutani Yaeko (1905–1979). Mizutani had attracted the attention of the critics for her performance of Tyltyl in a *shingeki* production of Maeterlinck's *L'Oiseau Bleu* in 1920 and was seen often on the *shingeki* and *shimpa* stages throughout the 1920s. Another young actress soon to be famous in Japan was playing in *shingeki* at the time. This was Okada Yoshiko (1902–1992), a disciple of Nakamura Kichizō and active in *shingeki* in the 1910s. In 1925 she devoted herself full-time to films, then briefly returned to the *shingeki* stage, and in 1936 achieved fame as a *shimpa* actress.

If watching Mizutani Yaeko and Okada Yoshiko had inspired our theatre-goer to survey the progress made by actresses in the post-Matsui Sumako period, he might have been surprised at the number of female performers active on the stage in the early 1920s. In particular the Imperial Theatre was continuing its policy of regularly mounting productions performed principally by its own affiliated actresses. While these actresses were often used in specially written vehicles that made no pretence of giving them scope to show their acting skills, many productions, especially at this time, were of plays by the new playwrights of the 1910s.

Another programme that would have caught his or her attention in this respect was the appearance in June of the Flower Troupe (Hanagumi) of Takarazuka Girls Opera (Takarazuka Shōjo Kageki). While male characters in the dramas played by the Imperial Theatre actresses had generally been given to *kabuki* actors, in Takarazuka all the parts were played by women. At this time Takarazuka programmes were mainly built around sentimental playlets consisting for the most part of dancing and singing in both Western and Japanese style, and someone looking for satisfying and involving theatre might have been disappointed. On the other hand the technical standard of the Takarazuka troupes (there were two, this Flower Troupe and the Moon Troupe - Tsukigumi) was very high and this itself must have been impressive.

TAKARAZUKA

Takarazuka shared with the Imperial Theatre a management ethos that did not derive from practical experience in the theatre. It was the creation of a former banker named Kobayashi Ichizō (1873–1957), who after a period of unemployment became involved in railway construction in the Osaka region. In 1912 he raised the finance to build a railway from Osaka to a small hot-spring resort called Takarazuka. Japan is blessed with many such hot-springs and they have historically been places of rest and relaxation for large numbers of city dwellers. It made sense to build a railway to one, but Kobayashi also had his eye on the possibility of constructing housing estates along the railway to provide more customers for it.

One other way to increase custom for the railway was to build up the entertainment side of the resort. In the twentieth century travelling performers of many kinds made part of their living from performing at hot-spring resorts. Such entertainment was part of the hot-spring experience and people could be attracted to Takarazuka (in Kobayashi's railway carriages) if this aspect of the resort could be developed. Kobayashi was especially keen to attract families to the resort. The customers taking the waters were traditionally male, in that prostitutes were always expected to be available, but Kobayashi was principally interested in increasing custom for his railway and he therefore targeted more than single males. He tried a heated indoor swimming pool, but the technology at his disposal was not equal to the temperature requirements. He also tried exhibitions. The 1910s saw many ambitious exhibitions in the main cities, mainly organised and housed by the new department stores. (Yoshimi 1995) Kobayashi's exhibitions were successful in bringing more family groups to Takarazuka, but something more was needed. Department stores competed against each other fiercely during this period, and Mitsukoshi hit upon the idea of organising a band of child musicians which could be sent to provide entertainment for important corporate customers. Kobayashi says openly that he copied this for his first Takarazuka company. (Ōzasa 1985: 102)

Originally, the group consisted of sixteen girls between the ages of ten and fourteen and they gave their first public performance in April 1914 in a theatre made by covering over the swimming pool and reconstructing the rest of the building. Kobayashi himself wrote much of their early material and he was concerned to create a completely uncontroversial, wholesome atmosphere. In this he succeeded, and the group's performances were written up in a leading Osaka newspaper as entirely suitable even for school parties. They became a tourist attraction associated with Osaka and Kobayashi was soon enjoying increased patronage for his railway. Within a few years the enterprise had its own librettists and composers, who were writing the sentimental music dramas and arranging the large-scale dance pieces that have become the hallmark of Takarazuka. Its success fostered other theatrical ambitions in Kobayashi, and he took his group to perform at the Imperial Theatre in Tokyo in 1918. This too was a great success and led to annual performances there until 1923.[1]

Anyone looking for comedy who remembered the Soganoya brothers in their heyday about a decade earlier would have been disappointed when surveying the theatrical scene in 1923. The brothers had split up in 1914; Gorō, who had found himself always having to adapt on stage to his brother's easy, natural style of comedy acting, wished to develop on his own. Jūrō found it difficult to succeed without his brother and only appeared sporadically in the early 1920s. He died at the end of 1925. Gorō, by contrast, persisted with his ambition to create comedy that offered moral guidance to its audiences. In 1915 a singular success with a play entitled *Jūrokugata* (*Sixteen-sided*), in which a workers' leader bests a factory-owner who has tried to seduce his sister and thus averts a strike, drew the attention of Sakai Toshihiko, a leader of the incipient labour union movement. A subsequent association with

Sakai led Gorō to emphasise the social movement in his plays and even to rename his company Heimin Gekidan (Commoners' Company). While his audiences had had no objection to having right and wrong pointed out to them before, the elimination of the name Soganoya from both the company and the actors, who played under their real names, was not to their liking, and Gorō's support dropped considerably. Within three months 'Soganoya Gorō Company' reappeared on the billboards and Gorō's popularity returned. In August 1920 his company was granted the ultimate accolade of a run in the Kabuki-za in Tokyo, a performance discussed in a major theatrical magazine by a group of leading theatre critics, and regular Tokyo appearances followed. (Ōzasa 1985: 133-45)

There were also full programmes of *kabuki* throughout the first half of 1923 with ample opportunity to watch either classical or modern plays. Both Kikugorō and Sadanji were active in this area and Ennosuke II was also continuing his experiments with dance. There is, however, a consensus among theatre historians that the rest of the decade belonged to *shingeki* and one reason for this was the Great Kantō Earthquake of 1 September 1923.

The earthquake struck at noon and caused immense loss of life and destruction. Every sizeable theatre in Tokyo, bar one rather minor venue, was burnt down. The shock to major commercial theatre – *kabuki*, *shimpa* and the Imperial Theatre – was great. *Shingeki*, however, which had never had a purpose-built theatre building, benefited greatly from the lax building regulations that followed the earthquake. Initially, land was cheap and the construction of flimsy buildings was allowed in order to give Tokyo the semblance of a city again.

THE TSUKIJI LITTLE THEATRE

The first theatre building to be erected after the earthquake was the Tsukiji Shōgekijō (Tsukiji Little Theatre). It was so flimsy that one chose one's theatre-going evening with some care: if it was raining, the words of the actors from the stage would be inaudible because of the noise of the rain on the roof; if it was a cold evening the stalls would often be empty while the audience huddled around the inadequate heaters set against the side walls, not that the intellectuals who supported this new venture would have avoided any hardship if it meant missing the latest exciting show.[2]

The Tsukiji Little Theatre building and company (referred to here either as Tsukiji Shōgekijō or the Tsukiji Company) were the responsibility of six men, referred to as partners (*dōjin*). It was common for literary and artistic enterprises to be headed by a group of partners, and in the case of literary magazines, of which there were many, publishing and distribution expenses were usually borne jointly by the partners. Tsukiji Shōgekijō was rather different. Only one of the six partners had the money to build a theatre and launch a regular programme of plays performed by paid actors and actresses. One other of the six partners had far more experience in the theatre than all the others. The one with money was Hijikata Yoshi (1898–1959) and the one with the experience was Osanai Kaoru. Their first-hand familiarity with Western theatre was about equal in quantity, but Osanai's was with the Moscow Art Theatre and Stanislavski, while Hijikata's was in Berlin, then in the throes of theatrical Expressionism, and also in Moscow where by contrast he had been overwhelmed by the theatre of Meyerhold.

Hijikata came from a well-known aristocratic family and he was sent for his university education, as most male aristocrats were, to the Peers School (Gakushūin). While staying at his family's country retreat he had made friends with a boy one year his junior called Tomoda Kyōsuke and together they had put on amateur theatricals for the local people. Tomoda later became a *shingeki* actor in Tokyo and he was one of the first to be invited by Hijikata to join the partners' group at Tsukiji Shōgekijō. Hijikata set up a small theatrical study centre in the family compound in Tokyo and there studied scenery and lighting with friends using model stages. Through a family acquaintance Hijikata had gained an introduction to Osanai and he became Osanai's disciple. Under him he studied theatre direction and they became as friendly as such teacher/pupil relationships allowed. In the early twenties Hijikata's name occasionally appears with Osanai's as joint director.

Before Hijikata set off for Europe, Hijikata and Osanai had planned to open an acting school together. Hijikata was abroad at the time of the Great Kantō Earthquake and cut his trip short when news of the disaster reached him. On the way home Hijikata decided to use the considerable funds that were remaining from his curtailed stay abroad to found, not a drama school, but a theatre. He consulted Osanai as soon as his boat arrived in Kobe, but his offer to Osanai was for him to be an adviser not a full partner.

Theatre historians have speculated on the reasons for Hijikata not wanting Osanai to be a partner. With hindsight we can see that the pace of development in European theatre during the previous ten years may well have been a strong factor. Hijikata may well have sensed that he and the other partners, who were all his age and of like mind, would not see eye to eye with Osanai on artistic policy. Osanai was still committed to the establishment of realism on the Japanese stage and, for all his current writing which was introducing the work of the Expressionist playwright Georg Kaiser to Japanese readers, he still regarded a credible set of fundamentally realistic conventions to be the principal goal. Hijikata was impatient for Japan to be part of a fast developing world theatre. He had observed Meyerhold's actors with their training in bio-mechanics and he had seen the constructivist sets in which they played. His Moscow experience had convinced him that there was no time for the patient cultivation of a Japanese form of realism.

In addition Osanai was thoroughly disillusioned with the state of Japanese theatre and had severed his connection with Shōchiku, which had at least given him access to some of the facilities that they monopolised. His outspokenness on a number of theatrical issues had also made him many enemies in the worlds of theatre and literature. In other words he would come to Tsukiji Shōgekijō with too much baggage and Hijikata was probably worried about this. He wanted his new theatre to be judged for what he and the other partners would make it, without the complication of the passions that might be aroused against it by the full participation of Osanai.

Osanai, however, was adamant that he wanted to be a partner and Hijikata felt he had no option but to include him in the group of six. The result was that Hijikata and Osanai were regarded as the joint leaders of the enterprise and major decisions were reached by whatever accommodation could be made between them. This happened in the case of the character of the new theatre. The views of Hijikata and Osanai appear to have differed on this important point and the design finally accepted was as Osanai wished.

A site was selected in the Tsukiji area of Tokyo (from which the name was taken), not far from the Kabuki-za. The relaxation of building regulations after the Great Kantō Earthquake meant that building could be put up very fast and the Tsukiji Little Theatre was ready for its formal opening in June 1924, just over six months after Hijikata's return from Europe. Its physical properties showed the desire of the partners to incorporate what they could of the latest European ideas on theatre architecture. It appears that there was a difference of view between Hijikata and Osanai on the capacity of the theatre, Hijikata wanting a small auditorium of about 250 capacity, modelled on the 'chamber theatre' of Max Reinhardt, and Osanai pressing for something about twice that size. Osanai's view again prevailed, but in the event average audiences for productions in the theatre were nearer to Hijikata's planned figure and some of the enterprise's later financial difficulties resulted from the ambitious auditorium capacity.

Outside and inside the the decor of the theatre was uniformly grey. This rather forbidding environment for watching theatre was intended to create an atmosphere of serious dedication to the task in hand: the creation of a new drama for Japan. The layout of the auditorium ensured that all would have equal access to this drama. Much attention was paid to sight-lines and as far as possible each seat commanded a good view of the stage. This too reflected some of the concerns of younger theatre directors in Europe, and one of the Tsukiji partners explained in the first issue of the house magazine that those with money would not be able to purchase a superior theatrical experience.

The stage facilities also drew on contemporary European practice. The rear of the stage itself was enclosed by a magnificent *kuppelhorizont*, and this word entered Japanese theatrical terminology at this time. The *kuppelhorizont* was a white stage backing, often rendered in plaster, which curved into a dome over the stage. The potentiality of indirect stage lighting, then being actively explored in Europe, could be fully realised through a *kuppelhorizont* and the Tsukiji Little Theatre audiences were amazed by the effects that could be achieved by this first Japanese example. The stage itself was designed to be flexible, and the ratio of width to depth again emphasised that the drama to be performed here would have the closeness of focus of European drama rather than the tendency to diffuseness of performances that spread across a wide stage opening. Japan now had one of the most modern theatres in the world, even if its construction was somewhat flimsy.

The Tsukiji Shōgekijō aroused wide interest in the intellectual community and a 'Lecture Meeting on Drama on the Occasion of the Founding of Tsukiji Shōgekijō,' organised at Keiō University in May, attracted a capacity audience to the university's great hall. Included in it were many eminent *shingeki* personalities, many of whom were connected with a newly founded and already influential theatre magazine, *Engeki Shinchō* (*New Tides in Theatre*). Both Hijikata and Osanai spoke. Hijikata impressed everyone with his passionate statement of the artistic and social principles that were to govern the activities of Tsukiji Shōgekijō. Osanai was more controversial and, entitling his lecture 'Tsukiji Shōgekijō and I,' made a highly personal announcement about future artistic policy. For the foreseeable future the company would select only foreign plays in translation for production; Tsukiji Shōgekijō would not stage the works of Japanese *shingeki* playwrights because their plays did not excite his interest as a director.

Osanai's blunt rejection of Japanese plays aroused a furore within the Japanese theatrical world and caused a great deal of offence. What he appeared not to realise was that some of the playwrights sitting before him were themselves desperate to write plays suitable for the intimate atmosphere of a theatre like the Tsukiji Little Theatre. It was hardly their fault that they had adjusted their playwriting to take account of the fact that a wide stage was the norm in existing theatres. As articles by them in issues of *Engeki Shinchō* that summer made very clear, they were bitterly disappointed at having been denied the opportunity of seeing the plays that they wished to write performed at the new theatre.

Some clues to the reasons for this uncompromising approach on the part of the new theatre may be gleaned from the manifesto that was published in the August issue of *Engeki Shinchō* under Osanai's name. Divided into three sections, it declared that Tsukiji Shōgekijō existed for 1. Drama, 2. The Future and 3. The People.[3]

In the first section a clear distinction was drawn between plays as literature and drama as the total experience for all concerned in the performance of a play in a theatre. 'The best place to appreciate plays – literature – is a quiet study. Theatres are organisations which present drama. Theatres are not places where plays are introduced.' and 'The value of Tsukiji Shōgekijō will be the value of the drama it presents. It will not be the value of the plays it uses.' Ironically this is a distinction which, if anything, would have had less relevance to Japan than to many countries in Europe, if one is considering the whole spectrum of theatre. There had been a great production of *lese-drame* in the 1910s by Japanese novelists who were experimenting with the play as a means of expression, but the impact on the development of the theatre had been minimal. It was probably this that Osanai and the others were thinking of. The history of *kabuki* was replete with plays that had existed solely through their realisation on stage, but Osanai was so set against the classical theatre that he chose to overlook this uncomfortable fact.

It is interesting that the company also set itself against 'introducing' plays. Osanai was probably remembering with frustration the general mood among audiences to Jiyū Gekijō and Bungei Kyōkai that they had come to the theatre to learn about the translated Western play being performed. There are frequent references to this effect in autobiographical writings about the period. Both Osanai and Tsubouchi had on occasion found it necessary to give a lecture before a performance of a translated play, in the hope that if the audience had at least some of the background knowledge that a Western audience would bring to their appreciation of it, they could react more naturally to the action on the stage and thus help the actors. In the end Tsukiji Shōgekijō ensured by its selection of plays for performance that many of its productions did 'introduce' plays and the attitude of its audiences was often similar to that of their predecessors.

The section entitled 'The Future' is self-explanatory and the following passage makes the ambitions of the Tsukiji partners clear:

> It exists for those who come after us. If it does exist for us, it is not us as we are now but as we shall be in the future.
> The reason for Tsukiji Shōgekijō using only Western plays for a certain period is not a love of novelty. It is not adulation of the West. It is not despair of Japanese plays.
> Tsukiji Shōgekijō is working hard to create a future dramatic art for future Japanese plays.
> The problems of presentation involved in present-day Japanese plays – in particular, those of established playwrights – can be solved by the training in pictorial technique associated with *kabuki* and *shimpa*. The proof of this is surely in the fact that *kabuki* and *shimpa* actors

who have a smattering of the new knowledge perform [such plays] without much difficulty and are even achieving great successes. The future Japanese plays for which we are waiting and hoping must contain problems beyond the scope of *kabuki* and *shimpa*. For the sake of these future plays we must develop our new dramatic art. (Powell 1975a: 76)

From today's perspective, when acting styles like that of *kabuki* are being reevaluated in the West, this looks a little simplistic. *Kabuki* actors in the 1980s and 1990s showed themselves able to adapt to new media, and it seems unlikely that in the 1920s actors such as Sadanji and Ennosuke, who had after all been to the West, would have been as unsophisticated in contemporary plays as the declaration suggests. For Tsukiji Shōgekijō, however, a clean break with traditional theatre and its derivatives seemed absolutely necessary and Osanai's dictum to his actors for a 1926 production: 'Get away from *kabuki*. Ignore tradition. Don't dance, move. Don't sing, speak' indicates how strongly he felt this even after the enterprise was well established. (Mizushina 1954: 138)

These words were uttered during the rehearsals for the first Japanese play to be performed by the company. The period of productions of solely Western plays lasted two years and the range of playwrights performed is impressive by any standards: it included Andreiev, Björnson, Karel and Josef Capek, Chekhov, Goering, Gogol, Gorki, Hasenclever, Hauptmann, Hirschfeld, Ibsen, Kaiser, Maeterlinck, Meyer-Förster, O'Neill, Pirandello, Rolland, Schnitzler, Shakespeare, Shaw, Strindberg, Toller and Wedekind. It was in the selection of plays that the generation gap between Osanai and Hijikata was most obvious. For example in the first year Hijikata chose the new European drama (Kaiser, Rolland, Capek), while Osanai chose plays of realism from a slightly earlier period (Chekhov, Björnson, Gorki). (The selection of plays for performance was nominally done at meetings of the partners, but in practice the director's wish was paramount.) There thus developed quite early an artistic divergence of a fundamental kind, and *Engeki Shinchō* focused on this in some of its criticism of the venture. Such a rich variety of drama need not have prejudiced the ambitions of the group, as set out in the manifesto; it could even have contributed positively to the establishment of a 'drama for the future'. This would depend, however, on the quality of the acting that Tsukiji Shōgekijō achieved through systematic and regular training.

The Tsukiji partners had made considerable efforts in this direction between the decision to found the company and the opening night. Osanai had visited the Dalcroze school in Vienna on his European trip and had susequently observed this fashionable system of eurythmics being used for the training of actors at the Moscow Art Theatre. The Dalcroze system was employed for actor training by the Tsukiji Shōgekijō, but such training had to fitted in between rehearsals of the plays to be offered in the opening season. Once the theatre was open and trying to keep to a very busy repertory schedule, good intentions sometimes had to give way to necessity. The partners organised a summer school for aspiring actors in 1924, but the study centre that was planned for 1925 never materialised. Increasingly Tsukiji actors and actresses had to learn to act through rehearsals, and the dichotomy of realist and experimental drama made this task more difficult.

Much, therefore, in turn depended on the directors, both of whom had the advantage of having observed actor-training or rehearsals in the West, to give as much basic guidance to their Tsukiji actors as possible. In effect neither Osanai nor Hijikata seems to have identified this as a primary responsibility. They were both caught in a dilemma. Their concept of a new drama was holistic and they were in a hurry. They were committed to the period of translated drama, but the alienation from leading figures in the *shingeki* world that this policy had provoked could not be allowed to last long. In the interests of creating an overall effect detailed instruction was neglected, and some of the actors in published reminiscences of this time regretted the lack of contact between themselves and the two leaders.

Soon after the start of Tsukiji Shōgekijō's activity a third director emerged. His name was Aoyama Sugisaku (1891–1956) and he later became an important figure in *shingeki* history. Leaving university (Waseda) part way through his English literature course Aoyama had been associated as an actor with a number of *shingeki* groups in the 1910s. He joined Tsukiji Shōgekijō as an actor but was persuaded to try directing and soon proved his abilities in this area. He directed his first Tsukiji production in October 1924 and his name appears frequently as a director in records of productions thereafter. The qualities of leadership that were to mark his later career were already showing themselves at Tsukiji. Even in the early months he often took over rehearsals in the absence of Osanai, who still had publishing commitments in the Kansai area. Aoyama knew the *shingeki* actor's problems and he was far more patient than Osanai and Hijikata, who were prone to become temperamental and demanding in rehearsal.

The third section of the declaration stated that the drama at the Tsukiji Little Theatre would be for the benefit of the 'people'. 'The Tsukiji Little Theatre exists for all ordinary people for whom drama is as necessary as food. It exists to make ordinary people happy, to give them strength, to instil them with life.' Unbeknown to Osanai these references to 'the people' may have helped set the course of Tsukiji Shōgekijō's development.

The Japanese word Osanai chose to use for 'people' makes it clear that he was echoing the use of this word in the 'popular arts theory' to which Sawada Shōjirō had appealed when popularising *shinkokugeki*.[4] Osanai went much further than Sawada and he did not approve of the commercial hype that surrounded Shinkokugeki once it had become famous. Later in the declaration Osanai specifically committed the Tsukiji Little Theatre to opposing the large theatres – such as the Imperial Theatre – in which Shinkokugeki, along with *kabuki* and a variety of other theatrical entertainment, was performed. One of the main proponents of the theory of popular arts in the 1910s had been the anarchist Ōsugi Sakai, and the publication of the declaration may have led some to conclude that this new theatre also had a left-wing stance. The choice of repertory may have reinforced that impression, in that German expressionist drama was known to be associated with left-wing intellectual movements. Much of what Osanai wrote on the subject had strong echoes of Romain Rolland's *Le théatre de people* in the sense of a welcoming, uncondescending theatre that would provide creative relaxation and unprescriptive education. But this looked like idealism in mid-1920s Japan, as intellectuals were widely embracing Marxism and art was beginning to be discussed in terms of serving political ends. Such intellectuals crowded into the Tsukiji Little Theatre and gazed in amazement at the Constructivist sets of Murayama Tomoyoshi (1901–1977), no doubt aware that theatrical Constructivism was intended to reflect the cultural preferences of Soviet Communism.

Whether the *Engeki Shinchō* playwrights liked it or not, Tsukiji Shōgekijō attracted more attention than any other part of the theatre world in Tokyo up to 1926. While steady if gradual progress towards a theatre culture adjusted to the new age had been made in the later 1910s and early 1920s, the Great Kantō Earthquake severely interrupted this process and, in the opinion of one theatre historian active in theatre at the time, set it back by at least a decade. (Miyake 1943: 336)

OTHER POST-EARTHQUAKE THEATRE

Institutionally, the recovery after the earthquake was remarkably rapid. Ōtani Takejirō immediately sent his leading *kabuki* actors down to the Osaka-Kyoto area, where some played alongside the *kabuki* stars of the Kansai entertainment world, which was controlled by his brother. An arrangement was also made with Kobayashi Ichizō, and other *kabuki* actors were able to use one of the Takarazuka theatres. In Tokyo others of Ōtani's actors were already performing in the Minami-za, the only theatre to escape destruction. By March of 1924 the Hongō-za, home of *shimpa* in its *floruit* period in the early 1900s and after that always counted as one of Tokyo's main theatres, had been rebuilt and Sadanji was playing there. Other theatres were springing up out of the rubble in the early months of 1924. The biggest theatres took a little longer, with a new Imperial Theatre opening in November and a magnificent new Kabuki-za opening in January of the next year. The Shintomi-za, with its history stretching back to 1872, could not be rebuilt and its place was taken by a new theatre given the name Shinbashi Enbujō. The Shinbashi area of Tokyo had a famous pleasure district and, as the name Enbujō implies, this building was intended to provide a performance space where the Shinbashi geisha could demonstrate their skill at traditional dancing. The Shinbashi Enbujō also contained a fully equipped theatre, however, and it has a noted history as one of the major theatres of central Tokyo.

It appears that the character of the audiences changed at the large theatres after the Great Kantō Earthquake. Commercially these theatres prospered, as before, but the core of the audiences for *kabuki*, still the most frequently performed genre, ceased being fans from families with a long tradition of theatre-going behind them. With the destruction of central Tokyo, land prices rose in the suburbs and a new prosperity in these areas encouraged their inhabitants to spend their money on visits to the theatre. They were not aficionados, however, and classical *kabuki* still required considerable practised participation from its audiences to be satisfying to all concerned. In effect the theatres had to adapt to their different audiences and for some years after 1923 actors could not rely on the traditional instinctive reactions from the auditorium.

In terms of vitality and visibility the mid-1920s belonged to *shingeki* at the Tsukiji Little Theatre and to what is known as 'proletarian drama'. Other genres produced individual eye-catching productions from time to time – such as Sawada Shōjirō's performance as the nineteenth-century political leader Sakamoto Ryōma in the play of the same name by Mayama Seika – but for provoking sustained interest and debate about theatre nothing approached *shingeki* during these years. Much of this debate was political in nature, and indeed the precise meaning of the very term 'proletarian' was hotly disputed during these years as Marxist theory developed in Japan. The focus here is mainly on the place of left-wing drama in the history of theatre in modern Japan, and the practice of most Japanese theatre histories will be followed in using the adjective 'proletarian' to describe left-wing drama from 1926 onwards.[5]

PROLETARIAN DRAMA

The left-wing drama movement arose from two sources: performances by groups of worker actors before worker audiences in workplaces, and groups founded by left-wing intellectuals with an interest in drama, whose productions were always aimed at, if not always attended by, worker audiences. The latter were more organised and sustained. The former were so sporadic as hardly to merit mention outside a specialist history of Japanese left-wing theatre, but a small number of these performances acquired great importance through the effect they had on the intellectuals who attended them.

One in particular caught the attention of the future leaders of the *shingeki* movement in 1921. The group concerned had the name Rōdō Gekidan (Work[ers] Company) and was led by a man of extraordinary talent and drive, Hirasawa Keishichi (1889–1923). Hirasawa had left school at fourteen to become a trainee smith, but afterwards he seems to have been driven by an ambition to better himself in his spare time through further education. He gained qualifications in iron founding, but his interest soon moved in the direction of literature. He became a member of the first labour union federation in Japan and began contributing pieces to the literary column of the federation's journal. In the meantime his mission to open the eyes of the Japanese industrial workers was becoming increasingly clear to him. He was passionately angry at the misery he saw around him every day. He saw people brutalised by their environment and wrote that during one walk through a slum area he had seen not one human being. Gradually he concentrated his efforts on utilising drama to achieve his objective.

Rōdō Gekidan's opening performance was given in February 1921. The cast contained both workers with no experience of the stage and members of a small *shimpa* troupe. The short plays performed were either written by Hirasawa himself or compiled by members of the group. The leader of the *shimpa* troupe played a capitalist and Hirasawa, as in real life, the part of a leader of a workers' negotiating committee.

The list of intellectuals and *shingeki* people who gave Rōdō Gekidan their support is impressive. The opening performance was attended by many of them and there are scattered references in the autobiographical writings of other intellectuals later connected with left-wing drama that testify to the deep impression made on them by this group's performances. The overwhelming impression experienced by them all was of the rapport between the actors and their audience. Akita Ujaku (1883–1962), already noticed as a *shingeki* playwright by this time, admits to a feeling of superciliousness as he set out from home but says he returned overcome with emotion. The audience was nearly all workers and their frequent cries of 'Yes! Yes!' gradually turned the theatre into a seething crucible. The effect on Hijikata Yoshi was no less intense. He wrote: 'That evening was to me like a bolt from the blue, I was so moved with admiration and wonder. . . . There was a lively and vigorous rapport between the stage and the auditorium, and waves of joy, sorrow and anger rolled to and fro. I experienced deeply the joy of having found what I had been looking for in drama for so long, what I had hoped to see in the theatre.' (Hijikata 1947: 295)

This can be interpreted as a vindication of left-wing drama, but in the context of Japanese theatre of the time it may also be seen as an admission of how far *shingeki* still had to go. Hijikata and the others might have seen similar enthusiasm at performances of classical *kabuki* by famous actors. The identity of the actor had been so important to *kabuki* history that much of the rapport between stage and audience that had existed when the society portrayed on the stage was recognisable to the fans, still continued into the modern age even when the social assumptions behind *kabuki* plays may have seemed obsolete to many. *Shingeki* had never been able to recreate that. Its actors had not developed the charisma of the great *kabuki* actors and in many cases the plays performed required too much intellectual engagement to be appreciated fully. For Hijikata, the identification of stage action with everyday life and the uninhibited responses of the worker audience that he saw in Rōdō Gekidan represented a theatrical experience that, perhaps in a different form, he aimed to recreate.

A momentum for politically-related drama had been started, however, and the potential of such drama for definite political ends was quickly recognised by progressive theatre people. There was an air of political liberalism abroad, which had originated in serious discussion of democracy within the still tight framework of Japanese political structures in the mid 1910s, and by the early 1920s it included aspirations for a radical reform of Japanese society. The early labour union movement, in which Hirasawa had participated, had stressed capital-labour harmony, but this moderate viewpoint was now being challenged. The success of the Bolshevik revolution in Russia had inspired a number of politically aware intellectuals, and an incipient Communist movement, which was illegal from the first, started activity in 1922. On the arts side, the foundation of the Nihon Shakaishugi Dōmei (Japan League of Socialism) in 1920 was important in focusing attention on left-wing arts of all kinds. Many established Japanese writers became members of this league after coming under the influence of the times and embracing some form of socialism. Within a year of its foundation the league had been banned, but before that happened a magazine had appeared which was later to be acknowledged as the initiation of the left-wing literary movement in Japan.[6] One of the partners who ran the magazine was a young man named Sasaki Takamaru (1898–1986). He contributed articles on drama and reviews and in 1922 organised a production of Rolland's *Danton* (banned by the police before it could be performed) planned as part of a day seminar. He also took part subsequently in a small *shingeki* group named Senku-za (Pioneer Theatre), whose activities further reinforced the idea of radical intellectuals concerning themselves with drama.

In December 1925, the founding meeting of Nihon Puroretaria

Bungei Renmei (Japan League for Proletarian Arts and Literature – usually abbreviated to Puroren, which will be used here) took place. It was decided at this meeting that the league should have three sections: literature, art and drama. Sasaki was elected chairman of the league and he was also made responsible for the drama section, whose core members came from Senku-za. The objective required of these three sections was that they should make their respective arts useful to the labour movement. The labour movement was highly politicised by this time, and the passing of the Universal Manhood Suffrage Law this year with the promise of a general election soon meant that the level of political activity was high. In this situation drama was now being given a specific function.

The drama section formed themselves into an acting group and gave themselves the name of Toranku Gekijō (Trunk Theatre, which will be used here). The name had been suggested in a recent article by Osanai Kaoru, in which he had written of a group that would put all necessary equipment into a trunk and be free to perform where it liked. Having formed itself, the group waited for invitations to come in, and it was not long before the chance came to show that the group was actively fulfilling its mission.

In January 1926, a large-scale printing strike, led by a union federation controlled by Communists or Communist sympathisers, broke out in Tokyo. It is famous not only for its importance in Japanese labour union history, but also because it became the subject of one of Japan's best-known proletarian novels, *Street without Sun* (*Taiyō no nai Machi*). The author of this novel was a printing worker and one of the leaders of the strike. His name was Tokunaga Sunao (1899–1958) and he was an acquaintance of Sasaki.

After the strike had dragged on for more than a month, Tokunaga visited Sasaki and asked that a performance be given to raise the flagging spirits of the strikers. The request caused some consternation, as, in spite of the existence of the Trunk Theatre and its awareness of its duties, nothing had been prepared and there was no time for rehearsals. According to Sasaki they did not even have a trunk. So packing their effects in *furoshiki* (wrapping cloths) they went to a hall in the strike area and performed two short plays. Once again the atmosphere was electric, as reported in a left-wing newspaper, which concluded its jubilant review:

> [The actors'] spirits soared at the complete identity of the stage and auditorium, and they contributed very successfully to keeping up the morale of those exhausted by the continuing struggle and to the strengthening of the organisation. Further, we understand that the Drama Section has decided that in future, apart from of course being active at the time of strikes, it will maintain close links with the recreation sections of the unions and support the movement of the proletarian class. (Powell 1971: 111)

This performance by the Trunk Theatre not only served to bring together political activists and artists. Several students from Tokyo Imperial University were there, including one named Hisaita Eijirō (1898–1976) who had already tried his hand at playwriting and was destined to be a major playwright in the 1930s. These students were members of a student organisation called the Society for the Study of Marxist Arts (Marukishizumu Geijutsu Kenkyū-kai), which was a radical group within the already radical main student club in the Imperial University, the Shinjin-kai (New Men Society). The significance of the presence of some of its members at this Trunk Theatre performance lies in the fact that this society was to provide the next generation of leaders of the left-wing cultural movement.

It was at about this time that the character of the left-wing drama movement changed. In the two performances described above there was a tension inherent in the audience's situation, and the tapping into that tension by the actors created a highly charged atmosphere, irrespective of how good the acting was. The challenge for the practitioners of left-wing drama was to develop this into something more organised and disciplined without losing the atmosphere.

A complicating factor was the harsh censorship regime under which all left-wing drama had to operate. As had been the case since the 1880s, all scripts had to be presented to the police censors prior to performance and in practice this meant not long before. This could often result in a play being banned the day before the premiere, thus occasioning great financial loss for the group concerned. In the same year that the Universal Manhood Suffrage Law had been passed the government also enacted the Peace Preservation Law, which made it an offence to advocate any fundamental change in the state system. It was difficult to be a Marxist without implying that the imperial institution should at least be questioned and the censors were therefore doubly vigilant with left-wing groups' productions. There was at least one occasion where a play passed by the censor was interrupted and banned during performance by a policemen who said that the censor had got it wrong.

Also from this time begins the proliferation of names of factions within the left-wing arts movement and the theatre groups attached to them. Theory was assuming increasing importance in the political and arts movements and hence names were a very important indication of factional affiliation. The student from the Imperial University Marxist study society who had been present at the printing strike performance joined the Trunk Theatre, as did two actors in the Tsukiji Company who had walked out of the company in protest at what they saw as too little commitment to the left-wing arts cause. One of the latter was Senda Koreya (1904–1996), who was to become a leader of the *shingeki* movement for over fifty years. Marxist theory was particularly divisive in the mid-1920s and this was reflected in the splits and realignments that took place in all quarters of the socialist movement.

By the end of 1926, Tsukiji Shōgekijō had been forced to let its theatre building out to other companies while the main Tsukiji company went on tour or played in other theatres in Tokyo. There was by now a policy of appearing at least once a year at the Imperial Theatre – according to the left-wing group within the organisation, this was just to make money – and in a large theatre in Asakusa. The Tsukiji Shōgekijō's own rationale for this was to bring *shingeki* to both bourgeois and popular audiences. While the main company was away, it was mostly left-wing groups that took over the theatre building. In December 1926, an acclaimed performance of Lunarcharsky's (Lunarcharsky, not well-known in world theatre history, was Soviet Commissar for Education at the time) *Don Quixote Liberated* took place in the Tsukiji Little Theatre. The theatre was also hired out for meetings of left-wing societies. In this way the Tsukiji Little Theatre quite quickly acquired a reputation for being a centre of activity for those working in left-wing arts organisations.

The Tsukiji Company was very active itself in 1927. At the end of 1926 it had set itself four goals: 1) to produce as many original Japanese plays as possible, 2) to perform socialist plays by foreign playwrights, 3) to mount annual productions in a large commercial theatre and 4) to go on tour several times each year. These goals were amply fulfilled in the succeeding year. Twelve new productions of plays by Japanese playwrights were mounted, including Mushanokōji Saneatsu and a new playwright Fujimori Seikichi (1892–1977), and left wing plays, by both foreign and Japanese playwrights, were prominent. Ambitious tours took place and theatre-goers who went regularly to the big commercial theatres at least had the opportunity to watch this little theatre company in action. The company's profile rose. Its membership increased, and so many applicants came forward aspiring to membership of the group that regular auditions had to be instituted. During June and July its actors were giving full-scale performances in the evenings and putting on small-scale, experimental, performances of different plays in the afternoons. During the remainder of the day many of them were also energetically performing in one of Japan's first talking films.

TENSION WITHIN TSUKIJI SHŌGEKIJŌ

Tsukiji Shōgekijō was, however, subject to two different types of pressure in the second half of 1927. Firstly, criticism from the left of those productions, mainly directed by Osanai, which could not be defined as socialist, mounted in rapidity and intensity. Chekhov and Shakespeare were not acceptable. Those who were cast to act in such productions were constantly called on to justify their appearances. Within the company two clandestine societies had been formed, and one of them had direct links with the main proletarian theatre group. The second pressure was financial. Out of sixty-three productions – a considerable achievement in itself – up to August 1927 only fourteen had achieved audiences of over 50% capacity, and more than half the remainder attracted less than two hundred people. The theatre was running at a continuous and substantial monthly loss and this had to be made good by Hijikata out of his own money.

The artistic difference Hijikata had with Osanai and the financial anxiety finally proved too much for him and at the end of October he threatened to resign and take his money with him unless some viable financial plan was devised by the end of the year. Osanai had been invited to the USSR for the celebrations of the 10th anniversary of the October Revolution, but these problems within Tsukiji Shōgekijō detained him, and he left Japan in November greatly fearing that he would return to find a group rent by internal dissension.

Such was Tsukiji Shōgekijō's disarray at the end of 1927 that it seemed the brightest future was waiting for overtly left-wing *shingeki*. The two main left-wing companies had suffered heavily at the hands of the censors and in early 1928 it became even more difficult for them to carry on what they regarded as their normal activities, but in spite of this the future held promise. The movement had been weakened by violent ideological quarrels and these were now over. The first general election under the Universal Manhood Suffrage Law was due to take place in February 1928 and this was a potent unifying factor. Some successful productions of left-wing plays written by Japanese playwrights had been mounted and a number of playwrights were now writing in this genre. In the first two months of 1928 proletarian theatre people had good reason to hope that, provided a workable accommodation could be made with the censors, their art might mature into the new drama to which they were dedicating themselves.

TSUKIJI SHŌGEKIJŌ STARTS PERFORMING JAPANESE PLAYS

The original plays that were most noticed in the press between 1926 and 1928 were almost all left-wing. The one exception to this was *Aiyoku (Passion)* by Mushanokōji Saneatsu, which was the second Japanese play to be performed by the Tsukiji Company after its policy of performing only Western plays had been relaxed.

Aiyoku was performed in July 1926, four months after a rather anti-climactic production of Tsubouchi Shōyō's play *En no Gyōja*

(*En the Ascetic*). Tsubouchi had written this play in 1915 and it had aroused much comment at the time. No-one, however, had been tempted to produce it and it remained unperformed until the Tsukiji Company took it on. A monumental play, in the sense that the main character has speeches of immense grandeur and towers above mere mortals, *En no Gyōja*'s depiction of the legendary ancestor of the Japanese mountain ascetics (*yamabushi*) and his nurture of his *übermensch*-type self seems to have frightened directors off. It was a strange choice for Tsukiji Shōgekijō in that it required acting which ran counter to the whole direction of the company's artistic policy and had received scant support in a questionnaire sent to the theatre's supporters in advance of the abandonment of the no-Japanese-play rule.

This might have been seen at the time as an opportunity to ameliorate the tactlessness of Osanai's statement about original Japanese plays, but it seems no attempt was made to do this. Not only that, but Osanai probably managed to offend Tsubouchi. Hijikata had been particularly active in the preparations for the production and busied himself especially in the various contacts with Tsubouchi. He was anxious to bring together the two great pioneers of *shingeki*, Tsubouchi and Osanai, and he persuaded Tsubouchi to attend one of the performances of *En no Gyōja*. Tsubouchi was not impressed. In his work he had been concerned to preserve Japanese tradition and Osanai was well aware of this, but it was in the rehearsals for this production that Osanai had told his actors to move and speak rather than dance and sing. When pressed by Hijikata for an opinion, Tsubouchi grudgingly admitted that he liked the scenery, but he would say nothing more. Hijikata's attempt to bring him and Osanai together had failed. (Ozaki and Ibaraki 1961: 124)

Mushanokōji's play, by contrast, caused a sensation. The passion of the title is the passion felt for the same woman by two brothers. The elder, after his affair with her is over, has contrived that she (her name is Chiyoko) should become the wife of his brother Eiji, who is a painter and physically deformed. The elder brother's passion is not dead, however, and Eiji conceives an inordinate jealousy that eventually leads him to murder Chiyoko, by whose ghost he is subsequently haunted. The love between the brothers, made complex by the repect due to an elder brother which Eiji certainly feels, gave great depth to the realisation of the passion in the eyes of the Japanese audiences. Comments on the performance suggest that the theatricality of certain parts, like the hiding of Chiyoko's body in a chest, which would not have been out of place in *kabuki*, were ignored or filtered out by the audiences. Mushanokōji seems to have brought a new emotional intensity to the Japanese stage.

PROLETARIAN PLAYS MATURE

The second Japanese play to cause a sensation during these two years was not performed in the Tsukiji Little Theatre, although subsequent plays by the same playwright were. The playwright's name was Fujimori Seikichi and he had started a career as a fiction writer while in the German Literature Department of Tokyo Imperial University. Idealist in inclination, Fujimori became interested in socialism and joined the Socialist League in 1920. In 1924 he (unwillingly) attracted much journalistic attention by taking various labouring jobs, including a spell in a soap factory and in a spinning mill. In this way he had more contact with actual working lives than any other of the prominent intellectual socialists of the period.

Fujimori's first play was entitled *Haritsuke Mozaemon* (*Mozaemon Crucified*) and was a historical drama set at the end of the seventeenth century. It concerns a farmer, Mozaemon, who manages to present a petition to an imperial prince with the result that the oppressive and cruel lord of the region is punished. But Mozaemon has broken the feudal code in petitioning above his lord, and he and his wife are crucified. From the cross Mozaemon stops his fellow farmers starting a revolt and dies.

The play was given its premiere not by *shingeki* but by *shimpa*. It was performed in June 1926 by Inoue Masao's company in a large Asakusa theatre owned by Shōchiku. Very little was cut by the censor. However, when in 1928 a new proletarian company tried to perform it, the play came back from the censor with so much cut that the production was abandoned. This was one of the earliest indications to the left-wing movement of the determination on the part of the government to assign guilt by association. The play was harmless in the hands of Inoue Masao, who had no political affiliations, but it acquired a perniciousness when taken up by a left-wing company. There were sensitive lines in the play that could be highlighted on the stage, but Inoue could be trusted not to do this. *Haritsuke Mozaemon* was closer to *shimpa* in its technical aspects than Mushanokōji's play *Aiyoku*. For example, climaxes are artificially created and often depend on coincidence, the *hanamichi* raised walkway is specifically mentioned in the stage directions and there is a similar use of natural phenomenon to emphasise the mood of individual scenes.

Fujimori's next play was immediately taken up by Tsukiji Shōgekijō but was banned by the police after rehearsals were well under way. There were a number of reasons for the banning. The play concerned the writer Arishima Takeo, one of Mushanokōji's Shirakaba (White Birch) group, who apart from his novels is known for two events: the making over of his extensive estates in Hokkaido to the farmers who had rented plots on them and his love suicide with a married woman in 1923. On both moral and political grounds the play was suspect to the police, who were no doubt aware of the developing left-wing trend within Tsukiji Shōgekijō.

From about the middle of 1926, the history of proletarian drama is punctuated by the appearance of articles on the theory of proletarian art that are regarded as authoritative and therefore binding on writers who subscribed to the aims of the movement. One such appeared in the autumn of 1926 and required that creative works should be written with a conscious objective in mind. There was now an increasing trend towards criticising plays according to how well they conformed to the latest theoretical statement. It is not proposed here to do more than briefly mention the most important of these theoretical milestones, but the phenomenon does require comment. Firstly, as the next few years were to show, the most prominent playwrights were content to accept such political direction. Secondly, however inappropriate this theory looks in the context of the whole sweep of modern Japanese theatre history (much of it was written by people who had little knowledge or experience of the theatre), it did provide a critical framework for the drama to which it was applied and this drama happened to be the leading drama of the time.

Looked at in this way Hisaita Eijirō's *Giseisha* (*Victim*, 1926) is a significant play. With it proletarian drama reached maturity at a stroke. Not only was it about a worker's death leading to the formation of a union, but it was structured in such a way that the climax – the formation of the union – seemed to be the inevitable conclusion of the play's development. Outside the context of proletarian drama, however, it would be difficult to range it alongside the plays discussed above. This tends to be the trend for the next three years: many plays were written, often by playwrights who had no career outside proletarian drama, but they were judged by how well they conformed to whatever proletarian arts theory was accepted as authoritative at the time. Very few had any printed existence outside the ephemeral left-wing magazines in which they were published.

There were, however, some spectacular exceptions. One such was Fujimori Seikichi's *Nani ga Kanojo o Sō Saseta ka* (*What Made Her Do It?*), first performed under the title *Kanojo* (*Her*), as required by the censor, in April 1927 by the Tsukiji Company. This was a wild success and had ramifications far beyond the proletarian drama movement. The plot of the play is simple. The heroine is a young girl, Sumiko, who is forced into a succession of degrading situations in which she is maltreated by typical representatives of the class that Marxists were defining as the bourgeoisie. They include her uncle, the owners of a small theatre, workhouse authorities, the family of a member of a local assembly, a music teacher and the directors of a Christian home for girls. At the home

Sumiko is required to make a confession of her wicked past before the whole congregation in chapel on Sunday. She refuses to be publicly humiliated and denounces the home as based on lies. In the last scene she has set fire to it, and when she is arrested and taken out, there appears in the sky reddened by the flames an electric sign which reads 'What made her do it?'.

This play was extravagantly praised by left-wing critics, although in some ways it falls short of what the theoreticians were requiring of drama. The succession of misfortunes that Sumiko encounters and her final lashing out at the society that has allowed or caused them to happen struck a chord in the Tsukiji audiences. The production was revived in May 1929, when it was performed in the Imperial Theatre. The next year it was made into a film and contributed largely to a new genre of 'tendency films' (*keikō eiga*).

Helped by successes like *Kanojo* and in the heady atmosphere of preparation for the first general election under the new voting law due in February 1928, the left-wing theatre movement urgently discussed a unification of their effort. Finally after the election, in which the party supported by the proletarian arts movement did relatively well, the existing two left-wing theatre companies merged to form the Sayoku Gekijō (Left Theatre) in March of that year. Sayoku Gekijō achieved a psychologically important success with its opening production in the Tsukiji Little Theatre and this put further pressure on the Tsukiji company. For the next five years Sayoku Gekijō was the main left-wing theatre group and even survived beyond the end of the proletarian drama movement.

TSUKIJI SHŌGEKIJŌ SPLITS AND DISBANDS

1928 was a difficult year for Tsukiji Shōgekijō. On the surface it had a number of artistic and cultural successes. Its Ibsen Festival, to mark the centenary of Ibsen's birth, brought badly needed money into the organisation. But commercial success only compounded Tsukiji's problems, as the company came under greater fire from the self-confident proletarians that this was compromising with the enemy. This provoked a number of meetings within the organisation in September and these revealed the presence of three groups: those who were uncompromising in their belief that drama should serve political ends, those who were equally uncompromising that artistic standards should come first, and those – the majority but not as vociferous as either other group – that a social alignment for the theatre was acceptable but their theatrical activity needed to have a firm artistic base. In the end the company left it to Hijikata and Osanai to sort out, with the result that Hijikata again deferred to Osanai, who insisted that the original task of Tsukiji Shōgekijō – to grasp the fundamentals of drama – was still unfulfilled. To emphasise his point, Osanai chose an adaptation of a *kabuki* classic for the opening production of the new theatre building, next door to the old one, that had been constructed for the company. He followed this in November with a high-profile production of a play by a playwright who had always been opposed to a political role for drama.

This was Kubota Mantarō (1889–1963), who during the 1910s had been associated with a Romantic literary journal. He also joined *Engeki Shinchō* and had been one of the playwrights who had protested at having been excluded from the Tsukiji Little Theatre. *Ōdera Gakkō* (*Ōdera School*) concerns the owner (Ōdera) of a small private school whose existence is threatened by a plan to build a state school nearby. Ōdera maintains rigidly traditional standards in the school curricula and in personal relationships between the various members of staff. He tries to save the school by appealing to outside individuals on the basis of such relationships, but he is overtaken by progress. The play demonstrates the meticulous attention to the technical aspects of playwriting – for example, the sound quality of the words – for which Kubota later became famous. If it had appeared and been produced two years earlier, it could have been a model play for *shingeki* playwrights with its sustained atmosphere and characterisation and might therefore have had a lasting effect on *shingeki*. In late 1928, however, a play such as *Ōdera Gakkō* could only be derided by the left-wing drama movement, already almost monopolising the development of *shingeki* at the time.

Osanai was not to live to experience the upheavals in the Tsukiji Company that were to come. On 25 December 1928 he collapsed at a theatrical party and died soon afterwards. He was just 48 years old. Every major figure in Japanese artistic and literary circles paid tribute to him. His achievements had been great and he had persisted with his conviction against all opposition, but the times had overtaken him and even had he lived longer, it would only have been in bitterness and despair.

JAPANESE THEATRE TOURS ABROAD FOR THE FIRST TIME

He did, however, have the satisfaction of assisting in the great success of Japanese theatre's first tour abroad. After having talks in Moscow about the possibility of performances of *kabuki* there, Osanai tried the idea out on Sadanji, who was enthusiastic, and Ōtani who, somewhat to his surprise, also approved and even gave his full support. This was the first visit of a major foreign theatre company to the Soviet Union and it therefore had symbolic as well as artistic importance. Within Japan there was opposition from right-wing groups and the departure of the company on 12 July 1928 had to be carefully handled. For some months after Sadanji's return to Japan later that year his performances were occasionally interrupted by demonstrators opposed to the visit. In the USSR, however, there was general excitement, with receptions and protracted welcome speeches at the many stops along the Trans-Siberian Railway. The performances of classical and new *kabuki* in Moscow were sold out well in advance and the planned run of twelve days was extended for five more. Leningrad audiences were no less appreciative. A group of leading writers and intellectuals in Leningrad were so concerned at the possible dilution of the art of *kabuki* by Western influence that they sent a message to Sadanji urging him to preserve it at all costs. (Saeki and Kano 1981: 398–420)

The tangible results of the visit are hard to assess. Eisenstein was very impressed and was reported as having said that his artistic aims and those of *kabuki* were similar. Meyerhold watched the *kabuki*, and the *kabuki* actors went to see some Meyerhold productions. In the next year after the tour to the USSR a left-wing tendency among *kabuki* actors became apparent. Most of the actors involved had not been to the Soviet Union, but one had and he was to be a founder and leader of a *kabuki* company which joined the Japan Communist Party *en masse* after the Pacific War.

RADICAL *KABUKI*

The name of this actor was Kawarasaki Chōjūrō (1902–1981). He was the son of the younger brother of the famous Meiji actor Ichikawa Danjūrō IX and was therefore not excluded by birth from a good *kabuki* career. He had joined Sadanji's company in 1919, but even working with as innovative a *kabuki* actor as Sadanji did not satisfy him and with some friends he had founded in 1925 a playreading group that became Kokoro-za (Soul Theatre: the name was taken from Evreinov's play *The Theatre of the Soul*). This was a mixed *kabuki* and *shingeki* company, which was also internally divided into three factions by 1927. Murayama Tomoyoshi led a group that became increasingly committed to proletarian drama; the *kabuki* group, devoted to performing new *kabuki* plays was led by Kawarasaki, and there was also a group trying to adhere to artistic principles. Murayama was eventually forced out in May 1927, and two years later Kokoro-za went out of existence. Chōjūrō comments on himself at this time as having been completely caught up in the *avant garde* atmosphere but not possessing any systematic knowledge of socialism. (Toita 1961:175-81)

The global economic crisis of 1929 affected the entertainment industry in Japan as it did other parts of the Japanese economy, and Shōchiku required some lower ranking *kabuki* actors to accept cuts in salaries which were already far from large. These actors formed a society to protect themselves and then renounced all links with commercial *kabuki* by founding a new company, to which they gave the name Taishū-za (Theatre for the People). Some of the ex-members of the Kokoro-za, including Chōjūrō, joined after their own organisation collapsed. As far as acting talent was concerned, Taishū-za was similar to the Soul Theatre in that its members came from both *kabuki* (the majority) and *shingeki*. The group was later strengthened by the addition of more *kabuki* actors when a similar protest against Shōchiku, this time led by Ennosuke II no less, collapsed very quickly and not all the protesting group followed Ennosuke back into Shōchiku. What resulted from all this was a company called Zenshin-za (Forward Advance Theatre) that played a distinctive role in the theatre culture of 1930s Japan.

TSUKIJI SHŌGEKIJŌ SPLITS AND DISBANDS

Thus the ramifications of the confident rise of proletarian drama were widespread and a company like Tsukiji Shōgekijō was very vulnerable. Discussion within the group became increasingly bitter after Osanai's death and the company split up in March 1929. Two companies were formed from its ex-members. One was expressly non-political in outlook, the other intended to increase its politically aware productions. In April a national organisation to oversee proletarian drama, called the Japan Proletarian Theatre League (abbreviated name: PROT) was established. This successfully marginalised the first of the two new companies so that it disappeared the next year. PROT then set about exerting control over the second. This latter group had named itself Shin Tsukiji Gekidan (New Tsukiji Company) and it did not keep its independence for long in the circumstances of 1929. It hired the Imperial Theatre in July, intending to perform an adaptation of a proletarian novel that had been the publishing sensation of 1929. Hiring the Imperial Theatre was a costly business, and PROT members interrupted the performance soon after the curtain had gone up. They insisted that the conditions made by the author when he had given permission for the adaptation had not been met and refused to allow the performance to continue until ShinTsukiji Gekidan put things to right. After fifty minutes, during which time the audience became increasingly restless, the company agreed to accept two PROT representatives as full members, and the performance began again. The adapted novel, *Kani Kōsen* (*Crab Cannery Boat*) by Kobayashi Takiji (1903–1933), was a model of current proletarian literary correctness and Shin Tsukiji Gekidan were showing their commitment to the proletarian cause by performing it. The presence of these PROT members at meetings thenceforth would ensure that this commitment continued and changed in character if that was what was decided for the whole proletarian theatre movement.

BŌRYOKUDANKI

The high point of proletarian drama so far had come the month before, in June, with the production of a new play by Murayama Tomoyoshi that seemed to fulfill all that could be expected of a proletarian play. The play's title was *Bōryokudanki* (*Account of a Gang of Thugs*). It was set in China in 1923 and based on a strike which had taken place on the Beijing Hangzhou railway. Local gangsters are cooperating with the owners of the railway and the police in trying to prevent the railway workers forming a union. The founding meeting of the union goes ahead in spite of a banning order by the police, and the gang vandalises the room in the union building after the meeting has finished. The building itself is now under siege by the police, but the union continues its work of setting up the necessary organisation to prosecute the strike. A series of incidents connected with the strike follows, each emphasising the strength that can be found in adversity. A train approaches – the sound of a moving train is a terrible blow to the striking railway workers. The train is filled with soldiers. The final scene of the play takes place on the station as the strikers and military police confront each other. Someone announces that a striker who had earlier been tortured by the police has now been murdered by the gangsters behind the police station. The strikers surge forward and the soldiers shoot. Darkness. A voice cries out that their strike has failed in that it has been defeated by violence, but it has also succeeded because the basis for a national union has been created.

Bōryokudanki was praised greatly by the leading theorist of proletarian literature at the time, Kurahara Korehito (1902 –1979). Kurahara had published an article in the previous year which had set the course for proletarian literature into the 1930s. '*Puroretaria Rearizumu e no Michi*' ('The Road to Proletarian Realism') had defined this realism as one by which the individual is described from a social point of view. In it the proletarian writer was urged to look at the world and describe it with the eyes of the proletarian vanguard in the revolution to come. In Kurahara's eyes, Murayama had fully achieved this in *Bōryokudanki*. Another review mentioned the balance between the individual and the group, always a problem for writers who were trying to suggest that individual characters represented groups in society. The production of *Bōryokudanki* by the Sayoku Gekijō in the Tsukiji Little Theatre was a remarkable success. The theatre was full to overflowing every night with many turned away. The atmosphere in the auditorium was fervent, and the audience, which was reported as being 50% workers, engaged themselves fully with the action on the stage.

Bōryokudanki raises an interesting problem in the context of modern Japanese theatre. Although the situation changed again in the 1930s, the development of modern drama in Japan from the founding of Tsukiji Shōgekijō in 1924 seemed to be leading to this point. The atmosphere generated by the simple but theatrically involving productions of Hirasawa Keishichi that had so excited Hijikata and Osanai had now been replicated in a large theatre by the production of a play that answered the demands of the left-wing arts movement. In one sense *shingeki* had achieved what it had been aiming at. In the early 1920s there had been no consensus over the goals of a modern Japanese theatre. Gradually those goals had been identified and had now been demonstrated as attainable, but the process by which this had happened had involved criteria that had never applied before. For *Bōryokudanki* there was a congruence of factors, economic, social, political and theatrical, that aided the success of the production, but in the political circumstances of late 1920s Japan it had created theatre which could not be developed further. *Bōryokudanki* had solved some problems for *shingeki*, but it had raised many as well. It had created a theatrical environment that paradoxically shared some characteristics with its arch enemy *kabuki*, but unlike *kabuki* it was not offered the possibility of adjusting its parameters in a way that would enable it to survive the social changes to come.

For a short while, proletarian drama continued its triumphant progress. In February of the next year, 1930, the Sayoku Gekijō achieved another great success, again in the Tsukiji Little Theatre, with its adaptation of *Taiyō no nai Machi* (*Street without Sun*), the novel describing the printing strike for which the Trunk Theatre had performed in 1926. Once again the theatre was full to overflowing for the whole run.

From 1930 onwards, however, theatre was required to contribute much more directly to the political struggle. Productions of full-length plays in theatres were vulnerable to police action and to avoid this while still carrying out its political tasks the proletarian drama movement evolved various types of small-scale performance. Senda Koreya was now in Germany and he sent home accounts of a form called Living Newspaper used for propaganda purposes by the German Communist Party. The Living Newspaper was essentially a collage of short items, including dramatic sketches, songs, speeches, and choral speaking (*sprechtchör*). The latter especially fired Senda's imagination and he was deeply impressed by the dramatic effects it could achieve. Other names were subsequently given to this type of entertainment, but basically the principles were the same. Ideally the individual items of a programme of short pieces should create an overall propaganda effect, but however harsh the censorship of single items, others could always be substituted and the show could go on in some form. It was also possible for the printed scripts to be innocuous while elements added in performance – salutes, flag-waving, etc – increased the propaganda potential.

Such political activity could only make the police more suspicious of *shingeki* as a whole, particularly as its skilful infiltrators had discovered how the illegal Japan Communist Party was increasingly exerting direct influence over proletarian drama. The police began more systematic harassment of theatre people and there were frequent arrest of actors. They also began a practice that was to become commonplace later in the 1930s, that of taking the names and addresses of members of the audience. This was a potent method of reducing worker attendance at the theatre and it was successful. Theatre activists from good families were allowed to go abroad, as the police could have had difficulty dealing with them as harshly as they were wont. Hijikata Yoshi was a case in point. Being a scion of an aristocratic family he could not be arrested, and it was a considerable relief to the police when in 1933 he applied to be allowed to leave Japan. He went to Moscow and stayed there until the end of the Pacific War.

Other parts of the left-wing movement were also under great pressure. Intellectuals were constantly being arrested, held in prison, released and sometimes arrested again within a short time. For those who were suspected of links with the Communist Party interrogation was very harsh. Kobayashi Takiji, the author of *Crab Cannery Boat*, was beaten to death in police custody in February 1933. Soon afterwards, two Communist activists issued recantation statements (*tenkō*) which, whatever the intentions of their authors, were interpreted as denying Communism. It became a major goal of the police to obtain as many of these recantation statements as possible, and a variety of pressures was exerted on those in custody to write them. Murayama Tomoyoshi was the first prominent theatre person to write one. In the statement he handed to the police he reaffirmed his belief in Communism but contracted not to engage in direct political activity. He also issued notice of his withdrawal from membership of the Communist Party. He was released and within a few months had written the first of his agonised 'recantation novels'.[7]

Proletarian drama could not survive these concerted attacks. While the Shin Tsukiji Gekidan managed to continue performing plays throughout the 1930s, from 1934 onwards there was no possibility of performing anything with an overtly left-wing message. Sayoku Gekijō (Left Theatre) temporarily continued producing plays, but in May 1934 it changed its name to Chūō Gekijō (Centre Theatre). Proletarian drama had established its place in modern Japanese theatre history, but it had denied the theatre in Japan the fruits of its success through willingly accepting the imposition of aims that no Japanese theatre genre had previously entertained.

4
Diversity in Adversity

The end of the 1920s and the beginning of the 1930s were certainly a dynamic period in Japanese theatre history, but they were dynamic in a limited sense. The energies of a great number of very talented theatre people were spent on the development of proletarian drama. If proletarian drama was what Japanese theatre needed, PROT was a resounding success, and the English language materials distributed internationally by the Comintern at the time praised the Japanese movement above all others. Japan led the way in the world according to these articles – heady praise for the *shingeki* movement, which only a few years previously had decided that only an exclusive repertory of Western plays could teach the actors how to act and the playwrights how to write.

In the event, for a variety of reasons, the proletarian drama movement petered out, and one is left with the question why directors and actors who had been introduced to the riches of modern and classical Western drama had been persuaded to reduce theatre to something so poor in artistic content. The fact that someone with as varied and bohemian a background as Murayama Tomoyoshi could accept the tenets of successive Marxist theorists, who had little apprecation of theatre, testifies to the force of the momentum in Japanese theatre that proletarian drama had set up. Once that momentum was brought to a halt, a kind of languor seemed to pervade the *shingeki* world for a short while. (Ōyama 1969: vol. 3, 49) Novelists who had written plays out of interest stopped doing so and even some committed playwrights began to give their time to writing novels.

The social environment for theatre was not friendly. Beginning with the depressed economic situation carrying over from the 1920s and gradually worsening, Japan entered a period of economic and political uncertainty which saw her increasingly isolated on the international scene. As the military hold on domestic politics tightened and expansion continued on the mainland of China, many areas of Japanese society were affected by the general war atmosphere. Censorship increased in severity and many theatrical, literary and artistic people found their professional and, in some cases, personal liberty curtailed. Considering the publicity given in the newspapers to Japan's international isolation, one should not be surprised at the surge of national pride that occurred or the jingoistic mood that made itself felt on many occasions. It is perhaps also not surprising that the world of entertainment, which depended largely on the good will of its audiences, should respond to this in some ways.

KABUKI FLOURISHES

In spite of the seemingly unfavourable social and political circumstances, which even led to rumours that *kabuki* might go out of existence, Shōchiku built two new theatres during the decade. In 1930 it built the Tōkyō Gekijō (Tokyo Theatre), a Western-style theatre, within sight of the Kabuki-za, which was the company's main *kabuki* base in the Tokyo area. The new theatre was launched with a programme of grand classical *kabuki* performed by its most famous actors, including Onoe Kikugorō VI, Ichimura Uzaemon XV and Onoe Baikō VI, but it later became the base for Ichikawa Sadanji II, a *kabuki* actor who built up a wide following for his productions of *shin-kabuki* through the 1930s until his death in 1940.

Great celebrations of *kabuki* were to be a feature of Shōchiku policy for this genre in the 1930s. In 1932 it mounted an all-star *kabuki* extravaganza to commemorate the 30th anniversary of the great Danjūrō IX's death. Such was the success of this programme that other anniversaries were similarly observed. Shōchiku had a large number of very talented *kabuki* actors at their disposal during the 1930s. Apart from the core group of senior actors, such as Utaemon V, Uzaemon XV and Chūsha VII, they were able frequently to arrange for Kikugorō VI and Kichiemon II to appear together, a combination – referred to affectionately by the fans as the 'Kiku-Kichi combi' – that guaranteed full houses. Kichiemon's mature, uncompromisingly traditional approach to acting contrasted very effectively with the virtuoso range of Kikugorō.

SHŌCHIKU'S GRANDEST THEATRE

The second new theatre that Shōchiku built in the 1930s was the Kokusai Gekijō (International Theatre) in Asakusa. This mammoth theatre opened in July 1937 and was the biggest in Asia. It had a capacity of nearly five thousand and was intended to develop a taste for large-scale theatrical entertainment among the inhabitants of Asakusa. Theatre was thriving in Asakusa at the time, but mainly on a comparatively small scale. Much of the Kokusai Gekijō programming consisted of well-publicised film screenings, mostly of the latest American films, and shows by Shōchiku's answer to Takarazuka, the Shōchiku Shōjo Kageki (Shōchiku Girls' Opera). There were by this time two Girls Opera troupes belonging to Shōchiku. One had been started in Osaka in 1921 expressly to rival Takarazuka and the second in Tokyo in 1928. The tone of Shōchiku's Girls Opera was somewhat lower than that of Takarazuka; the shows were deliberately targeted at a more popular audience and Asakusa was their usual venue. The Kokusai Gekijō could easily be filled for performances of operettas, musicals, song and dance routines by the company.

The theatre also mounted high-profile productions of *kabuki* and other live theatre. Later in 1937 Sadanji and Ennosuke II performed a programme of established *kabuki* classics and the same year both *shinkokugeki* and *shimpa* also attracted capacity audiences. Kokusai Gekijō was financially very successful for Shōchiku and the economic gloom of the early 1930s seemed finally to have been dispelled. It is possible, however, that at least some of the attraction to audiences of the *kabuki* classics was due to a deliberate government encouragement of traditional values as Japan began large-scale military operations in China.

In spite of two restructuring exercises in the changing economic climate, Shōchiku had control of all the six main theatres in Tokyo in 1930. There were few major *kabuki* actors who were not under contract to it. This near-monopoly of Japan's most vigorous traditional theatre genre did not go without challenge. Ennosuke II left Shōchiku in 1930 in order to pursue an independent career which combined his new *kabuki* dance with proletarian plays, but in the event this was a short-lived challenge to the organisation, as he reverted to being a Shōchiku actor in mid-1931. Of more concern to Shōchiku was competition from Kobayashi Ichizō, the founder of Takarazuka. Kobayashi, who was an adviser to Shōchiku in the early 1930s, had long wanted to extend his own entertainment operations to Tokyo and in 1934 he constructed the Tōkyō Takarazuka Gekijō (Tokyo Takarazuka Theatre). Although a large part of his intention was to promote regular performances of his very successful Takarazuka Girls Opera, he realised the potential draw of *kabuki* and needed to recruit *kabuki* actors as well. He could only poach them from Shōchiku, which he did with some success. The venture, at least on the play production side, proved not to be financially viable, however, and came to an end in 1939.

ZENSHIN-ZA AND RESISTANCE TO SHŌCHIKU

While Tōhō (the abbreviated designation for Takarazuka's Tokyo operations) put Shōchiku on the defensive temporarily and has been credited by some as having introduced welcome competition into the *kabuki* world, more sustained defiance came from some low-ranking *kabuki* actors who had resigned from Shōchiku at about the same time as Ennosuke. Zenshin-za emerged as a hybrid company of thirty *kabuki* and *shingeki* actors in May 1931 and was soon the focus of widespread attention.[1] '*Zenshin*' means 'marching forward' or 'advancing' and from the first the new company set itself against the prevailing conventions in the *kabuki* world. At the founding meeting a number of iconoclastic measures were passed, including the abolition of the traditional status system among actors and a transparent policy with regard to the general finances of the company including actors' salaries. The principle of equality among all members, whatever their function, was also affirmed. (Powell 2002: 174)

Zenshin-za had three acknowledged leaders, all *kabuki* actors. Kawarasaki Chōjūrō was the only one from a major *kabuki* family. He had been trained by Sadanji II and might have expected to become a famous actor in his own right. Nakamura Kan'emon (1901-1982) and Kawarasaki Kunitarō V (1909-1990) were different. Kan'emon had been born into a minor acting family and Kunitarō was the son of an artist and therefore an outsider. Neither could have had much expectation of playing sustantial parts in the world of traditional *kabuki*. Their position within Zenshin-za, however, would have entitled them to star billing on posters advertising the company's performances, but this would have been contrary to the spirit of the three resolutions passed at the founding meeting. For the rest of 1931 actors' names appeared in alphabetical order.

Cast lists in alphabetical order were the most obvious sign to the outside world that Zenshin-za intended to distinguish itself from established *kabuki*. No less radically, but less obviously, the adoption of the principle of *a priori* equality within the company meant that the atmosphere in which the members worked was something unknown to the general run of commercial theatre in Japan. In effect Zenshin-za was denying practices involving the showing of respect that would have been the norm in any artistic grouping, and not everything implied by this idealistic beginning survived. The earliest casualty was the star-billing system. Whether connected to the posters or not, audiences were very poor for the early productions of Zenshin-za and when the Ichimura-za, which could offer the company financial security, insisted on star-billing as part of a package in early 1932, the posters were changed.

In the 1930s, Zenshin-za drew most attention to itself by its productions of classical *kabuki*. Many of the most famous *kabuki* classics were regarded as the preserve of certain mainstream *kabuki* families, who monopolised productions of them. Zenshin-za had declared themselves against the whole structure of the *kabuki* theatre, but they recognised the worth of the plays which had stood the test of time. Beginning with a highly successful production of *Kanadehon Chūshingura* in early 1932, which the management of the Ichimura-za had forced on them, Zenshin-za challenged the *kabuki* establishment head-on in 1933 by deciding to perform *Kanjinchō* even though the play itself, and especially the leading role of Benkei, was regarded by the main Ichikawa family of *kabuki* actors as their monopoly. *Kanjinchō* was one of the Eighteen Favourite Plays of the Ichikawa family.[2] Chōjūrō performed Benkei without obtaining permission. Again Zenshin-za's performance proved to be a great success among *kabuki* fans and the company boosted its recognition in the *kabuki* world. Subsequently the Ichikawa family gave permission for other plays from the Eighteen to be performed by the company.

In the first half of the 1930s, *shingeki* plays on historical subjects figure prominently beside productions of classical *kabuki* in Zenshin-za programmes. Most of them were by playwrights formerly associated with proletarian drama and thus can be seen, at least by association, as a kind of counterbalance to the feudal ethic informing classical favourites such as *Kanadehon Chūshingura*. 'Popular drama' (*taishū engeki*) formed a third category of play regularly performed by Zenshin-za. This grew out of a boom for historical novels of a fast-paced and often repetitious type that occurred soon after the Great Kantō Earthquake in 1923, stimulated by advances in printing technology that allowed enormous print runs. Hasegawa Shin (1884–1963) was a leading pioneer of popular literature and he was active over the whole range of the media which provided it, writing novels, plays and film scenarios. His main subjects were the *yakuza* gamblers of the Tokugawa period, in particular the loners who toured the country offering their services temporarily to different local *oyabun* or bosses. Into the obligation-based morality of this grim, but easily romanticised society, Hasegawa injected a humanitarian ethos that had appealed earlier to Sawada Shōjirō, who created one of this writer's most famous characters not long before his death. Hasegawa was later closely associated with Zenshin-za during its first two years of existence, and one of his plays appeared in well over half of the monthly programmes during that period.

Given the dominance of *kabuki* actors within the company and its progressive-sounding name and professed outlook, one might reasonably expect Zenshin-za to have encouraged new playwriting from writers working in *shin-kabuki*. There were indeed many *shin-kabuki* plays in the company's production lists and few of the monthly programmes during the decade did not include one play that could be put into that category. On the whole, however, it was the well-established playwrights that Zenshin-za performed. In 1932 Kawatake Mokuami's plays were prominent and this connection with the Meiji pioneer of reformed *kabuki* was maintained with sporadic productions later on. Tsubouchi Shōyō was also performed. From 1934 Okamoto Kidō's name appeared regularly in Zenshin-za programmes. One of the most famous names in *shin-kabuki*, his plays figured frequently in production lists of mainstream *kabuki* during this time. No-one has suggested, however, that Kidō was moving *shin-kabuki* playwriting forward during this time. He was enormously prolific, but he never reached the heights of the earlier plays, in particular *Shuzenji Monogatari*.[3] His plays in the 1930s were redolent of pre-Meiji *kabuki* and permeated by standard conflict situations that were resolved in predictable ways. It was much to Zenshin-za's advantage to enjoy the support of this popular playwright, but in performing his plays they were only giving their audiences a slight variation on what would have been available at any Shōchiku-controlled *kabuki* theatre.

Films were also an important part of Zenshin-za's varied activities. Ten were shot between 1935 and 1940 under contract to Japan's two largest film companies, Nikkatsu and Tōhō. One film made for Nikkatsu and released in 1935 was voted second in its Best Ten list by *Kinema Junpō*, the leading film journal at the time. (Engeki Hakubutsukan 1962: vol. 3, 389)

Zenshin-za was by now financially secure and it was able to contemplate fulfilling one of the dreams it had entertained at its founding – the creation of an artistic community which would live together as well as acting together. In 1937 Zenshin-za achieved this by the construction of a large-scale study centre, with rehearsal rooms, offices and living accommodation. As the company's success continued, this was enlarged in 1940 and 1942. A community life was established in which everything was decided by general debate. Everything one might need for everyday life was available on site and everyone, including spouses and children, partook collectively in the activities of the company.

While Zenshin-za challenged some of the basic principles on which *kabuki* as a theatre genre was based, the struggle to create a theatrical identity outside that framework seems to have left little opportunity for promoting new *kabuki* playwriting. Somewhat paradoxically this function was fulfilled by someone within the Shōchiku organisation, namely Mayama Seika, whose contribution to *shimpa* playwriting was noted in Chapter 2.

ICHIKAWA SADANJI II AND MAYAMA SEIKA

Sadanji II came into his own as a *kabuki* actor in the 1930s. After early problems with his technique and his struggle to win any kind of acceptance from the *kabuki* establishment, he had gradually matured through the Taishō period as a result of the stability afforded by Ōtani's faith in him and through his collaboration with Okamoto Kidō. He was more suited both by inclination and acting style to new plays and during the 1930s he branched out from the now somewhat predictable plays of Kidō and moved closer to Mayama Seika. Seika, also enjoying the patronage of Ōtani, needed an actor to whom he could respond fully as a playwright after the death of Sawada Shōjirō and he wrote some of his best plays for Sadanji during the 1930s.

Ōtani was instrumental in setting up this partnership, in particular by commissioning a series of plays from Seika specifically for Sadanji. Although Ōtani used Sadanji in several Tokyo theatres in the early 1930s, he became convinced that *kabuki* would benefit from some clear indication that Sadanji was regarded as having his own identity as an actor. While the other famous actors of the time had different strengths in the more presentational aspects of *kabuki* acting and could be reviewed on that basis, Sadanji had usually suffered in comparison when appearing on a mixed programme with them. From 1935 Shōchiku pursued a policy of contrasting Sadanji's ability at acting and interpreting new plays with Onoe Kikugorō VI's pre-eminent skills in performing the classics. Henceforth Kikugorō's base was to be seen to be the Kabuki-za and Sadanji was to reign at the Tōkyō Gekijō across the road.

Reigning with him were Mayama Seika and Okamoto Kidō, although in terms of innovation and variety Mayama was by far the more active. As Mayama progressed in his career through the 1930s, he moved from a period of intense experimentation through solid historicity to a major re-dramatisation of the Chūshingura story. During these years Sadanji played more lead roles in Mayama premieres than any other *kabuki* actor, thus incidentally confirming his own flexibility as an actor.

Although plays about *yakuza* were the forte of Hasegawa Shin, Mayama Seika also tried his hand at them in the early years of the decade and Sadanji played the lead in two such plays. They told the story of Kunisada Chūji (1810–1850), a popular Robin Hood figure of the first half of the nineteenth century whose exploits had invited a number of dramatisations. The first of Mayama's two plays on Kunisada was premiered in 1932. Kunisada started in on a gambling career at nineteen and soon established a position of undisputed authority as *yakuza* boss (*oyabun*) in his area (in modern Mie Prefecture). In 1834 he won a notable victory in a battle against the forces of a rival *oyabun*. He spent the rest of the decade on the run, as the authorities had condemned him to death in his absence. In 1843, as the search for him intensified, he transferred to Shinshū (present Nagano Prefecture) and *en route* he sacked a border post. After three years in hiding in Shinshū, he returned to his home area, where, after suffering a stroke, he was arrested and crucified.

Kunisada Chūji had usually been presented as a swash-buckler whose main dramatic interest was his exploits, but Mayama's Kunisada was a rather reflective hero, an aspect of Mayama's treatment of him that was immediately picked up by the critics. Like some previous Mayama lead characters, Kunisada is anxious to achieve a particular objective, needs power to do so, but is wary both of acquiring the power and then, once having acquired it, of using it. Sadanji's acting style was ideally adapted to such a part and his interpretation was praised. Not that the plays lacked action. Again, as in previous Mayama studies of heroes torn within themselves, Kunisada's inner conflict is projected onto two trusted lieutenants, and one of them, the more cautious one, is dramatically cut down on stage by Kunisada.

As a playwright Mayama is noted for his play series and this dramatisation of what he saw as the salient elements of Kunisada's life was spread over two plays. He wrote a number of studies of famous historical figures in a two-play format, with each play able to stand on its own but the two of them together achieving a complementarity that has impressed some critics. Mayama also wrote a three-play series and a ten-play series based on the same principles. The trilogy concerned the handover of Edo castle, which effectively meant the surrender of the huge city of Edo, to the victorious imperial troops, which ushered Japan into the modern age. Mayama was thus using the multi-part format to chart the activities of those most concerned in the resolution of this epochmaking conflict. Sadanji, ably supported by Ennosuke, played both the character with the most power (Saigō, leader of the imperial forces) and the character with the least power (the surrendering shgun, Yoshinobu).

The first play of the trilogy, *Edo-jō Sōzeme* (*General Attack on Edo Castle*) had been written and premiered in 1926, also with Sadanji and Ennosuke in the leading roles. When it starts, the last shogun, Yoshinobu, has already surrendered to the imperial anti-*bakufu* forces led by Saigō, and the chief *bakufu* minister sends an emissary to Saigō's camp to plead for the life of Yoshinobu. It is at this point that the second play, *Yoshinobu Inochigoi* (*Pleading for Yoshinobu's Life*, written in 1933) begins. In some ways the emissary, Yamaoka, is a more satisfying part than that of Saigō, to whom he is passionately appealing for his master to be spared. Mayama, like all *kabuki* playwrights, had to some extent to write with certain actors in mind. Sadanji had great stage presence in modern *kabuki* plays, especially those involving dense dialogue like Mayama's, and Mayama needed to give Yamaoka, whom he knew Ennosuke was going to play, some passages of high dramatic intensity to counterbalance Sadanji's gravitas as Saigō.

Mayama's plays were sometimes criticised at the time for being too wordy and the first act of the third play *Shōgun Edo o Saru* (*The Shogun Leaves Edo*, premiered 1934) contains some of the longest speeches Mayama ever wrote. It was a *tour de force* for Sadanji to deliver them. Later in the play, however, Mayama shifts his style more towards what *kabuki* fans were used to – actions which spoke louder than words. After Yamaoka, again played by Ennosuke, has made a deliberately emotional appeal to Yoshinobu (also played by Sadanji) to leave Edo and thus spare the bloodshed that his continuing presence might occasion, the dialogue becomes more sparse and the symbolism of the last shogun leaving the castle built by his family nearly three centuries before is created mainly through the body language of the characters concerned.

Mayama's contribution to *kabuki* playwriting is usually summarised under two heads: his historicism and his use of language. He was passionately interested in Japanese history, to the extent that he spent much of his time and most of his money on his historical research. The fruits of this research were mainly incorporated into his plays, but the edition of his collected works published between 1975 and 1977 also contains some substantial articles on historical topics. The trilogy mentioned above was written after exhaustive research by Mayama both in contemporary sources and through interviews with people involved in the events described.

There are many aspects to Mayama's use of language. *Kabuki* actors describe it as uncompromisingly packed with meaning and therefore difficult to paraphrase if their memory fails them on stage. It is rich in metaphor, and it can switch abruptly from being pedantically detailed to being grippingly vivid. All these qualities, in addition to a historicism sometimes very apparent and sometimes moderated in the interests of drama, were strongly present in Mayama's last great dramatic statement made in collaboration with Sadanji and Ennosuke.

MAYAMA SEIKA'S *GENROKU CHŪSHINGURA*

This was his Chūshingura cycle written between 1934 and 1941 and given the overall title of *Genroku Chūshingura* (*A Treasure House of Loyal Retainers in the Genroku Period*). This series of ten plays provided Sadanji with some of his finest *shin-kabuki* roles. Furthermore, its adoption by Zenshin-za during the war after Sadanji's death links Mayama with post-war *kabuki*, where his plays are still performed.

An outline of the events comprising the Chūshingura story was given in the Introduction. Mayama was by no means the only post-Meiji playwright to use its material for plays. From Mokuami onwards the human issues and the stirring deeds in the Chūshingura story, not to mention the tenacity with which it maintained its hold over audiences' imaginations, had commended the story to playwrights and especially impresarios. It was Ōtani who suggested to Mayama that he should write his own Chūshingura for Sadanji and he eagerly accepted the challenge.

Of the Chūshingura plays that Mayama wrote during Sadanji's lifetime two have established themselves as *shin-kabuki* classics. These were the first, in 1934, and the last but one, in 1940, and they are quintessential Mayama. The intervening plays generally follow a chronological sequence and are more obviously part of a continuing historical narrative. Perhaps for that reason, and also because most of them challenge the romantic image of the forty-seven *rōnin*, they have been individually less popular, only coming into their own when the whole series of *Genroku Chūshingura* plays is presented together.

The first play, *Ōishi Saigo no Ichinichi (Ōishi's Last Day)* dramatises the very end of the sequence of events that make up the Chūshingura story. It is Ōishi's 'last day' because, as leader of the vendetta group, he receives the final judgement of the military government, and he and the others file out before the last curtain to commit the honourable suicide that they have been granted as punishment for their crime of killing Kira. The play centres, however, on the love of one of the younger *rōnin* for a girl who manages to infiltrate herself, disguised as a page, into the residence where he is being kept prisoner. For her to persuade Ōishi to allow her to see her lover involves a range of emotional appeals and the demonstration of great strength of character on her part (as a woman disguised as a man, but played by a male actor). Nowadays audiences will sometimes clap as Ōishi signals his consent for the two to meet and the scene clearly has dramatic force.

It was reported that on occasion when Sadanji was acting his part in the penultimate *Genroku Chūshingura* play there were tears in his eyes. (Powell 1990: 176) It was the last play he appeared in before he died in February 1940. His role was Tsunatoyo in *Ohama Goten Tsunatoyo-kyō (Lord Tsunatoyo at his Hama Estate)*, a future shogun conscious of his delicate political position but wishing the revenge on Kira to take place and willing one of the conspirators to tell him that indeed a revenge is planned. A series of male and female characters have reasons to be afraid of divulging a piece of information that they hold but yet want to use that information for the end that they all desire – a successful vendetta on the part of the forty-seven *rōnin*. As a blend of all the elements that define Mayama's playwriting, with the bonus of a strong female character,

Ohama Goten is known as Mayama's masterpiece.

SHIMPA IN THE 1930S

On the whole *kabuki* fared well in the 1930s. Its classical repertory was served by some superlative actors, while it was not short of new plays of high quality which challenged established and aspiring actors alike. There was thus much within the *kabuki* world itself to keep its actors busy. *Shimpa*, by contrast, still seemed to feel that it was hovering between *kabuki* and *shingeki*, and at several points in the decade tried to reposition itself within the wide spectrum of theatre active at the time. The movement of *shimpa* actors about that whole spectrum tended to give the impression that *shimpa* simply meant the coming together of certain actors for a production. It also showed that actors and actresses primarily associated with *shimpa* had the flexibility of technique to please audiences with widely differing expectations.

Shimpa had revived in the second half of the 1920s, helped greatly by the popularity of new stars like Mizutani Yaeko and the *onnagata* Hanayagi Shōtarō (1894–1965). Although most of the well-known actors led their own *shimpa* companies, from 1929 onwards there were frequent high-profile grand productions of *shimpa*, for which all the stars assembled. The success of these gave *shimpa* the boost it needed and the emergence of a new and very popular playwright at the beginning of the 1930s ensured an audience base for the genre for the rest of the decade.

In 1931 a company which included Hanayagi alongside older stars such as Ii, Kitamura and Kawai performed a play entitled *Futasuji-michi* (*Forked Road*) by Seto Eiichi. Seto (1892–1934) was Osaka born and he had become one of the playwrights attached to Ii's company in 1922 after having dropped out of formal education. There he learnt to write parts for specific actors and, unlike Mayama Seika, he seems to have accepted the prevailing ethos of the *shimpa* world. *Futasuji-michi* is in the mould that is stereotypically *shimpa*; indeed the title itself is a commonly used metaphor expressing the standard conflict between personal feelings and obligation. A tale of three *geisha*, one now respectably married, one with spirit, and one in love with a businessman on the brink of failure, the play focuses on the familiar choice that the lovelorn woman has to make. As such characters usually did, she renounces her love.

The setting of the play – the world of the *geisha* – was one common to all his previous plays. The outcome was only to be expected. The box-office potential for familiar themes in Japanese theatre has been noted before in this book, but for some reason *Futasuji-michi* was an unusual success. Seto seems to have taken particular care over the part – young, intelligent and quick-tempered – that he wrote for Hanayagi and it is likely, given Hanayagi's popularity, that this added an extra lustre to the performances. (Ōyama 1969: vol. 3, 210) Whatever it was, it was capitalised on by Shōchiku and *Futasuji-michi* eventually had seven sequels, including one that was performed in the Kabuki-za at the end of 1932, the first time for twelve years that *shimpa* had performed in Shōchiku's flagship *kabuki* theatre.

Futasuji-michi and its sequels might have continued beyond 1932, but Ii Yōhō died and the series concluded with a play that was his memorial. In the short space of little over a year *Futasuji-michi* had given some stability to *shimpa* by laying the foundations for a lasting popularity. While the world of the *geisha* had been staple fare for *shimpa* since its inception, Seto injected into his plays on the subject a sincere sympathy for what was in many ways a harsh way of life. Plays with *geisha* as heroines continued to be popular after *Futasuji-michi*.

Seto died in 1934 and his place as leading playwright for *shimpa* was taken by Kawaguchi Matsutarō (1899 –1985). Kawaguchi had in his younger days been a pupil of Osanai Kaoru and was well aware of the aspirations of the modern theatre movement. He was also, however, involved in the business side of entertainment in the 1930s and the need for commercial success shaped many of his plays. His interests were broader than Seto's, but many of his successes shrewdly utilised the familiar elements that *shimpa* audiences appreciated. He was frequently commissioned to write the second play on a *shimpa* programme (the *nibanme-mono*). It was often this play that decided the commercial fate of the whole programme and he did not let Shōchiku down. Several Kawaguchi plays have become *shimpa* classics in the postwar period.

INOUE MASAO'S 'MIDDLE-OF-THE-ROAD THEATRE'

While *shimpa* was steadily gaining audiences with the plays of Seto and Kawaguchi, Inoue Masao was entertaining doubts about whether it had really achieved its true potential. In the 1910s he had tried to pull *shimpa* in the direction of the new medium of film and now he determined that *shimpa* was too near *kabuki* in its approach to its audiences. In 1936 he proposed a new category of theatre to which he gave the name 'middle-of-the-road theatre' (*chūkan engeki*), and his intention was that it should be half-way between *shimpa* as it was at the time and *shingeki*. He formed a company to perform this new genre and in June 1936 in the Kabuki-za they mounted a production of Hisaita Eijirō's *Dansō* (*Fault Line*) directed by Murayama Tomoyoshi. Hisaita (1898–1976) was well known as a playwright who had been associated with left-wing theatre a decade earlier and this play had itself been premiered by one of the leading left-wing companies of the 1930s. Similarly

Murayama was thought of as clearly belonging to the left-wing camp, although by this time he had publicly renounced his Marxism under police duress. Perhaps more important than the political affiliation of some of the personalities connected with Inoue's company at this time was their image as the leaders of new drama in Japan. While Seto and Kawaguchi were certainly commercially successful, Inoue was performing playwrights like Hisaita, Miyoshi Jūrō (1902–1958) and Mayama Seika, whose plays would attract intellectual interest for their potential to bring something new to Japanese culture. Inoue's company (Inoue Engeki Dōjō: Inoue's Theatre Gymnasium) regularly performed new plays by such playwrights over the next five years.

SHIMPA FLOURISHES

Shimpa was now on offer to Tokyoites almost every month and as 1937 progressed there was even a choice of *shimpa* productions in some months. In February the 50th Anniversary of the start of *shimpa* was imposingly celebrated in the Kabuki-za. Over 170 actors and actresses were mobilised and each performance started with a line up of actors formally attired, bowing low to the audience. One by one they announced their names, thanked the spectators for their past patronage and expressed the hope that this patronage would continue into the future. This was a direct borrowing from the traditional theatre where such ceremonies had been practised since the early seventeenth century. *Kōjō*, as they were called, were frequently utilised by Shōchiku to draw attention to special productions of *kabuki*. This golden jubilee *kōjō* and its location – the Kabuki-za – illustrated vividly the dilemma of identity that *shimpa* faced. Shōchiku was packaging it as if it was *kabuki*, whereas some of its leading actors were more anxious to present it as a type of theatre significantly more in touch with the times.

Shimpa's fortunes improved steadily during the next two years. At the end of 1937 Hanayagi enjoyed great success as Komako in the first stage adaptation of Kawabata Yasunari's novel *Yukiguni* (*Snow Country*) and then in September 1938 Shōchiku gave over the whole of the vast Kokusai Gekijō to a *shimpa* programme, granting Hanayagi the use of nine microphones, more than double what they usually provided for other companies. Hanayagi, now at the height of his powers, made a request to Ōtani for him and his closest co-actors to be treated as an independent artistic unit. Ōtani agreed to regular spring and autumn programmes by Hanayagi's group and in November 1939 this was formally graced by the name of Shinsei Shimpa (Reborn Shimpa). Although Shinsei Shimpa only achieved formal recognition from Shōchiku at this time, it can also be seen as the culmination of efforts, started in the early 1920s, of a group of actors and writers to revitalise *shimpa*. Shinsei Shimpa aroused the interest of many in the theatrical and intellectual worlds. It attracted the leading playwrights of the day and performed adaptations of novels by famous novelists, such as *Gan* (*The Wild Geese*) by Mori Ōgai and *Shunkinshō* (*The Tale of Shunkin*) by Tanizaki Jun'ichirō.

Shimpa ended the 1930s on a high note. Shinsei Shimpa won an important theatrical prize in1940, although Shinkokugeki and Zenshin-za were also in contention. Its success had prompted Kitamura and Kawai to form their own identifiable group, to which they gave the name Honryū Shimpa (Mainstream Shimpa). By choosing such a name they set out to contrast their company with Hanayagi's by emphasising a policy of continuing in the main to perform plays on the subjects regarded as central to *shimpa*. Together with Inoue's Engeki Dōjō and the company that had earlier been formed around Mizutani Yaeko, four separate *shimpa* companies were regularly performing in major theatres in Tokyo and other large cities.

Thus the 'dark valley,' in the phrase coined to designate the political situation during this period, was at least illuminated a little by theatre. The commercial theatre – that part of Japan's theatre activity that was dominated by commercial considerations – thrived and diversified, continuing its classical repertory while supporting innovation in several ways. Its productions caused little worry to the censors, for it concentrated most on providing entertainment of a high technical standard in effective theatre spaces. It was perhaps a measure of the control that the authorities had already established over theatre that in these spheres previous association with anti-establishment activities did not invite extra-vigilant attention from the censors. Ennosuke performed throughout the 1930s, several former proletarian playwrights contributed regularly to commercial repertories, the whole of Zenshin-za was known to be progressive, and even as substantial a work as Mayama's *Genroku Chūshingura* had aspects that have been interpreted as left-wing, but commercial theatre in 1930s Japan sailed serenely on, supported by theatre-goers who preferred not to see anything that might remotely have been thought to be subversive in the plays they were watching.

SHINGEKI VIGOROUS BUT UNDER SUSPICION

Such courtesy from the censors was not extended to *shingeki*, most of whose practitioners had to be very wary of the police during this period. In terms of playwriting and acting – the practicalities of theatre – there was much genre boundary crossing during these years, but in the minds of the authorities *shingeki* had a distinct character and needed close supervision. Throughout the 1930s the main *shingeki* companies were regarded with suspicion and, apart from being subject to a censorship system which had not changed since the previous decade, their performances were regularly watched by police auditors who would now quite frequently take down names and addresses of members of the audiences.

This was hardly surprising given the way that *shingeki* had developed in the early years of the decade. Overt political propaganda was not possible in the theatre after 1934, but the authorities were not unaware that *shingeki* was still a powerful symbol for many intellectuals and students, who had no means of expressing their opposition to the advance of militarism. Simply to attend a performance of *shingeki*, even of a politically innocuous play, was thought of as an act of protest, and one would always find like-minded people there. The politicised workers had disappeared from *shingeki*'s auditoria, but politically frustrated intellectuals were there in force.

It was not only proletarian theatre that had been compelled to discontinue activities in 1934. A similar fate had met proletarian artists over the whole range of the left-wing arts movement, in particular in the sphere of the novel. The novelists' organisation (Nihon Puroretaria Sakka Dōmei, the Japan Proletarian Writers League) had always had a central part to play in this movement and much theoretical debate had taken place among its members. It too was forced to disband in 1934 and this took place amid vigorous debate over the type of theoretical stance that would allow its members to continue writing.

The debate over theory revolved around the recommendation in 1932 from the Union of Soviet Writers, looked to as a main source of theoretical inspiration by left-wing Japanese writers, for the new stage of the literary movement to adhere to 'socialist realism' as the methodology behind all literary works. This formulation implied that one stage of the socialist revolution had been achieved and the resulting changed society should be described as it really was. While this could be justified in the USSR, 'socialist realism' was manifestly irrelevant to Japan's social circumstances in the early 1930s. Now that there was no question of the police allowing any literary slogans that even hinted at a political agenda, Japanese writers and theorists addressed the problem of what kind of realism would be suitable for Japan.

Four theatre people took part in this debate. From the plays that were written later it would seem that their individual formulations at this time only affected dramatic writing in a very marginal way. Most uncompromising was Kubo Sakae (1900–1958) in his call for anti-capitalist realism, later embodied in the most famous play of the period, which ironically suffered no problems with the censors.[4] Murayama himself preferred the more flexible 'developmental realism', which allowed him some scope in his fiction writing. He did not, however, produce a major play for *shingeki* during this period, instead concentrating his playwriting energies on historical plays for *kabuki* and *shimpa*. His importance in 1930s *shingeki* was more as a director and organiser.

Soon after his release from gaol he took the lead in trying to resurrect the left-wing drama movement. In July 1934 he published an article entitled 'The crisis in *shingeki*' in a major intellectual monthly, in which he called for cooperation between the various *shingeki* groups.[5] Here he argued, or rather passionately pleaded, for a large unified *shingeki* company which would be progressive yet commercially viable, with an artistic conscience and a unified directorial style. This 'Great *Shingeki* Union' would have the power and influence to rebuild *shingeki* into a major force in Japanese theatre.[6]

Murayama's dream was not realised. A new company did result from the grandiose plans to unite everyone involved in *shingeki*, and this in itself must be accounted something of an achievement, but the overarching organisation that Murayama had hoped for never materialised. The new company, given the name Shinkyō Gekidan (New Cooperative), mounted the most celebrated *shingeki* productions of the next six years. Its membership at its foundation in November 1934 consisted mainly of former members of Sayoku Gekijō, with the addition of a number of disaffected Shin Tsukiji Gekidan actors and members of a smaller group which had only been formed at the beginning of the year.[7] Many leading *shingeki* personalities from the 1920s were associated with Shinkyō Gekidan and it started life as a potentially authoritative presence. Shin Tsukiji Gekidan, however, in spite of the defections to Shinkyō, was still very much a viable company and remained the principal rival to Shinkyō until 1938. These years are often referred to as the Shinkyō-Shin Tsukiji Era.

Shinkyō's first production, in the month of its foundation, was a great critical, if not financial, success. It was an adaptation by Murayama of one of the last novels of Shimazaki Tōson, *Yoake-mae* (*Before the Dawn*). Tōson was still serialising it at the time of the Shinkyō production, and so it shared with *Konjiki Yasha* in the Meiji period the dubious distinction of being adapted for the stage before it was complete. By this time, however, the main lines of the plot had been laid down and Murayama could write Part I of this two-part play with some confidence that he could convey what Tōson intended. The novel spans a number of years (1853–1866) of great political change in Japan and is set in a village which though remote is uniquely situated to learn about, reflect and be affected by those changes. The main character, Hanzō, is torn between his inherited duties under the feudal system, which involve financial levies on local hard-pressed farmers, and his aspirations for the new age – the 'dawn' of the title – that Japan stands poised to enter. The strong possibility of an allegorical interpretation was no doubt not lost on the rather small audiences of intellectuals who watched this first production. There was nothing overtly political in the text, however, and true to the new emphasis on a less politically directed realism, the sets, costumes and production were scrupulously authentic in the sense that they reproduced 1850s daily life in great detail. Shinkyō Gekidan lost money on this and many future productions. It was always in financial trouble, but Murayama had at least succeeded in restoring some of the lost pride of the politically committed wing of the *shingeki* movement.

Left-wing *shingeki* had enjoyed a period of dominance in the late 1920s, and Shinkyō and Shin Tsukiji's vigorous activity in the mid-1930s ensured that it maintained a high profile even during these troubled years. During 1934, however, a theatrical event had occurred which had suggested that the formerly repressed side of the *shingeki* movement might become a force to be reckoned with. While the playwright concerned, Mafune Yutaka (1902–1977), had a left-wing past and most of the remembered *shingeki* successes of 1934–1938 were associated with the left, the extraordinary reception given to the production of his rather apolitical play *Itachi* (*Weasels*) in September 1934 seemed to confirm the staying power of those who had stood apart from proletarian theatre. The actors who performed *Itachi* all came from the professedly artistic wing of the *shingeki* movement. The director, Kubota Mantarō, had achieved success as a playwright in the 1920s with non-political plays.

The play concerned a remote village in the deprived Tōhoku (northeastern) area of Japan and a family business in that village in a severe state of decline. The young head of the household has gone off to make his fortune, but now the debts are being called in, with the main creditor being his aunt whose relationship with his mother is one of intense mutual hatred. The play seems mainly to be saying, with occasional touches of humour, that a harsh environment brutalises human beings, but the effects of this brutalisation are depicted with such intensity through the dialogue that audiences at the time were greatly moved. Even left-wing critics, while decrying the lack of an obvious political standpoint, acknowledged the dramatic power that Mafune had achieved. *Itachi* brought Mafune, a playwright with no previous successes, into the limelight and ensured that he did not lack offers to perform his plays for the rest of the decade.

Shinkyō Gekidan's next success shows some similarities to *Itachi*. This was Hisaita Eijiro's *Dansō* (Fault Line), first performed in November 1935. Like *Itachi* it was set in northeastern Japan, an area that was becoming almost a dramatic cliché for poverty and what it can do to human beings. While the social and economic level of the family at the centre of Hisaita's play, however, is considerably higher, the action of the play is driven by the individual characters' mutual hatred and need to get money out of each other, so that again the spectator wonders whether any values at all have survived the financial break-up of the family. The dearth of common standards is made more poignant by the fact that two characters have embraced Christianity. Hisaita was committed to left-wing drama, but here he seemed to be adopting a similar dramaturgical method to Mafune in concentrating on the portrayal of morally depraved characters without directly suggesting the source of their depravity. What seemed to be significant about *Dansō* at the time, however, was that here the focus was on a bourgeois family and their problems, whereas previously Hisaita's plays had been primarily concerned with those affected by the financial behaviour of such families.

If the Shinkyō and Shin Tsukiji groups could not openly profess their political beliefs on the stage, in other respects 1936 was a year of great achievement in all other aspects of their theatrical activity. This was in spite of unprecedented social tension occasioned by a rebellion by army officers in February. Both groups mounted productions regularly during the year, Shinkyō nine in total and Shin Tsukiji ten. Almost all were performed in the Tsukiji Little Theatre, which could be said finally to be fulfilling its promise as a venue for high quality productions of plays by both Japanese and foreign playwrights. Fujimori Seikichi was now turning his hand to historical dramas and his play about the mid-nineteenth-century intellectual and reluctant political activist Watanabe Kazan ushered in a period of intense interest in the potentiality of historical drama by the two main *shingeki* companies. Foreign playwrights included Gorki and Molière, and Senda Koreya's productions of the latter were well received. Comedy had not featured much in the rather earnest 1920s repertory in the Tsukiji Little Theatre, and Shin Tsukiji's productions reflected a growing appropriation on the part of *shingeki* practitioners of a dynamic comic tradition that had so far been relatively free of Western influences. Thus the varied activity centred on the Tsukiji Little Theatre was characterised by vigour and self-confidence, to such an extent that it was hailed as the 'revival of *shingeki*'. (Sugai 1973: 48)

The person who made this claim for 1936 *shingeki* was himself at the time the head of Shin Tsukiji's governing body and he was thinking of a revival of *shingeki* as performed by groups and actors associated with proletarian drama a decade earlier. This was not unreasonable even at this time, because non-political groups achieved little prominence in the mid-1930s. This was partly due to their rejection of the Tsukiji Little Theatre as a venue because to them it was still too closely associated with the political theatre of the 1920s. Thus their productions were often given in the Hikōkan (the intriguingly named Hall of Flight), a theatre important in the history of *shingeki* but at this time lacking the charisma of the Tsukiji Little Theatre. Also personality clashes may well have played a part in weakening a movement dedicated to artistic aims in theatre that might be thought to have naturally benefited from the suppression of the left. The group that had performed *Itachi*, for example, had been founded by some actors who had taken issue with the leadership of the main non-political group of the early 1930s, Tsukiji-za (Tsukiji Company). That group went out of existence in March 1937, as did Tsukiji-za itself in February of this year.

ALTERNATIVE *SHINGEKI*

Tsukiji-za's brief existence belies its importance in *shingeki* history. Although never contemporaneous with either the Tsukiji Shōgekijō or the company that was to champion non-political theatre in the postwar period – Bungaku-za (Literary Theatre), it had links with both through the trio of people who founded and sustained it. These were an actress, a director and a playwright. Tamura Akiko (1905–1983) had been one of the two first actresses in Tsukiji Shōgekijō and was by now well-known on stage and screen. Her husband, Tomoda Kyōsuke (1899–1937), had also been a member of Tsukiji Shōgekijō, and the two of them had precipitated the split in the company by being the first to resign in 1929. In the heated meetings that had led up to the split over the previous year, Tomoda had on several occasions stated his strong conviction that drama and politics should be kept separate. He was a man not afraid to fight his corner when the odds were against him, and it seems likely that his forceful personality may have contributed to several of his actors leaving to found yet another company. The third person who had taken a lead in the founding of Tsukiji-za was a young playwright named Kishida Kunio (1890–1954).[8] Kishida too had been deeply unhappy at the way Tsukiji Shōgekijō had developed and had been seeking the essential wellspring of drama in something other than the ideological orientation of the playwright.

Tomoda was a vigorous leader and over the four years from the first production in February 1932 he directed no less than twenty-eight plays, most of them by Japanese playwrights. Some of the Japanese playwrights performed had established reputations, like Kubota Mantarō who was a firm supporter of the venture, while others were at the beginning of their careers. Many of the latter were being published in a new drama journal founded by Kishida also in 1932 and entitled *Gekisaku* (*Playwriting*).

Tomoda and Tamura had stated at the foundation of Tsukiji-za that they wanted *shingeki* to make a fresh start; they wanted to return to 1924 – the year in which Tsukiji Shōgekijō had been formed – or even to the period before the *shingeki* movement had been centred on that company and its purpose-built theatre. It was something of a personal quest for the two of them to develop their art free from what they saw as imperatives extraneous to drama. Kishida provided the theoretical backing to their practical theatre, as well as contributing to the practice by his own plays. He had been developing his own ideas on drama in published articles from the mid-1920s. (Rimer 1974: 79-105) While acknowledging the power of modern Western drama, as Tsukiji Shōgekijō had, he differed from the latter in believing that *shingeki* had to be developed in a thoroughly Japanese context and would not be served by productions, such as Osanai's and Hijikata's, that in effect reproduced Western theatre in Japan. Like Tsukiji Shōgekijō he rejected classical Japanese theatre as constituting a viable basis for modern drama, and what he then had left to work on was Japanese modern life as expressed in the modern Japanese language. Kishida's efforts became focused on the Japanese language and he urged playwrights to concentrate on realising the full potential of the language to express emotional change both abrupt and gradual, extreme and subtle. Drama had beauty – again something not much in evidence in left-wing theatre – and this was to be sought through words.

Tsukiji-za performed four of Kishida's plays and he wrote two others in 1935 that were intended for production by the group. Kishida is recognised as one of the most important *shingeki* playwrights and much of his reputation depends on the plays he wrote in the 1920s and early 1930s. His earlier plays, such as *Chiroru no Aki (Autumn in the Tyrol*, 1924), have an air of diffidence about them, as if Kishida was probing the possibilities of his playwriting style just as the characters are gently probing each other's feelings. By the thirties he knew what he was doing and his characters act with more certainty towards each other, although for a while this primarily illustrates rather unpleasant sides of human nature. This is particularly so in the case of *Mama-sensei to sono Otto (Teacher and her Husband*, 1930), where the motives revealed in others by Kishida's dialogue are generally selfish and inconsiderate ones. At this level there are superficial parallels with other plays of this period mentioned here; whether one entertained a certain view of historical and social development or not, it was distrust and hatred that found the most effective dramatic expression. Kishida moved beyond this in his 1935 play *Sawa-shi no Futari Musume (Mr Sawa's Two Daughters)*, whose eponymous lead he wanted Tomoda to play. Here a variety of motives are displayed and the context is a dramatically paced revelation of personal secrets, also something that had interested other playwrights confronted with the challenge of creating characters that are almost wholly themselves rather than being constructs of society.

The artistic activity and financial management of Tsukiji-za had been sustained almost entirely by Tomoda. He and Tamura had hoped that regular productions free, at least internally, of ideologically inspired pressures, would enable them to develop their acting skills and significantly increase their knowledge and awareness of Japanese theatre's needs. The production record of Tsukiji-za was remarkable in the circumstances, but by early 1936 Tomoda was beginning to feel that the burden was too great and the company was disbanded in February, ostensibly to allow him and his wife to concentrate their efforts on increasing their knowledge of theatre in general rather than having their time taken up with administrative matters.

The disbanding of Tsukij-za was something of a blow to the group of playwrights who had been given hope by the uncompromising artistic stance of the company and its leaders. Tomoda had hinted that he might attempt a relaunch at a later stage and Kishida was determined that this should happen. Kishida and Kubota set about organising the new company, which they planned should begin regular productions the next year, 1937.

The year 1937 has been mentioned several times in this chapter as one in which theatrical successes were achieved and new ventures initiated. The opening of the Kokusai Gekijō and its capacity *kabuki* performances, the 50th anniversary performances of *shimpa*, the construction of Zenshin-za's permanent home – these and other events in the theatrical world testified to a self-confidence that seemed much at odds with the worsening political situation. 1937 is also the year in which Japan's war in Asia started, as the attack by Japanese forces at the Marco Polo Bridge Incident in July began hostilities in China, which continued until Japan's surrender in 1945. It is not unknown for theatre to flourish in time of war, if economic conditions permit, for it offers solace when the latter is sorely needed, and temporarily Japanese theatre enjoyed a period of intense activity.

The history of Japanese theatre in the mid-1930s has been presented here in terms of two dichotomies – between commercial theatre and *shingeki*, and within *shingeki* between the politically committed and the artistically dedicated. It has been noted that while the boundaries between these categories were fairly clearly drawn, a significant number of active theatre practitioners chose to move between them. There was less such movement on the part of the audiences. On the whole commercial theatre attracted audiences from a wide social spectrum while *shingeki* relied on students and intellectuals to be its core supporters. There were exceptions to this, as intellectuals were certainly attracted to the *kabuki* of the Mayama Seika/Ichikawa Sadanji team in the Tōkyō Gekijō. One other area where commercially controlled theatre proved attractive to intellectuals was comedy.

COMEDY COMIC AND SERIOUS

Non-commercial theatre had also shown interest in comedy during this period. Shin Tsukiji Gekidan's productions have been mentioned. In addition a small *shingeki* group devoted to comedy, specifically translated French comedy, had been active in the first half of the decade. Teatoro Komedī (Théatre Comédie) had been founded in 1931. It had no theatrical agenda (only to raise money for the Keio University baseball team) and performed plays that took its fancy. It was a very young company and was said to be largely free of hierarchy in its organisation. (Toita 1961: 206) Its productions were sporadic, to say the least, but it is accorded a role in Japanese theatre history in that it brought attention to contemporary European comedy by such playwrights as Ferenc Molnár, whose gentle satires on bourgeois life revealed a concern for humanity that had not been perceived as possible in Japanese comedy.

In general comedy had been a low priority for *shingeki*. Teatoro Komedī was criticised by those involved in the powerful *shingeki* groups as not being serious, and of going no further than providing titillating entertainment for well-to-do audiences. The prevailing image of comedy was that it was something that had originated in and belonged primarily to the Kansai area and was closely associated with the somewhat vulgar world of Asakusa entertainment. As we have seen in earlier chapters, the Soganoya line of comedy was not as one-sided as this snobbish view suggests, and there was even less reason to dismiss comedy as the 1930s progressed.

Soganoya Gorō maintained his popularity through the 1930s performing in the Shinbashi Enbujō for several months of each year. His reforming days were over, however, and and he became more conservative in his espousal of social norms that by now many had questioned and if anything more insistent on commending them to his audiences through his plays.

As actor-playwright star of comedy, however, he was joined at the end of the 1920s by two other personalities who dominated this sphere of Japanese theatre in the early 1930s. These were Enomoto Ken'ichi (1904–1970) and Furukawa Roppa (1903–61). Both became household names, enormously popular wherever they performed their farcical revue sketches. Enoken (as Enomoto was affectionately known by his fans) had originally hoped to become a film star but instead started his career in show business in Asakusa opera in 1919. In 1929 he was one of a group of revue enthusiasts who founded the Casino Follies in Asakusa. Their programmes of song, dance and sketch items were immediately popular, apparently meeting the need for consolation at a time of great economic hardship. Enoken's popularity caused Shōchiku and Tōhō to vie for his services. At one point there was suspicion that Shōchiku was subsidising its financially precarious *kabuki* and *shimpa* operations with comedy. Furukawa Roppa, by contrast, came into comedy through the cinema, where he had earned a living as a *benshi* (film commentator). In the early 1930s the increasing penetration of talkies into films threatened the *raison d'etre* of the *benshi* and a group of them decided to try their hand at comedy. Roppa emerged above the rest as a comic superb at fast-paced repartee but also in tune with the concerns of a society determined to enjoy itself despite the uncertainty of the future. The mid-1930s onwards in comedy are often referred to as the Roppa-Enoken Period because of the dominance of these two performers.

What Enomoto Ken'ichi and Furukawa Roppa performed is variously put into the category of *kei-engeki* (light theatre) or *shinkigeki* (new comedy). The term 'light theatre' is often used to distinguish the two main types of comedy being performed at the time, of which this was one. Essentially it was centred on star performers who generally wrote their own material, and the financial health of the groups that performed it depended much on the continuing popularity of the stars. Enoken and Roppa are sometimes included in 'new comedy' because they were more sensitive to the contemporary concerns of their audiences than Soganoya Gorō, but neither of these categories has very firm boundaries.

It is, however, generally recognised that the comedy which one could watch in Shinjuku in the thirties at the Moulin Rouge was qualitatively different. To some this is the true 'new comedy'. This judgement tends to be based on how near comedy was to *shingeki*. The Moulin Rouge, which was founded in 1930 and lasted (with a change of name) until the last months of the Pacific War, provided entertainment which in some ways conformed to intellectual expectations of *shingeki*. It was, for example, playwright-centred, at least during the early years, and had a formally constituted literary section along the lines of *shingeki* companies. Its audiences contained a high proportion of students, and established writers and academics were often seen there. While standard comedy fare was available at the Moulin Rouge to those who were looking for this, the theatre also acquired a reputation as a place where subtle minds – and even on occasion not so subtle minds – could detect and applaud indirect criticism of the way in which Japanese politics and society were developing at the time. Thus to intellectuals worried about the political situation and convinced that they were powerless to affect it, the Moulin Rouge offered a chance to make a symbolic protest simply by their presence. There were many other opportunities to do this by attending *shingeki* performances, but the combination of comedy and the *frisson* that some plays could offer seemed more attractive. One well-known intellectual of the period is quoted as saying that he would attend *shingeki* productions if he were offered a free ticket, but if he had to pay for himself he would choose the Moulin Rouge. (Miyoshi 1980: 239)

Much of the success of the Moulin Rouge coincided with the time there of the playwright Ima Uhei (later, and better, known as Ima Harube). Ima, together with other young aspiring playwrights, joined the Literary Section of Moulin Rouge when the company was first organised. He stayed with Moulin Rouge until 1936 when he and others left. Ima's plays changed during these years. His early works were gentle in tone, almost celebrating the foibles of those whose status in life involved them in rather repetitive occupations but provided them with enough leisure to indulge in hopes for and even moves towards something economically, socially or romantically better. Such people are referred to in literature on new comedy as the 'petit bourgeois'. Ima, in such plays as *Kagerō wa Haru no Kemuri desu* ('Brume' is Smoke in Spring; 1934), described with affection the aspirations of his characters and the silliness which invariably resulted from pursuing them. Later, as in *Hei no Isshō* (Life of a Fence, 1936), he began to question whether all was well with that lifestyle, whether the prevailing social and political ethos did not rather force his characters into degrading situations. He himself expressed the view that playwrights like him had a role in being the mouthpiece of intellectuals who were being demoralised by the increasing restrictions on freedom of speech.

HEYDAY OF SHINKYŌ AND SHIN TSUKIJI

As new comedy faltered at the beginning of 1937, large-scale *shingeki* seemed to go from strength to strength. 1937 and 1938 saw two of the most celebrated prewar *shingeki* productions and, beginning in April 1937, the two competing entertainment conglomerates, Shōchiku and Tōhō, took notice of the commercial potential of *shingeki* by inviting *shingeki* companies to perform in their large city-centre theatres. This level of activity did not go unnoticed by the authorities, who were aware of the high profile that *shingeki* was acquiring through its performances in large theatres and were suspicious of the vigorous involvement of former proletarian theatre people. There was thus a brief period of triumphant success on the part of the Shin Tsukiji and the Shinkyō companies before both were forced to disband in 1940. In the meantime they were joined by the Bungaku-za, which became the major *shingeki* presence through the war years, however regrettable that seemed to disapproving and now dispossessed supporters of committed theatre.

At the beginning of April 1937 Shin Tsukiji Gekidan performed a play by Kikuchi Kan in a Shōchiku theatre located in the

Marunouchi main business district of Tokyo. Later that month Shinkyō performed Wedekind's *Spring Awakening*, by now a *shingeki* classic, in another Shōchiku theatre, and by the end of the year both companies had performed in such theatres for a second time. Their forays into these bastions of commercial theatre did not, however, diminish their loyalty to their Tsukiji Little Theatre patrons and between them they also mounted twelve productions in their home theatre. Two of these, as it happened one by each company, achieved great critical success and because of their subject matter may well have fuelled the suspicions of the Justice Ministry officials that *shingeki* was not adequately controlled.

The first of these, Hisaita Eijirō's *Hokutō no Kaze* (*Northeast Wind*), was performed by Shinkyō in March and, unusually, repeated at a different theatre in December. It has the reputation of being one of the two greatest plays of socialist realism, although as we have seen this was something of a misnomer. With *Hokutō no Kaze* Hisaita continued the process noted earlier of seeing dramatic potential more in characterisation than in social class. While the political message of the play is clear, all the main characters in *Hokutō no Kaze*, whatever their social background, engage his attention, and consequently ours, as human beings with strengths and weaknesses. Not only the characterisation, but also the setting is studiedly realistic, being based on an aspect of labour-management relations that would have been familiar to its audiences. The industrialist/politician on whom the central character is modelled was well known in Japan.

The argument of the play revolves around Japan's return to the gold standard in 1930 as a method of countering the effects of the world depression. As exports of luxury goods slumped, this measure caused great losses to the textile industry and extreme hardship in the countryside where raw silk production was a cottage industry of vital importance to poor farmers. In the latter half of *Hokutō no Kaze* Toyohara, the head of a large textile firm, goes into the Diet to lead opposition to government economic policy. At the beginning of the play, set in 1901, he is shown pacifying, indeed shaming, a group of female workers who are complaining of their working conditions. This he does by expounding, not for the first or last time, his views on the management ethic that he is convinced is right for Japanese industry. Expressing sympathy and fellow-feeling for them – itself very persuasive in a hierarchical system – and emphasising how much effort he puts into looking after their welfare, he compares his firm with others that are laying off their workers and reduces his listeners to tears as he promises to do all he can to protect their own jobs. Thus, in Act I his brand of management paternalism is appreciated by his employees and Toyohara is almost heroic as he persists with it in the face of major shareholders who want firm action to be taken. The rest of the play, however, is set in 1929 and 1930, when economic pressures are seen to be too great to be resisted by paternalism of this kind. The firm is in turmoil and political action is now the only way forward. The striking employees of his firm have helped to get Toyohara elected to the Diet and at the end of the play they are noisily looking to him to represent their interests.

Hokutō no Kaze is full of detailed discussion of management practice and economic policy. The list of characters is long and the various strands of the plot are intricately woven together. Hisaita could not be called a lively playwright on the basis of *Hokutō no Kaze*, which is generally recognised as his greatest play. His playwriting style is deliberate and even heavy at times. In the postwar period *shingeki* has often been criticised for its excessive seriousness and this play contributed to this image. It required considerable concentration on the part of its audiences, although this was often taken for granted anyway, and an engagement with political and economic problems. In spite of some moments of high drama, *Hokutō no Kaze* was a thinking person's play and it was greeted enthusiastically by its student and intellectual audiences.

Hokutō no Kaze was directed by Sugimoto Ryōkichi (1907–1939), one of the most active directors in Shinkyō, who was by this time recognised for his exceptional talent. Inoue Masao had also been employing him as a *shimpa* director from the previous year and Sugimoto was therefore associated with both *shimpa* and *shingeki* successes. While working in *shimpa* he met and fell in love with Inoue's leading lady, Okada Yoshiko, who at this time was wishing that she could be free of commercial pressures and work more in *shingeki*. Sugimoto proposed to Okada that they flee together to the Soviet Union. The fact that Hijikata Yoshi had been in Moscow since 1933 helped to reinforce Sugimoto's idealistic hope that his drama could be nourished in Russia until such time that he could return to Japan. In January 1938 Sugimoto and Okada crossed the border between Japan and the USSR on Sakhalin in deep snow, and thereby caused a sensation. They were parted and never met again. Sugimoto was shot a year later, but Okada was never told of the fate of her lover.

With the production of *Hokutō no Kaze* as a powerful contributory factor, *shingeki*'s profile as part of Japan's theatrical culture was significantly raised in 1937. Not only Shōchiku, but also Tōhō (in the next year, 1938) invited *shingeki* companies to use its theatres. If Shinkyō and Shin Tsukiji had wanted to be part of the theatrical establishment, it looked as though early 1937 might have been their chance, but suspicions of the government's wish to control the arts ran very deep. As it happened, the Diet had in the previous year passed a proposal to found a national theatre for Japan, and although this was enthusiastically welcomed by some, many *shingeki* people feared that such an institution would only provide an opportunity for further ideological interference. In 1937 the establishment was nearer than at any previous time to subsidising the best of Japanese theatre, as several earlier proposals had come to nothing, but while many favoured the stability that this would give the classical art of *kabuki*, few thought it would widen access to the theatre in the way they wanted.

So vibrant was *shingeki* activity in 1937, and also in 1938, that the China Incident seemed not to have much impact on it. While many commercial theatre productions were suspended in September and October and Shōchiku hastily set up screenings of newsreel footage, *shingeki* productions at the Tsukiji Little Theatre continued as normal, even registering another sensational success in October. This was a production of a stage adaptation of a novel entitled *Tsuchi* (*Earth*, by Nagatsuka Takashi).[9] Written in 1910 and based on the native area of its author, *Tsuchi* described the grinding poverty of the countryside and the actions it forced on human beings, against the background of some nostalgic evocation of the surrounding scenery and the festivals observed by the local people. Although the novel had not been inspired by any political ideology, no doubt the Shin Tsukiji Gekidan audiences who watched the adaptation in 1937 took what they wanted from it, some of them mindful of the fact that the adaptor had himself been active in the proletarian drama movement. But *Tsuchi* escaped the censors and took its place alongside *Itachi* and *Dansō* as plays whose subject matter were a severe indictment of Japanese society without indicating who might be to blame.

The success of *Tsuchi* was soon matched by a Shinkyō production of a play that has come to define 1930s *shingeki*. This was Kubo Sakae's *Kazanbaichi* (*Ash Terrace of the Volcano*) performed in June and July of 1938. Also about the countryside, this time of Hokkaido, this is a monumental play in two parts that has a cast of over sixty and takes roughly six hours to perform in full. Describing the play in terms of its main characters is to miss the point, because their concerns, emotions and interrelationships, although vividly depicted, constituted only part of Kubo's vision as the playwright. This is a play about Japanese agriculture at the time, about Japanese society as a whole, and about individuals who accept or stand against what is shown as the established order of things.[10]

The individual standing against the establishment is a young intellectual named Amamiya, who heads a team at the local agricultural research station. He is a good scientist, as is evidenced by the fact that he has married his professor's daughter, and he is also a thinking man deeply concerned at the plight of the farmers in his area, whose land is heavily contaminated with volcanic ash and needs extensive fertilisation just to enable them to make a bare living. Amamiya develops a fertiliser theory that runs counter both to the research of his father-in-law and to the fertiliser policy of the local hemp factory. Amamiya's wife sides with her father rather than her husband, and this emphasises his departure from social norms. The hemp factory can be taken to symbolise firstly the power of Japanese capitalism at the time, secondly the virtual colonial status of Hokkaido and thirdly, in that hemp had military applications, the dominant influence that militarism had on people's lives.

Stated like this, the plot of *Kazanbaichi* is a political allegory whose implications cannot have been lost on the censors. Similarly, Amamiya's horror at the direction his own political thinking is taking him – towards communism – is a subtle way, not unexploited elsewhere in prewar *shingeki*, of suggesting that the audience perhaps should also be thinking along those lines. If this had been the whole of the play, *Kazanbaichi* would probably have been banned, but it was not and the reason for this must lie in the way the plot is interrupted by numerous scenes from country life enacted by diverse social groups. Thus much of what could have been perceived as unacceptable political comment was buried in these meticulously researched vignettes of Hokkaido life. Kubo had set out to write a play that observed his ideological tenets and combined the results of scientific investigation with human interest. There has been much debate over whether he succeeded or not, but in the political circumstances of 1938 Japan *Kazanbaichi* was greeted with unrestrained enthusiasm by its audiences.

With the vigorous activity of Shin Tsukiji Gekidan and the individual successes of Shinkyō Gekidan, *shingeki*, particularly *shingeki* known to have previously had left-wing associations, was carrying all before it in the first half of 1938. Over the past three years it had been much more vigorous and organised than that part of the *shingeki* movement which took its stand on the artistic and dramatic worth of the plays performed, in spite of the fact that the latter had some fine actors and accomplished playwrights as supporters. In 1938, however, a group emerged that was to mount a concerted challenge to ideologically inspired theatre and become after the war one of the three leading *shingeki* companies.

BUNGAKU-ZA

Already in 1937 such an enterprise had been planned. In early September of that year a meeting had been arranged by three playwrights – Kishida Kunio, Kubota Mantarō, and Iwata Toyoo (1893–1969) – to explore the possibility of founding a new *shingeki* company. The trio had in mind to build the group around the husband and wife acting team of Tomoda Kyōsuke and Tamura Akiko. In the event Tomoda received his call-up papers on 1

September and the meeting thus turned into a send-off party for him. Subsequently the three playwrights set up a 'three-executive system', whereby responsibility for running the company and overseeing all its productions would be their joint responsibility. Thus from the start the group had a simple and clear, if somewhat autocratic, arrangement for leadership and control from the top. During the initial years the three took it in turns to assume ultimate responsibility for periods of six months. As a trio they had considerable charisma, Kishida being a popular novelist as well as a playwright, Kubota being highly respected as a veteran playwright of great experience, and Iwata known as a successful playwright, essayist and translator of French drama. It seems that the young actors and actresses that made up the initial company were inspired by these leaders and happy to accept their leadership.

All did not go well for the group during the first months of its existence. Tōhō, well aware of the potential draw of actors as good as Tomoda Kyōsuke and Tamura Akiko but before learning of Tomoda's call-up, had agreed to provide the Yūraku-za as the venue for the first production for a two-day run starting on 30 November. In the event Tomoda was one of the first casualties of Japan's war in China and Tamura refused to appear on stage, objecting violently to the media interest which had suddenly made celebrities – not to say, marketable personalities – of two people who only wanted to be good actors. (Tamura and Koyama 1962: 276-7) She resisted all attempts to persuade her to appear, and Tōhō decided that without Tomoda and Tamura the production was not worth supporting. It withdrew its offer to rent out the Yūraku-za and the production had to be cancelled.

The shock of Tomoda's death and the cancellation of their opening production seems to have resulted in a loss of momentum, and some of the younger members of the company were irked that their new careers were not starting soon enough. There is a suggestion too that at this stage the leaders felt that the acting strength of the company had to be supplemented by guest appearances of established actors. (Kitami 1963: 111) Guest actors were not uncommon in early productions, but an ensemble spirit soon developed and from among the company's own group of actors emerged names, such as that of Sugimura Haruko (1909–1997), which would draw audiences and help to provide stability. Still, however, in the matter of public image, the leaders proceeded cautiously and the new opening production was not announced as a full 'public production' (*kōen*) but as a 'trial production' (*shien*).

This took place in March 1938. The name under which the company appeared was Bungaku-za (a literal translation would be 'literature company', but its official English name was Literary Theatre). (Rimer 1974: 118-9) Both the name and the policy statement issued by the three leaders presented an unequivocal challenge to all the companies, commercial or otherwise, engaged in performing contemporary plays, but in particular to the two left-wing *shingeki* companies. The three playwrights stated that the healthy development of Japanese theatre was being impeded and audiences' attention diverted by, in a strange phrase, 'decorative devices'. Whatever was meant by that – it could cover the detailed but inconsistent realism of *shimpa* production style or the ideological flourishes of left-wing *shingeki* – Bungaku-za was aiming to give 'spiritual pleasure' to the 'intellectual masses' through stage performances. Its appeal was to cultured adults who had kept away from the theatre until then. Above all Bungaku-za rejected the politicisation of drama. True to its word, Bungaku-za mounted regular productions of new plays by Japanese playwrights and quickly established itself as a viable alternative to the now very powerful Shin Tsukiji and Shinkyō groups.

The adjective 'powerful' needs to be qualified. Within the modern drama movement, which at this time effectively meant *shingeki* as little innovative was going on in commercial theatre, Shinkyō and Shin Tsukiji's influence was dominant. The scale and range of their theatrical activities in Tokyo far surpassed that of other parts of the *shingeki* movement, and their frequent tours had ensured that their brand of theatre had been experienced by many outside the capital and was widely known. They were also able to mobilise financial power. Early in 1939 it was proposed that the Tsukiji Little Theatre, still owned by Hijikata Yoshi now long in Moscow, should be floated as a joint stock company so that Hijikata could be bought out and some major reconstruction and refurbishment could be undertaken. Shinkyō and Shin Tsukiji became the largest corporate shareholders as a result of this flotation.

LEFT-WING *SHINGEKI*'S FALL

Thus, by the end of 1939, by which time the new Tsukiji Little Theatre was already in operation, these two companies were poised to take *shingeki* forward along their own lines, with the example of *Kazanbaichi* there to reassure them that in spite of the deepening war situation and its social implications drama that was left-wing in inspiration could play an important part in this. This was not, however, to the liking of the bureau within the Ministry for Internal Affairs charged with controlling potentially subversive activities. The latter's extreme measures against left-wing theatre in 1934 seemed now to have been ineffectual in the long run and it was reported in the press that a national conference had been organised to coordinate and standardise censorship of the theatre. Interference in individual productions had become more frequent from the beginning of 1939. The dress rehearsal of a Shin Tsukiji production was visited by the dreaded Special Higher Police, even after many negotiations with the metropolitan police and considerable rewriting of the play concerned. (Okakura and Kinoshita 1960: 177)

The final blow was to come on 1 August 1940, when over a hundred members of Shinkyō Gekidan and Shin Tsukiji Gekidan were arrested and those remaining were strongly encouraged to take the initiative and disband their respective companies. Murayama Tomoyoshi himself was arrested in the morning and released in the evening after being put under considerable pressure to lend his personal authority to the independent decision that was looked for from Shinkyō. (Ozaki 1956: 157–8) The heads of Shinkyō and Shin Tsukiji made their way to Metropolitan Police Headquarters on 22 and 23 August respectively and reported that their companies had passed resolutions to disband. The statements issued by the two companies referred to regret for past mistakes and expressed a resolve to work for the establishment of a 'national drama' (*kokumin engeki*) in the future.

It is with 'national drama' that the next chapter of this book will be concerned. In 1940 only the former left-wing section of the *shingeki* movement, which was itself a relatively small part of the total entertainment of the time, was denied the freedom to perform as it wished, but all sections of the entertainment world would soon be affected by the developing war situation. The events of August 1940 mark a break with the previous decade because they were the clearest sign yet that the arts, like every other element in society, were going to be expected to participate fully and unequivocally in the war effort. The 1930s had been a vibrant decade in Japanese theatre, which had flourished against a political background of increasing instability. Now political stability had to be imposed in the national interest and ideological diversity in the arts could not be tolerated. As we shall see, the heady achievements of the theatre in the 1930s would not be forgotten, but for the duration of Japan's wars on the mainland and in the Pacific drama would fulfill a function that was defined for it.

5

Theatre Mobilised

What happened to theatre in wartime Japan is hardly surprising. The Japanese state was well practised in controlling theatre and suppressing those elements in it which were seen to be hostile and potentially dangerous to the establishment.[1] As we have seen, the system of theatre censorship was constructed in such a way that it could inflict maximum financial damage on any company rash enough to risk rousing its ire. Theatre people with the temerity to hold left-wing political beliefs had been arrested in great numbers, some of them several times, during the 1930s. As an institution and as a collection of individuals, theatre was vulnerable at this time of increased emphasis on conformity to national goals. Those responsible for the various genres of Japanese theatre knew well how harsh their operating environment could be, even in peace time, and there was no incentive to transgress beyond what they knew would be acceptable. Perhaps Shinkyō and Shin Tsukiji, either by inclination or association, might have hinted to their audiences that the government's policies might be questioned, but they no longer existed. Of the large theatre companies only Zenshin-za had a comparable ideological background, but by 1940 it was no longer regarded with any suspicion by the authorities. In that year it participated in an extended drama festival to commemorate the 2600th anniversary of the founding of the Japanese state and won a number of prizes.

Not that an avowedly anti-left-wing stance guaranteed immunity from interference. Bungaku-za also took part in the drama festival, reportedly to the delighted approval of the Kanda police station in whose area the Bungaku-za office was located. (Kitami 1963: 112) (Incidentally, one of their performances in the festival was the first television outside broadcast in Japan.) Not only that, but when the

Imperial Rule Assistance Association (Taisei Yokusan-kai) was set up by the government in October 1940 to encourage support for national policies throughout the country, Bungaku-za's Kishida Kunio became the founding head of its Cultural Section. In spite of this apparent identification with wartime policies, a member of Bungaku-za was warned by someone from the Special Higher Police that they should not be complacent. They might not be left-wing, but they were liberals and that in itself was suspect. The French plays Bungaku-za performed, while seemingly innocuous, implied personal relationships and an outlook on life that were already unacceptable. Later in the war all foreign plays were frowned on and productions of them discouraged.

While the government was convinced of the potential subversive qualities of theatre, it also viewed theatre as something that could contribute positively to the social changes that were necessary in a time of war. The persuasive powers of theatre could be channelled to raising and maintaining morale. Even if not at that level, theatre could at least provide solace and comfort at a time when sacrifices were being required of everyone. Thus theatre had a role to play in wartime Japan.

THE JŌHŌKYOKU

The task of guiding theatre in that role was the responsibility of the Cabinet Information Office (Naikaku Jōhōkyoku, abbreviated here to Jōhōkyoku). The government had felt the need for direct access to a facility dedicated to the gathering and dissemination of information soon after the China Incident in 1937. What had been established then was reorganised and expanded in 1940 and its powers to encourage the flow of government propaganda and to control the flow of information from other sources were greatly increased. From the start the Jōhōkyoku took its responsibility for theatre very seriously. If one considers that ensuring the public was given appropriate information by the press was the Jōhōkyoku's major concern, it seems remarkable that so much attention was paid to theatre, which at the time was primarily an urban entertainment confined to the large cities and attended by a small number of people compared to the millions who read the newspapers every day. From the way the Jōhōkyoku was organised, it appears that only a small proportion of the six-hundred-strong staff comprised of Home Ministry and Foreign Ministry officials and military officers ever had anything to do with theatre. It had five sections of which one was given responsibility for culture; that cultural section had four departments of which one was designated for both film and theatre. Nevertheless, it is clear from contemporary theatrical sources that the Jōhōkyoku was a constantly felt presence to all those working in theatre.

The film and theatre department was given two main tasks. Firstly it was to ensure that films and theatre were instrumental in spreading propaganda and give film and theatre people guidance on how that should be achieved. Secondly it was to exercise supervision over, and again give general guidance to, any organisations concerned with film or theatre. To utilise these wide-ranging powers it needed a base and it requisitioned the Imperial Theatre in October 1940 in preparation for the formal announcement of the newly reorganised Jōhōkyoku in December. This rather grandiose gesture may have been symbolic of the Jōhōkyoku's hold over theatre, but the building itself, consisting mainly of a large unusable void, was manifestly unsuitable for housing a bureaucratic organisation and it was returned to its owners a year later.

Apart from enormous disbursement of money for the rent of the Imperial Theatre, the Jōhōkyoku had considerable sums at its disposal for the encouragement of approved drama. (Ōzasa 1995: 336) In 1941 it established a system of prizes that were to be awarded to the best productions over a period of time defined by itself. This was not an open competition, as the Jōhōkyoku designated only certain theatre companies as eligible to take part. For the first round these were fourteen in number; *kabuki* was prominent with four Tokyo companies and one based in Osaka, but the list also included *shimpa*, Shinkokugeki and comedy. Zenshin-za was a participating group, but Bungaku-za was not (although it joined in 1943 when the number of groups was expanded). (Ōzasa 1994: 256) The period during which productions were eligible for this first year was from September 1941 to March 1942. In the event Matsumoto Kōshirō's *kabuki* company won the Jōhōkyoku President's Prize of ¥3000, and further prizes of ¥1000 each were given to two *shimpa* companies. In parallel with this the Jōhōkyoku ran a competition for new plays. Here again, the prizes seem quite generous for wartime conditions. The President's Prize was for ¥1000 and there were to be two other prizes of ¥500 each. (Ōzasa 1994: 259) In January 1941 the Jōhōkyoku was reported as having offered to set up an actors' organization and guarantee all the actors a monthly salary of ¥120.

In this way the Jōhōkyoku made considerable efforts and committed considerable sums of money to give theatre and playwriting a function in Japanese society at a time of national emergency. Winning one of these prizes was for many a source of some pride. Two of the competing productions in the first round were of plays in the classical repertory. While not all classics were acceptable as they stood by any means (for example, a reference to the emperor in the *kabuki* classic *Kanjinchō* had to be deleted on one occasion), one can assume that a production entered in the Jōhōkyoku competition was competing on the basis of its technical rendering and judged according to the conventional standards of *kabuki* criticism. On the other hand, all the other competing productions were of new or recent plays and to be successful with one of those close attention to the content was required. The Jōhōkyoku's intention was to reward what it defined as National Drama (Kokumin Engeki).

NATIONAL DRAMA

What later became known as the debate over National Drama had been initiated after the China Incident of July 1937 by Iizuka Tomoichirō (1894–1983), whom the Jōhōkyoku included in the panel of judges for its prizes. Iizuka had revealed a talent for *kabuki* research during his days as a student in the Law Department of Tokyo Imperial University by writing a book distinguished for its close analysis of the elements of *kabuki*. He later gave up a career in law to pursue his interest in *kabuki* in an academic environment. (Engeki Hakubutsukan 1962: vol. 1, 106) The China Incident had been the occasion for a number of government measures designed to persuade the Japanese people that they were all involved in this war and should whole-heartedly support it. In October that same year Iizuka had made a radio broadcast advocating what he saw as the role of theatre in this endeavour. This was followed by another broadcast in August 1938 and from then on by numerous other contributions which culminated in a monograph on National Drama published in early 1941. (Iizuka 1941)

In the first broadcast Iizuka attacked the commercial nature of much contemporary theatre: instead of facilely performing plays glorifying the war, the theatre should consider carefully what its role should be in the new situation. A clear sense of purpose was needed to ensure that theatre took its place alongside schools and places of religion in contributing to the 'spiritual mobilisation' of the whole nation. Theatre and film should reflect the national spirit. In developing what he called a 'patriotic theatre' those involved in drama should reflect on whether any further study of Western drama was appropriate at this time in the nation's history. While Iizuka's deprecation of Western models was primarily aimed at *shingeki* (and film), he did not see much of a contribution coming from traditional genres such as *kabuki* and *nō*. As if to confound any later attempts to categorise him as a willing tool of an increasingly militarist government, he stated that he placed most of his hopes in Zenshin-za. He must have been talking in terms of a company of classically trained actors who had attempted to adapt to the modern age, but he cannot have been unaware of their ideological background. (Iizuka 1941: 31–7)

Iizuka developed these ideas in subsequent broadcasts and publications. He was disenchanted with the world of *kabuki* as he saw it in the 1930s from two points of view. Firstly, while France might be content with Molière and Britain with Shakespeare, *kabuki* did not have the ability to reflect the changing circumstances of life in Japan at the end of the decade. Secondly, the entrepreneurial aspect of *kabuki* displeased him and he attributed much of the ills, as he saw them, of contemporary theatre to the pursuit of profit on the part of those who financed it. Thus if the dominant theatre form – *kabuki* – along with *nō* and *bunraku*, was unacceptable, theatre as a whole had to be reformed. The morality of the emerging new Japan was a national morality and this must be clear in its drama. A national drama could not devote itself to pursuing artistic ends; it had to help to realise the goals set by the state. So theatre could not be allowed to go its own way; instead it had to be controlled. Iizuka compared drama to a chess piece, which like all the other pieces was dedicated to protecting the king, and to a good wife or *geisha*, who while not taking a prominent part should exert subtle guidance. Iizuka was also concerned that theatre should no longer be concentrated in the large cities, as it had been. He was anxious to foster amateur drama of many kinds, in particular drama performed by children and by students, which could take place anywhere in Japan, and theatre which was performed in agricultural villages by members of the farming communities.

By the end of 1940 Iizuka was writing articles sprinkled with the now familiar slogans of militarist Japan. He was openly advocating totalitarian policies under which theatre would be completely reformed and be totally subject to politics, which he defined as the means of skilfully conducting national life. He thought that theatre was behind other areas of society, such as religion, in reforming itself and firm measures were necessary. Drama had a welfare function and must be forced to fulfil it. To accomplish this he advocated a firm government policy for theatre with much strengthened control over all theatre buildings; in practical terms this could be a national company to supervise all performances, with carefully controlled magazines which would only print plays that had been passed for performance by the censors.

Others took up Iizuka's ideas and expanded them over the next two years. The central concern, however, remained much the same: that drama might not change quickly enough to reflect the shift in national consciousness. There was no suggestion that theatre might question that shift, nor was there any doubt that the shift involved the whole nation. The new political order was a given and theatre had to find ways of expressing its essence. Discussion of National Drama also focused on the various forms that it could take. Japanese theatre was already, as we have seen, rich in genres, and National Drama could utilise them all. Beyond this new forms could be developed which were better suited to the aims of National Drama. There were also some exchanges of ideas on the identification of theatre and politics, although again the type of politics that should have primacy in this relationship was not in question.

Such discussion of National Drama was inevitably one-sided as the case for freedom from state control was never an issue. Complying with the wishes of a totalitarian government in time of war is not so surprising, but the fervour with which the contributors to the National Drama 'debate' commended their ideas to their readers argues for more than mere subjugation. It was perhaps Miyake Shūtarō (1892–1967), already by now a prominent and respected theatre critic, who voiced most clearly what lay behind this. Writing in 1942 he reminded his readers that never before in its three hundred year history had Japanese theatre attracted such attention – friendly, supportive attention – from the powers that be. Theatre had come into its own, for it was finally being offered a recognised place in the culture of the country and a role in the national destiny. Unlike the considerable government interest in theatre in the 1880s, which attempted to reform the conventions of *kabuki*, productions of classical plays performed to the highest technical standards were also part of the wartime government's programme for theatre and Miyake could not but approve of that. (Miyake 1943: 394–7)

The efforts of the Jōhōkyoku and the publicity given to National Drama by the writings of people prominent in the theatre spurred a number of playwrights to write plays answering to the new situation. Many of these plays had the predictable characteristics of much artistic work produced to a narrow political agenda. Heroes were always great heroes, and rarely were they allowed to have any weaknesses, especially decadent weaknesses like feelings of affection towards partners. While the characters in these plays were painted with broad brush-strokes and primary colours, opportunities were found in the text to urge the audience on to greater loyalty to Japan and willing sacrifice to the national cause. (Ōyama 1969: vol. 3, 142–4) Many audiences may well have responded with enthusiasm to performances of such plays, just as worker audiences were fired with passion by many dramatically rather slight proletarian plays in the 1920s, but most National Drama has been forgotten.

Hōjō Hideji (1902 –1996) was one of very few playwrights who wrote acceptable National Drama pieces without apparently compromising himself, and he continued on to become one of the best known commercial playwrights of the postwar era. He did not escape interrogation after the war as someone suspected of being too positive in his support for wartime policies, but he seems to have impressed his interrogators by his open attitude. He said he was willing to go to prison, and he admitted to having written plays that helped promote the war effort, but his defence that he had only been doing what any ordinary Japanese would do in similar circumstances was accepted and he was simply urged to devote his playwriting talents henceforth to promoting peace. (Tanabe 1994: 97)

Hōjō had earlier worked under Okamoto Kidō and Hasegawa Shin and this may have been the reason for him choosing the commercial theatre above *shingeki* as his medium, unlike most of his friends. It was one of his first plays for the commercial theatre – for Inoue's *shimpa* company – that brought him lasting fame as a playwright. The title was *Kakka*, which is an honorific form of address used towards those of high social status, and the play was first performed at the beginning of 1940. The hero of the play is a captain of industry who, while on a business trip, visits a remote mountain village which holds memories for him. Much to his annoyance he is surrounded by local sycophants who are not used to entertaining such exalted personages. The memories that drew him there were of a love affair with a local girl while he was a student, and he ascertains that she is still in the village. Although these memories are fond on each side, the two are finally unable to bring themselves to meet. There was nothing startling or extraordinary about this play; Hōjō had written with a simple candour about deeply felt human relationships and this seemed to commend itself to his audiences.

This may be the key to Hōjō's success during the war and his survival afterwards. His plays are characterised by an open, uncomplicated attitude towards his subject matter. He wanted Japanese soldiers to fight bravely during the war, but was not afraid to have one character tell a loved one to keep out of the way of bullets; he wanted love to be deeply felt and genuine, and any characters who lacked sincerity in their relationships were presented in an unfavourable light. None of this, however, prevented many of his National Drama plays from being strongly affirmative in their treatment of the war and thereby occasioning his later interrogation.

Tanna Tonneru (*Tanna Tunnel*, 1942) is regarded as a model example of a National Drama play, but it also has the hallmarks of Hōjō playwriting. He himself set out to write a play that was even and restrained in tone and did not artificially try to fabricate climaxes. The appeal to the audience was to be its honesty towards its subject matter, a tunnel in Shizuoka Prefecture which took sixteen years to build and claimed the lives of sixty-seven construction workers. Towards the end of construction, when management wanted to bring in foreign engineers to finish the job, the workers insisted on completing the tunnel themselves, both to show that they could and to preserve the memory of their sacrificed fellow workers. Hōjō found in their spirit an inner strength that he thought should be praised whatever the political circumstances. (Tanabe 1994: 78–80)

ZENSHIN-ZA DURING THE WAR

Tanna Tonneru was performed by Zenshin-za in 1942. This company continued to mount productions throughout the war and has been criticised for being identified too closely with the war effort. The performance of a play entitled *Ohinata-mura* (*Ohinata Village*) in October 1939 signalled to the authorities that Zenshin-za was inclined to be docile and their active participation in the nation's 2600th anniversary celebrations confirmed that. The play, which retained its popularity through the war years, concerned an impoverished village in northeastern Japan, and the production was endorsed by several government ministries, including the Ministry of War. In June 1941 a party was held on stage before the scheduled performance of the second play in Mayama Seika's *Genroku Chūshingura* cycle. The play itself is the only one in the cycle that bears a nationalistic interpretation, and the party, to celebrate the tenth anniversary of the founding of Zenshin-za, included among its guests officials from the Jōhōkyoku and officers from the Ministries of the Army and the Navy. (Ōzasa 1995: 434)

It is intriguing to speculate on how Zenshin-za managed to move from the high ideals (for a while, even put into practice) of the early years of its history to being the darling of the militarist establishment during the war to being a Communist company a few years after the war had finished. It is ironic that the communal living, which was one of the main strategies of Zenshin-za for breaking down what its members saw as the stultifying hierarchy of the *kabuki* world, could in Japan also be seen as reinforcing the kind of group consciousness that the government was trying to foster. Kawarasaki Kunitarō, the leading *onnagata* of the company, recalls that Zenshin-za's collective life-style was commended by a Home Minister as a model for the whole of Japan. As we have seen, however, hierarchy was partially reinstated within Zenshin-za and it was the senior actors who played the leading roles. *Kabuki* itself reacted to the military regime in much the same way as Miyake Shūtarō, quoted above: it was glad to have been noticed and quite content to be identified with much of the Jōhōkyoku policy for theatre. Zenshin-za in effect operated largely like a *kabuki* company after 1938 and it is possible to suggest that there was little in its ethos then to lead it into even indirect conflict with the authorities. Its apparently more radical reversal of ideology after the war will be discussed in the next chapter.

SHINKOKUGEKI

Ōzasa Yoshio, so far the fullest chronicler of modern Japanese theatre, comments that of the independent companies Zenshin-za and Shinkokugeki seemed to be the most willing to follow and support government policy during the war. Both were predominantly male-oriented organisations, Zenshin-za in having become dominated by its *kabuki* component and Shinkokugeki by virtue of the onstage sword-fighting that had made it famous. Shinkokugeki also had a large body of members to support, as its numbers had crept up to around the hundred mark after a slump to around thirty soon after Sawada Shōjirō's death. Unlike Zenshin-za there was little in its history to give it pause on ideological grounds. Sawashō's original ideal of keeping 'half a step ahead' of his audiences had no ideological basis outside a conviction that audiences would enjoy theatre more if they were not simply fed the repetitive fare that the commercial theatre would serve up to them. Shinkokugeki was still performing Mayama Seika during the war and he had certainly represented the 'half a step', but the plays chosen could be, and were, judged not to be offensive to nationalist sensibilities.

By its own admission, Shinkokugeki had been very adept at catching a public mood and taking advantage of it. (Shikokugeki 1967: 162) It had timed the performance of a play about Charlie Chaplin to fit in with an eagerly anticipated visit of the film star, and the craze for *King Kong* was also rapidly reflected in its repertory. In the wake of the China Incident in 1937 it mounted numerous productions of plays about (and extolling) war and these were very popular with its audiences. By the 1940s it had taken its place alongside major *kabuki* companies as an organisation much in favour with the authorities, and when the Jōhōkyoku announced the companies that would be eligible to compete for its first round of prizes in 1941–2, Shinkokugeki was duly included. When the Jōhōkyoku handed the Imperial Theatre back to Tōhō in March 1942, it was Shinkokugeki that gave the first public performance in the newly reopened theatre, after *kabuki* stars had performed before a private audience mainly composed of Jōhōkyoku staff. This was in general the story of Shinkokugeki's war – regular, successful productions in major theatres, as long as the latter were available, including a number of plays commissioned from Hōjō Hideji, which were affirmative in their support for the war and government policies towards Manchuria.

KABUKI ENCOURAGED AND USED

Kabuki, too, did very well during the war. Full houses were frequently reported for 1942 and 1943, usually for performances of well-known classics, and average monthly attendance figures increased during these years. After 1943 the financial and artistic environment of *kabuki* changed markedly, but up to the end of 1943 the principal *kabuki* actors – Kikugorō VI, Uzaemon XV, Ennosuke II, Kōshirō VII – were able to perform much as they always had. Grand celebration programmes aroused as much, if not more, interest as before the war. The annual memorial programme for Danjūrō IX and Kikugorō V continued as before. Not only that but in June 1943 three rival productions of *Kanadehon Chūshingura* were playing simultaneously in three different theatres. This was a well-known but not very frequent phenomenon and theatre histories refer to such 'competitive performances' (a term – *kyōen* – was coined for them) in terms that suggest periods of some vigour in the *kabuki* world.

In November and December 1943, the programme to commemorate the 200th anniversary of the *haiku* poet Bashō's death, with its line-up of top stars playing two favourite classics, attracted capacity audiences in spite of an earlier increase in entertainment tax which had raised the prices of seats considerably. So memorable was this programme thought to be that the noted theatre scholar Kawatake Shigetoshi (1889–1967) proposed to the Jōhōkyoku that it should be recorded on film. This was at a time when there were very severe restrictions on film-making because of a shortage of film stock and it may have been a measure of the establishment's estimation of *kabuki*'s worth to the war effort that permission was given. The first showing of the resulting film was given in the official residence of the Minister of Education. (Ōzasa 1995: 263)

Thus *kabuki* basked in the warmth of official favour in spite of Iizuka's doubts whether its profit-seeking character and its inability to adapt could allow it a significant role in National Drama. Shōchiku had certainly made its intentions to support the war plain enough from the start. In the next issue of *Chūō Kōron* after Pearl Harbour Ōtani Takejirō, still the head of Tokyo Shōchiku, agreed with Miyake Shūtarō that the operation by the Navy deserved warm congratulations. Ōtani even went so far as to say that for the operation to have gone so well the Navy must have practised as hard as *kabuki* actors rehearsed a play. He went on to praise the Prime Minister, Tōjō Hideki, for the warmth of his affection towards *kabuki*. Official policy towards *kabuki* and *bunraku* was that they were welcome to perform provided their plays were wholesome. When leading *kabuki* actors invited the head of the Jōhōkyoku section responsible for drama to meet them at the end of January 1942, they were told that *kabuki*, provided it expressed the full beauty of Japanese traditional sentiments, was indeed regarded as a part – a magnificent part – of National Drama. *Kabuki* companies won more Jōhōkyoku prizes than any other competing genre.[2]

There was a price to be paid. On three occasions in 1942 *kabuki* companies were sent to Manchuria, where in 1932 the Japanese government had created the puppet state of Manshūkoku, to entertain the troops stationed there and Japanese immigrants who had moved there in response to government propaganda. The third visit was in September, when Kikugorō took part in ceremonies marking the tenth anniversary of the founding of Manshūkoku. In addition to this the Jōhōkyoku expected other practical manifestations of support in Japan itself. In the middle of 1942, for example, it suggested that all seven large theatres in Tokyo should devote one day per month to entertaining conscripted soldiers.

Furthermore, official indulgence towards *kabuki* could not last once the inevitable privations of war increased in severity. During 1942 restrictions on the use of textiles to make costumes were introduced, and this affected *kabuki* badly. It had long prided itself on the splendour of the costumes worn by its leading actors and had often spent huge sums of money creating new costumes that were not strictly necessary because similar ones remained from a previous production of the same play. The use of electricity also had to be substantially reduced. In October 1943 six theatre magazines were closed down because of paper shortages, including *Engei Gahō*, which in its thirty-seven year history had established for itself a reputation for authoritative views on *kabuki*. In February 1944 theatre restaurants were banned, as was all heating in theatre buildings. Finally at the end of this month the Jōhōkyoku closed all 119 large theatres in Japan for one year. Some became munitions factories; the Kabuki-za started a new existence as a public hall.

However, this was not the end of wartime *kabuki* by any means. The closure of the theatres had been at least partly a device to gain complete control over production schedules. Simultaneously six theatres were allowed to reopen under the Plan for the Reform of Productions issued by the Home Ministry. Low maximum ticket prices were established and among other restrictions the total length of performances was limited to two and a half hours, a far cry from the six hours that had been the norm before the war. This was all in the name of preparing for final victory: the theatres should not henceforth be the playground of the well-off but places where those who were actively working for Japan's victory – soldiers, the so-called industrial warriors, and their families – could relax in a healthy atmosphere and be confirmed in their resolve. Of the six theatres two – the Meiji-za and the Shinbashi Enbujō – were in Tokyo, two in Osaka, one in Kyoto and one in Nagoya.

Playing to industrial warriors was not a new experience for *kabuki* (or *shimpa*) actors, as the government had for several years been encouraging theatre owners to be conscious of their duty to this section of the populace. In October of the previous year (1943) Shōchiku had begun what it intended to be a monthly practice of providing five hundred cheap seats for industrial warriors at the Kabuki-za and this was extended to other Shōchiku theatres the next month. From March 1944, however, a large proportion of all audiences for *kabuki* was composed of people who might not otherwise have been able to afford to go to the theatre, and with the abolition of seat reservations they were often in the best seats. *Kabuki* actors were historically accustomed to playing before audiences who knew all the *kabuki* conventions and as this applied to very few of the industrial warriors, it was a shock to some actors not to be able to rely on the reactions of their audiences. Had the coming destruction of Tokyo not been so total or the restoration of normal life after the war not taken so long, this influx of new audiences into *kabuki* might have affected it permanently, but in the event the initiation of mainland bombing in June of this year meant that this theatre regime lasted less than twelve months.

Kikugorō experienced the first air raids, which were in Kyushu, and in August 1944 he gave a public lecture in Tokyo to those training for the air raids on the capital that were now inevitable. Kikugorō's robust attitude to the bombing is legendary. (Ōzasa 1995: 278–9) He was performing in the Shinbashi Enbujō in January 1945 when the Shōchiku Tokyo Headquarters nearby received a direct hit. Normal procedure was to postpone the start of a performance if the air-raid sirens sounded and to wait, up to a maximum of two and a half hours, until one hour after the all-clear had sounded. Theatres would be evacuated if the sirens sounded during a performance. In May 1945 Kikugorō, by now exasperated at the interruptions to his dancing, told his audience to ignore the sirens as he was going to continue regardless.

In the great Tokyo air raids of 9–10 March 1945 the Meiji-za and several other theatre buildings were bombed and in the raids of 25–26 May the Kabuki-za was burnt down. By this time *kabuki* had virtually ceased to exist. In June the only performance of *kabuki* in the whole of Japan was at the Minami-za in Kyoto, which escaped the air raids. In July no *kabuki* was performed. In August there was a programme in the Tōgeki, the only Tokyo theatre still standing, but even this came to a stop on 15 August when Japan surrendered.

STRAINS WITHIN *SHIMPA*

All four *shimpa* companies that were active at the end of the 1930s qualified to be considered for the first Jōhōkyoku competition of 1941, but three experienced problems during the year. Shinsei Shimpa, the company recently formed around Hanayagi Shōtarō, had mounted a highly successful first production in November 1939 and went from strength to strength during the year. The *Miyako Shinbun*, a newspaper with an authoritative voice in theatre matters, singled out this company as having mounted all but one of the most memorable productions in 1940, and Hanayagi was praised extravagantly for several performances in 1941. (Ōzasa 1995: 590) Shinsei Shimpa was very profitable and Shōchiku was well pleased.

Shōchiku was also pleased by the company led by Hanayagi's mentor, Kitamura Rokurō, but by the end of the year some rifts had appeared in the lute. Kitamura was a very senior actor and it seems that communication between him and the younger members of the company was becoming rather remote; the feeling was growing that the company was becoming unnecessarily focused on what Kitamura wanted to do. (Ōzasa 1995: 597) Shōchiku was considerably less pleased with Mizutani Yaeko's company, Geijutsu-za, and Inoue Masao's group, because at a time when almost any play seemed to draw capacity audiences, these two companies were not as profitable as their *shimpa* competitors. Shōchiku thought they would do better if they combined forces and in May 1941 they shared the Imperial Theatre stage. Other such joint productions followed.

This in itself caused tensions within the group. The younger members were still inspired with Inoue's vision of an independent company positioning itself somewhere between traditional *shimpa* and *shingeki*. The ideal itself had been considerably weakened by this time. Many of Inoue's productions between 1938 and 1940 had been directed by Murayama Tomoyoshi, whom Inoue considered the best director in Japan at the time. Murayama's arrest and imprisonment in August 1940 denied his talents to Inoue. There was another *shingeki* director in the company, Sasaki Takamaru, but he was deeply worried at Inoue's attitude towards his company over a play designed to encourage emigration to Manshūkoku, which Inoue and Hōjō Hideji had planned and compiled, apparently without the knowledge of the other members. (Ōzasa 1995: 527) Inoue afterwards regretted that the very quality of the play might indeed have persuaded some young Japanese to try their fortunes in Manchuria, but that the play was good did not lessen the problem for Sasaki. (Inoue 1946: 277)

Inoue was sixty in 1941 and felt he could no longer maintain a regular monthly schedule of productions by his company. (Inoue 1946: 280) He negotiated with Shōchiku for a reduction to four productions per year, and this was agreed. It meant, however, that he had to find work for his actors for the rest of the time and the easiest way to do this was by farming them out to Geijutsu-za, which they resented. As if to reinforce their conviction that too much of the company's independence was being surrendered, the director of a play which won one of the first Jōhōkyoku prizes was at Shōchiku's insistence named as a more established theatre figure, not Sasaki who had in fact done the directing. The accumulated resentment of this group exploded during a production – another joint production with Geijutsu-za – in February 1942 and a number of them, including Sasaki, withdrew from the company and formed a new company of their own.

This seemed to mark the end of Inoue's brave experiment in 'middle-of-the-road theatre'. Of all the various types of theatre in modern Japan *shimpa* had found it most difficult to establish a clear identity for itself. When it began, its only theatre referent was *kabuki* and it quickly developed into what many saw as a somewhat updated version of the senior genre. When it achieved popularity in the later 1910s Shōchiku began applying to the management of *shimpa* many of the same criteria it applied to *kabuki*, so that even had there been a will to move away from being a modern classical theatre, it was fixed in the same commercial framework. Inoue had tried to bridge the gap between this kind of theatre and the radically different *shingeki* by involving *shingeki* directors and actors in his productions. In his autobiography he also describes his fear that a continuation of regular monthly programmes would mean his *shimpa* was performing many inferior plays. While he selected plays by what one might term non-*shimpa* mainstream playwrights, such as Hisaita Eijirō and Mayama Seika, he thought that there were too few such playwrights to justify full-time production. Whether this was the major reason for his request to reduce the average annual number of productions by his company, or whether, as he also says, he was just very tired, the effect of the failure of the 'middle-of-the-road theatre' agenda was that *shimpa* indeed became a classical theatre after the war, and the middle ground, which could have produced modern plays conveyed in familiar emotional expression, never developed fully.

To his credit Inoue Masao persisted in his support for Murayama Tomoyoshi. While the latter was being held in detention, Inoue several times made representations on his behalf, something that required some courage as Murayama's offence, if convicted, was against the Peace Preservation Law. (Ōzasa 1995: 528) Murayama was finally sentenced in April 1944 to two years in prison deferred for five years, so he was free to leave detention. He was not free to resume his theatrical activities, but Inoue used him anyway. A production in November 1944, the last of Inoue's before the end of the war, was of a play written and directed by Murayama under an assumed name.

Murayama, like many *shingeki* practitioners, was devoted to the theatre and could not imagine life without it. However, if like Murayama one had a left-wing past and had been arrested, legal theatre work was impossible. All those connected with theatrical performances had to apply to the authorities – in most cases this meant the local police station – for an 'arts licence' (*gigei kansatsu*). No-one with Murayama's record could ever have obtained one openly, but in certain circumstances influential friends in the entertainment world could intercede on one's behalf. Susukida Kenji (1898–1972), an actor and director in Shinkyō Gekidan who had been arrested when the authorities closed the company but released without charge after a year, related in his autobiography how he was helped to obtain a licence by the head of the Daiei film company. (Susukida 1960: 222) Tōno Eijirō (1907–1994), a former Shin Tsukiji actor – later to be famous as an actor in many of Kurosawa Akira's films, tells how on his release after a similar period of detention he was summoned to the Home Ministry and told to use his real name, not his stage name, from then on. The Ministry apparently feared that audiences would connect the name Tōno with an undesirable political ideology and be negatively influenced by it. (Tōno 1964: 187)

Despite all the difficulties a number of former members of the proscribed companies were determined to keep *shingeki* alive during the war. They banded together in various groupings, to which they gave names suffixed by *-za*, as if they were regular *shingeki* troupes, but in effect this was a desperate attempt to put at least a few productions together. The three groups formed in this way in 1942 and 1943 only managed a handful of productions between them, and to exist at all they were forced to cooperate in the government's National Drama programme. Performing under the worst possible conditions, however, did have a certain symbolic value and was of great importance to them psychologically. Most of those involved were among the leaders of *shingeki* after the war.

BUNGAKU-ZA EXPLOITS ITS LIMITED FREEDOM

When the left-wing *shingeki* groups were banned in August 1940, Bungaku-za, which had been founded in 1937 on a strictly non-political basis, was still only a fledgling company that needed to involve guest actors in most of its productions. It was, however, properly constituted and could have been banned like the other companies. Fearing that this might happen, Bungaku-za took some precautionary measures in the second half of 1940 to try to ensure that its activity could continue. A play by the nineteenth-century romantic French novelist and playwright Prosper Meriméee that ridiculed government officials was hastily replaced, and the senior leaders of the company, all prominent playwrights, decided to withdraw into the background by redesignating themselves 'advisers' as opposed to 'managers'. (Sugimura and Koyama 1970: 120) It is not clear why the latter measure was thought to be necessary, as none of the personalities concerned held political beliefs that could have been regarded as dangerous, but it may have been that high-profile leaders would have attracted more attention and one misinterpreted remark could have been disastrous for the company. A more active way of, if not courting favour, at least allaying suspicion was participation in the celebrations marking the 2600th anniversary of the founding of the Japanese state, which were held in November of 1940. No-one of the left, however, could forgive Kishida Kunio for accepting an invitation from the government to head the Cultural Department of the Imperial Rule Assistance Association, which the government had established in October to coordinate all activities nation-wide that could contribute to the war effort.

Views of Bungaku-za are sometimes coloured by what is perceived as its collaborationist attitude during the war, but it is also possible to see part of its attempt to maintain its artistic integrity as a form of minimum resistance to the government's subordination of all artistic enterprise to narrow national goals. Several productions of French plays (by playwrights such as Marcel Pagnol, Paul Graldy and Charles Vildrac) took place during the period 1940–1943, although it was known that the interpersonal relationships portrayed in them were to the censors as problematical as a banned political ideology. The company was unsuccessful in obtaining permission to play *Marius* by Pagnol in Osaka because of erotic dialogue and a stage direction indicating a kiss. In general, plans for productions of foreign plays made the authorities suspicious. They told one of the small groups formed in 1942 that applying for permission to perform an enemy play like *Cyrano de Bergerac* (well known and often performed before the war) was like asking to be put back in prison. (Susukida 1960: 224)

On the other hand, the censors seem to have been less sensitive to satire, as Bungaku-za managed to perform two plays by Iizawa Tadasu (1909–1994), who is credited with laying the foundations of Japanese dramatic comedy with his ingeniously suggestive situations and witty dialogue. *Pekin no Yūrei (Ghosts of Beijing)*, performed in 1943, completely escaped official interference in spite of a trenchant look at the war in China and a sympathetic treatment of its Chinese characters. *Chōjū-gassen (Battle of the Birds and Beasts)*, which took the now wider conflict as the butt of its satire, fared less well in 1944 and on the day of the dress rehearsal a notice was served on Bungaku-za that it was unacceptable. Morimoto Kaoru (1912–1946), a younger member of Bungaku-za who was rapidly assuming a leadership position, was forced to appear at the Jōhōkyoku and plead its case.

Morimoto had been brought into Bungaku-za by Iwata Toyoo, one of its founders. By many accounts Morimoto's brilliance, dedication and energy as a theatre person and his ability to manage the harsh environment of the times in such a way that the company could operate effectively sustained Bungaku-za through the war. In the last months of the war he wrote and directed a play whose title almost became synonymous with Bungaku-za itself.

The play was *Onna no Isshō (Life of a Woman)* and the woman's part had been written for Sugimura Haruko, already the leading actress in Bungaku-za, who had worked closely with Morimoto throughout the war. Apart from the opening scene *Onna no Isshō* is a diachronic narrative tracing and commenting on the life of its main character, the woman of the title whose name is Kei. The play opens on Kei as an old woman (in fact she is not that old, but life has aged her prematurely) sitting blankly among the ruins of her house, which, along with all the others in the area, has been destroyed in the 1945 bombing. A slightly older man, Tsutsumi Eiji, comes picking through the ruins and eventually they recognise each other. At this point the narrative proper begins as the scene changes to 1905, when Kei as a young war (in this case the Sino-Japanese War of 1894–1895) orphan is taken into the prosperous Tsutsumi household. She flourishes there, initially as a servant only too eager to repay the debt of gratitude she owes to those who have saved her from a very unhappy life, and then later, after her untiring work on everyone's behalf has been recognised, as the wife of the eldest son of the household. He is weak and unsuited to running the family business, and Kei takes this over, very successfully. In the process, however, she loses some of the human warmth that the rest of the family, although they depend on her, still expect from her and gradually they all move out, including her husband, and she is left alone. The play ends again among the ruins with her musing on her life and Eiji trying to suggest that the future will be better.

Onna no Isshō was written and performed under the most appalling wartime conditions. Regular air-raids on Tokyo had already started when Morimoto started writing and his rather rapid composition was achieved against the background of touring activity outside Tokyo, official restrictions on performance-length and materials for building scenery, not to mention the constant fear of death in an air-raid. Getting the company together for rehearsals was a major problem and once the Tsukiji Little Theatre, which had been renamed the Kokumin Shingekijō (People's Shingeki Theatre) in 1940, was bombed in March 1945, there was no obvious venue for this production. Sugimura Haruko comments on the great sense of sadness among *shingeki* people at the loss of this theatre, as no-one could foresee when, if ever, another purpose-built *shingeki* theatre might be constructed. (Sugimura and Koyama 1970: 171) The premiere of *Onna no Isshō* took place in a cinema on 11 April 1945. The air-raids were so intense by this time that the company feared no-one would come to see it, but *shingeki* aficionados were clearly determined to make the most of what was probably their last opportunity to go to the theatre, and audiences were very good. After ten performances the run ended and the company was evacuated as a group.

Onna no Isshō is something of a phenomenon in *shingeki* history. Bungaku-za performed it more than 250 times between its premiere and the mid-1950s and it saved the company financially on several occasions. Its appeal over the first postwar decade may be due to its strong resonance with postwar changes in the position of women: its female characters are strong and the male characters, with the exception of Eiji, noticeably lacking in aptitude for the male lifestyles expected of them. There is a warning, however, that may have struck a chord – Kei's success in a man's world de-feminises and by extension de-humanises her, but just when she is about to address that problem, the war destroys everything. In the context of the mid-1940s the frequent and sympathetic references to China seem remarkable and one wonders why the censors apparently ignored the oft-stated insistence of Kei's husband that China must be understood, not just exploited for profit.

Onna no Isshō was Bungaku-za's, and *shingeki*'s, last full-scale performance before Japan's defeat and surrender in August 1945. The company was not allowed to be idle during its evacuation and the Jōhōkyoku required some touring activity as a continuing contribution to the war effort. Small scale touring theatre performances continued right up to the end of the war and one famous *shingeki* actor was killed at Hiroshima while on one such tour.

WARTIME TOURING THEATRE

While the leaders of *shingeki* and *shimpa* were most concerned that their art proper – the encouragement and performance of new full-length plays – should somehow survive wartime conditions, and the Jōhōkyoku was content to see this happen provided that the plays were acceptable to it, the government was also anxious that the persuasive power of drama should be utilised widely throughout the country. Unlike now, small towns very rarely possessed halls suitable for mounting productions planned for urban venues, particularly as the perception that elaborate scenery was necessary was pervasive throughout *kabuki*, *shimpa* and *shingeki*. Thus the Jōhōkyoku was determined to promote a type of theatre that could be taken anywhere in Japan.

This does induce a certain sense of *déjà vu*, as it was only ten years before that the proletarian drama movement had similarly been seeking to influence people's minds by taking its own type of drama to them in a highly mobile form. The experiences of one actress involved at that time sound similar to those of the 1940s actors, who would travel to remote areas prepared to create their own performance space and then perform in it before moving on. Some physical stamina was needed. (Sawamura 1969: 109-28) Politically the agenda was very different and this time the goal was not to change political opinions but to exert moral suasion.

Such theatre had been part of Iizuka's plan for National Drama and others had developed this element of his ideas. No form of theatre was excluded and even the entertainment conglomerates had their own touring theatre subsidiaries, but there was some feeling in articles contributing to the debate on mobile theatre that it should be anti-commercial and focused on developing new dramaturgical and performance modes to suit its new mission.[3] Both the Imperial Rule Assistance Association and the Jōhōkyoku were keen to promote *idō-engeki* (mobile theatre) as part of their drive towards the mobilisation of all aspects of the nation's life and they supported fully the establishment of an official organisation to coordinate mobile theatre activity. This was the Nihon Idō Engeki Renmei or Japan League for Mobile Theatre and its founding meeting took place in June 1941.

The principles by which the League expected its constituent groups to operate were predictable in the circumstances. It was not going to stop at just bringing wholesome entertainment to villages and towns throughout Japan; it must aim at elevating the national spirit and bring hope and joy to workers in factories, mines and agricultural and fishing villages. (Ōzasa 1994: 395) The plays written for mobile theatre should be technically not very demanding and should only require a small number of actors not including children. Scenery should be simple to erect and special lighting effects kept to a minimum. Plots should be easily understood and the preferred format was the one-act play. (Ōyama 1969: vol. 3, 146)

In practice this was not difficult to achieve, as so much of the social background to such plays was taken for granted. Although many of them were explicit in indicating what people should be feeling, as agit-prop drama had a decade earlier been explicit in telling their audiences what they should be thinking, most built on an assumed common consciousness that Japan was under threat and must be saved. One such was Miyoshi Jūrō's *Kan'eki* (*Cold Station*), said to be one of the best examples of its kind. (Ōyama 1969: vol. 3, 148) In it a poor, young migrant labourer is returning home with a little hard-earned money that he intends to give his parents before he goes off to fight at the front. At the cold railway station of the title he saves a young widow from pursuing, exploitative employers who will not let her go to her parents' home where her young son is seriously ill. While Miyoshi has been described as collaborationist and himself wrote later that he regretted his support for the war effort, this seems to have been an emotional rather than an ideological response to Japan's changing circumstances and the play, while faultless from the censor's point of view, has a human warmth that was unusual at the time.

Mobile drama was performed by many actors who had previously been members of the banned *shingeki* companies and a particularly tight rein was kept on them. In general the League maintained close control over mobile drama performances. It had offices in many cities and towns all over Japan and it was at these offices that touring groups would assemble before departing for their performance venue. An official of the League would often travel with them and either he or a counterpart from a local office would make a morale-boosting speech to the audience before the performance started. There was little or no possibility of circumventing this control, even if one's inclinations were to try to do so.

Maruyama Sadao (1901–1945), one of Tsukiji Shōgekijō's first actors, lost his life on a mobile drama tour. He and Tomoda Kyōsuke, who had been killed in the China Incident at the very start of Japan's war against China, are *shingeki*'s martyrs – powerful symbols of the sacrifice of artistic talent occasioned by war. Maruyama had been one of the most brilliant actors of the proletarian drama period. As a Shin Tsukiji member he had been deprived of a company to act with in 1940. Subsequently, like others, he did some film work, but live theatre was his first priority and in 1942 he joined four others in founding one of the several small groups that somehow kept acting during the war. This one was given the name Kuraku-za – the Pleasure and Pain Company – because the members were determined to bring some pleasure to their audiences beset as they were by pain. (Susukida 1960: 223) Kuraku-za inevitably suffered interference from the censors, but it managed to mount a few productions, including some mobile theatre, until the Tokyo air raids rendered any further activity impossible and it disbanded. Maruyama in the meantime had been invited to star in a Bungaku-za production opposite Sugimura Haruko, who praised him as one of the best leading men she ever had. (Sugimura and Koyama 1970: 134–6) After March 1945 Maruyama was determined despite everything to continue acting and he helped form the Sakura-tai (Cherry Blossom Unit), an active mobile theatre group that was a member of the Japan League for Mobile Theatre. This group was in Hiroshima on 6 August 1945 and nine of its members were killed in the atomic bombing.

Maruyama himself was badly injured when the building he was in collapsed. He lived until the day of the emperor's surrender broadcast on 15 August. Makimura Kōkichi (1915–2001), also a member of Sakura-tai, who nursed Maruyama during his last few days of life, remembers how he heard the surrender broadcast and started telling Maruyama about it but then realised that he had died. (Maruyama 1970: 337–8) Maruyama's writings on his theatre activity during the war testify to his utter dedication to acting. It is hard to imagine that there was a war on while reading them. It was partly this that has made his death seem so poignant in *shingeki* history, as it was his very devotion to theatre that led him into danger.

That *shingeki* survived at all is surprising, given that, apart from its ideological unsuitability in the widest sense, it always had to compete against a senior and far better funded traditional theatre, many of whose values meshed very well with official policy. Not only did it survive, but the vigorous activity shown by *shingeki* companies in the immediate postwar period demonstrates the preparedness of *shingeki* people to begin again at the high point where they had left off at the end of the 1930s. The case of Haiyū-za (Actors' Theatre) illustrates this very clearly. As early as the beginning of 1944 Senda Koreya was urging his actor friends from prison to form a group that would be ready to start *shingeki* productions as soon as the war finished. Ten of them (only nine were listed as Senda's name could not be used) founded Haiyū-za in February 1944 and in August managed to put together a programme of one-act plays that were performed in the Tsukiji Little Theatre. In September they even organised an actor-training course which lasted three months with thrice weekly sessions. In 1945 only mobile theatre was possible, but Haiyū-za met the end of the war with a production team and an incipient drama school already in place.

The story of Japanese theatre during the Pacific War is one of compromises, some of them more active than others. It is not unusual to want to be patriotic when one's country is at war, and not surprising that a state would want to use the theatre to encourage that patriotism. War inevitably has to appeal to values that circumscribe freedom of choice and it was quickly recognised by the Japanese authorities and by those who controlled the traditional theatre that at a very basic level the presentation on stage of a pre-modern society where many choices were made for one was not at all out of place in the society of a country at war. As has happened in many theatre cultures, however, the persuasive power of theatre was also perceived to have subversive potential, and it was relatively easy to control that part of Japan's theatre whose preferred production choices would have suggested a society politically or socially remote from present actuality. What does come through in all genres of theatre during the war is dedication to the art of theatre; in some cases this tends to look like a desperation to keep going whatever the moral cost, in others it resembles more a purposeful search for ways and means to preserve artistic integrity within a hostile system in the hope of better times in the future. Either way, while almost all buildings that could be used as theatres had been destroyed by the end of the war, theatre people themselves were ready and eager to resume their careers.

6

Consolidation

Japanese theatre had not enjoyed a quiet existence between the 1870s and the 1940s. Its most popular classical form had been subject early in this period to challenges from outside and from inside that it had never experienced before. The *shingeki* movement had early struggled to establish a viable artistic basis for itself before being assailed by demands that it assume a political role. And during the Pacific War all forms of theatre were required to participate actively in the war effort.

The first five years after the end of the war were times of great financial hardship for all types of theatre. Few theatre buildings in Tokyo were undamaged after the air raids. *Shingeki* was particularly badly affected by the loss of the Tsukiji Little Theatre, which had been the focus of the modern theatre movement since the mid-1920s. The struggle simply to survive engaged the energies and purses of a large proportion of the population, many of whom would need to make considerable personal sacrifice to buy a theatre ticket.

In the weeks after the emperor's surrender broadcast of 15 August 1945 there was also great uncertainty as to what the attitude of the first postwar government was going to be towards the arts. Theatre had been subject to comprehensive control throughout the war period and theatre groups had performed either what they hoped would not break the law or what they knew to be the positive desire of the government in power. This situation did not change at a stroke with the surrender. Many *shingeki* people greeted the end of the war with jubilation, but they also had to be aware that the Peace Preservation Law, which the authorities had used freely to prevent anything suspected of being even remotely subversive, was still in force. Many of them were outside Tokyo, still in the remote places to which they had been evacuated or had gone to perform.

The uncertainty had less effect on *kabuki*, which had been relatively free of official interference, and it is perhaps not surprising that the first postwar theatrical production should have been by *kabuki*. *Kabuki* also had the advantage that, although it might have to account for its willingness to compromise with a discredited and defeated government, the major concern of most of its actors had been the continuation of a long tradition. Ichikawa Ennosuke organised and mounted the first theatrical production of any kind since the end of the war. This opened on 1 September 1945 at Tōgeki, which had escaped major bomb damage, and consisted of two contemporary (1928 and 1939) pieces, a play based on a humorous work of the nineteenth century and a dance inspired by a famous *nō* play. In a newspaper article which Ennosuke wrote to coincide with the opening performances he made it clear that he realised the difficulties which *kabuki* might face. If American influence on Japanese theatre would mean that the ideology behind Chūshingura was unacceptable (Chūshingura was indeed banned soon afterwards), he would at least perform dances associated with it and he protested that his only motive was the preservation of the art of *kabuki* for posterity. (Kurahashi 1966: 10)

THEATRE AND THE OCCUPATION

Japan was occupied by the Allied Powers from the end of August 1945 until April 1952. In effect this was an American occupation, as virtually all the responsibility for planning and executing policies to ensure that Japan would not go to war again was in the hands of the American Army. General Douglas Macarthur, the Supreme Commander of the Allied Powers (often abbreviated to SCAP, which came to refer to the occupation authority as well as the man) was American, as was the overwhelming majority of his staff. Ennosuke's instinct had been right: it was an American view of theatre that was likely to hold sway when policies towards the performing arts were discussed and put in place.

Japanese theatre of all types had laboured under some form of censorship since the seventeenth century. Control of content had never been greater than during the four years of the Pacific War, and the narrow view of the world that the Jōhōkyoku had tried to force on the theatre had been totally discredited by the defeat. SCAP dedicated itself to rooting out anything that might have contributed to Japan's slide into war, and the ideology behind government policy from the mid-1930s was an obvious target. *Shingeki* people in general were not concerned about the censorship apparatus put in place by SCAP early in September nor by the enunciation of SCAP policy towards theatre and film made soon afterwards. The latter was intended to ensure that what were defined as 'feudal' values were not presented on the stage or through other media.

Most of the *shingeki* movement had followed quite a different agenda since the mid-1920s, but *kabuki* was specifically mentioned and it was likely that the use of the term 'feudal', however defined, signalled problems for much of the classic *kabuki* repertory.

SHINGEKI'S INITIAL EUPHORIA

The early years of the Occupation were a time when *shingeki* came into its own. Bungaku-za continued its activity much as before, once it was able to regroup. It was, however, those on the left of the *shingeki* movement who felt the greatest sense of liberation. While Bungaku-za had no more worries over censorship of scenes of moral decadence in its productions, those formerly involved in proletarian and socialist realist theatre had practically all their repertory freed up. Activists who had spent some or all of the war years in prison now found themselves being recognised for the courage they had exhibited in providing at least some resistance to the progress of militarism. Hijikata Yoshi, who had been in prison since his return to Japan from the USSR in 1941, was released in October. Murayama Tomoyoshi had exiled himself to Korea in March 1945 after being told that he risked imprisonment and possibly death in a camp being planned for dissidents and he now returned to Japan. (Toita 1961:244) Many others, such as Okakura Shirō (1909–1959), whose professional lives had been severely restricted by wartime police activity, were now able to contemplate being leaders in a *shingeki* revival.

To reestablish itself *shingeki* needed companies, performances and money. The pre-existing Haiyū-za and Bungaku-za were soon joined by a third company. This was the Tōkyō Geijutsu Gekijō (Tokyo Arts Theatre; the Japanese name is usually abbreviated to Tōgei) founded in December 1945 and led by prewar leftwing stalwarts such as Kubo Sakae and Takizawa Osamu (1906–). The latter had been an actor member of Tsukiji Shōgekijō and Shinkyō Gekidan and would later become one of postwar *shingeki*'s leading actors, his greatest triumph being Willy Loman in Arthur Miller's *Death of a Salesman*. Performances required a concentration of human, technical and financial effort that was simply beyond any individual company at the time and the first postwar *shingeki* production, which took place in December 1945, was a joint venture by the three companies. This production was sponsored by a major newspaper, but an unlikely source of *shingeki* finance became available from Tōhō and Shōchiku. Seeing the Occupation's hostile attitude towards *kabuki*, both of these entertainment conglomerates announced that in future they would be giving most support to modern theatre. Tōhō sponsored the formation of Tōgei. (Burkman 1984: 190) It also owned the theatre in which the December joint production was presented. In this, too, *shingeki*'s association with big business was useful at the time. Most *shingeki* productions during 1946 were mounted in Tōhō and Shōchiku theatres.

Postwar *shingeki* productions begin with Chekhov's *The Cherry Orchard*, for that was the play performed in December 1945. The theatre was packed every night and by all accounts the production was a great success. The event was heavy with symbolism. As Hijikata Yoshi noted, no-one killed anyone, no blood flowed, and the only person to die was due to die anyway. (Kurahashi 1966: 22) People were getting on with their lives in a village against a background of a landowner's decline and a capitalist's rise. The old order was crumbling and the new one was beginning to make itself felt. The run took in the seventeenth anniversary of Osanai Kaoru's death and Hijikata paid tribute to the great service Osanai had performed for *shingeki* by introducing the plays of the Moscow Art Theatre to the Japanese stage. Hijikata greatly liked Chekhov as a playwright, but others noted later that the new *shingeki* was starting off much as prewar *shingeki* had at the Tsukiji Little Theatre: with a foreign play. Although this production was very moving, some thought that it only served to show that *shingeki* was still alive and did little to mark out its future path. (Ibaraki 1956: 70–1)

The parallels with prewar *shingeki* were striking. Haiyū-za reflected the Tsukiji Shōgekijō/Shin Tsukiji Gekidan companies closely in personnel. Tōgei included several former members of Shinkyō Gekidan. Murayama Tomoyoshi assumed that his former status as prewar leader of Shinkyō would commend him as a senior figure of this new company, but he was only offered ordinary membership, which he refused. (Toita 1961: 246) Instead he reestablished Shinkyō Gekidan in its own right as a company dedicated to realising the artistic creativity of the mass of the populace and to fostering democratic drama with and from within the people. (Ōyama 1969: vol. 4, 31) He recognised, but found unsatisfactory, the gradualism of Haiyū-za, the attempts of Bungaku-za to adapt its preeminently artistic stance to the modern age, and the academic approach, as he saw it, of the group that had just snubbed him. There were variations of ideological nuance – although they seemed much more than that at the time – but Murayama regarded his new Shinkyō as much the most politically committed of the postwar reincarnations.

Shinkyō started off in a blaze of publicity, as Inoue Masao was accepted into the company at his request. For a prewar *shimpa* leader to join an avowedly left-wing company with a Communist leader caused a sensation. Murayama speculated that Inoue, who admired him greatly as a director, was not able to produce the plays he wanted while under contract to Shōchiku. He may have joined Shinkyō with high hopes, but Murayama only gave him a small part in Shinkyō's first production and in other ways failed to help him at a time when his type of *shimpa* was struggling to survive. Inoue soon left the company. Altogether the early existence of the new Shinkyō Gekidan was stormy. Several of the core members, probably because of disagreements that reflected tensions in the Japan Communist Party, also decided to pursue their theatre careers outside Shinkyō, thus weakening the company considerably.

At the start of 1946, however, *shingeki* presented the remarkable picture of four companies eager to begin regular productions after years of official interference that had affected almost every one of the people involved. By the end of March all four companies had achieved their individual first postwar productions. Murayama opened first, in mid-February. He also managed to produce a new Russian play rather than a revival as *The Cherry Orchard* had been. For this Murayama received some praise, but it was clearly a rushed production. In March both Tōgei and Haiyū-za performed translated plays that had venerable places in *shingeki* history. Ibsen's *A Doll's House* and Gogol's *Government Inspector* were solid choices that had a nostalgic appeal to some *shingeki* devotees but could still be seen as relevant to a younger generation wondering whether postwar Japanese society would change in any fundamental ways. Bungaku-za had wanted Morimoto Kaoru to write a new play for this first public production, but he was by this time too ill to do so. Instead it chose a poetic drama of the countryside in which the playwright, who had formerly been associated with proletarian drama, promoted his evolving ideas about community living, something rather different from anything Bungaku-za had done before. Audiences were poor and the reviews were unflattering.

In spite of the lack of suitable theatre space a *shingeki* fan would have been able to watch *shingeki* in eight of the twelve months of 1946. All groups managed at least two productions. Altogether Bungaku-za had a rather shaky year and this was reflected in its choice of production for a tour to Kyoto in December, when it revived *Onna no Isshō* in the hope of regaining some of its former self-confidence. In terms of personalities Shinkyō and Tōgei were the most clearly left-wing in inspiration and a joint production of Gorki's *The Lower Depths* was counted one of the few successes of the year. The most self-assured group seemed to be Haiyū-za and under the leadership of Senda Koreya and Aoyama Sugisaku it steadily acquired stature over the year.

While gathering inflation and high taxes on theatre admissions made profitable productions practically impossible in 1947, the various *shingeki* companies gradually consolidated the artistic gains that had been made the previous year and acquired the distinguishing characteristics by which they (or in the case of Tōgei its successor) would be known. Ozaki Hirotsugu (1914–2000), a major postwar *shingeki* critic and chronicler, encapsulated these at the end of 1948 as a series of nameplates hung at the 'gates' to each of the groups. For Haiyū-za he chose the 'Rediscovery of Humankind'; for Shinkyō 'Class-based'; for Mingei (Tōgei's successor) 'For the people'; and for Bungaku-za he chose a not very complimentary phrase suggesting audiences would be entertained with respectable plays that they would enjoy. (Kurahashi 1966: 139) Over the next few years each of these groups mounted productions or engaged in activities that confirmed the expectations or anxieties of those supporters who remembered the prewar period. Both the more left-wing groups – Shinkyō and Tōgei – were subject to the debilitating splits and realignments that had so weakened proletarian theatre, but what resulted finally in 1950 was a company that over the next decade contributed greatly to establishing *shingeki* firmly in postwar Japanese theatre. This was Mingei, one of the so-called 'three big companies' that defined *shingeki* for theatregoers in the 1950s and 1960s.

The other two were Haiyū-za and Bungaku-za. Both groups felt keenly the need to develop actor training and bring on new actors. The obvious commitment of Senda Koreya to do this within Haiyū-za seems to belie somewhat the characterisation of the postwar *shingeki* movement as a revived copy of its prewar manifestation. Senda's choice of repertory for his company was very varied and included Japanese playwrights who had openly rejected the premises of proletarian drama, and this was in the cause of giving his established and new actors as wide a range of experience as possible. His periods of enforced inactivity during the war had been spent reading as many of the Western manuals of acting as he could get hold of (the list is impressive) and from the autumn of 1947 he gave his company the benefits of his conclusions on the actor's art in a series of lectures averaging five or six hours per week over more than a year. In 1949 he wrote up this material into a two-volume work entitled *Kindai Haiyū-jutsu* (*Modern Acting*), the first comprehensive treatment of the subject in *shingeki* history. Essentially realist in thrust, which is not surprising for the time, there is considerable emphasis on the actor knowing and training his whole body and mind. That, plus a lifetime of experience, make for a successful actor. (Senda 1980: vol. 1, 294) The actor should train himself to be sensitive to the 'transmutations' (*hen'i* – Senda deliberately uses an unusual word) in characters' thoughts and motivations as shown through and behind the playtext. At that point the 'technique of saying things' (*mono o iu jutsu*) becomes preeminent and much of these two volumes is devoted to developing this technique.

Senda castigated too academic an approach to acting and hoped to bring on a new generation of *shingeki* actors through practical training along the lines proposed in his book. In 1949 Haiyū-za founded a Drama Study Centre, which incorporated an actor training school (Haiyū Yōseijo). The latter remained the only large-scale actor-training facility in Tokyo for many years. Some of its many graduates found places in the Haiyū-za company itself over the years, but such opportunities were bound to be few. Some tried to continue live theatre activity by founding their own Haiyū-za satellite groups, but many more were taken into the rapidly expanding broadcasting industry. The mismatch between numbers of actors and actresses trained at the Haiyū Yōseijo and the possibilities of an acting career in the theatre later contributed to the reaction against *shingeki* in the mid-1960s.

Part of Ozaki's implied criticism of Bungaku-za was justified as the company turned back to tried and tested favourites after the failure of its first production. *Onna no Isshō*, apart from being revived in late 1946 with performances in Kyoto, was taken on tour in the middle of 1947 and performed in Tokyo in August of the same year. There were further extensive tours with this play in 1948 and a triumphant production in Tokyo in December, which achieved 110% capacity audiences. This play ensured that Bungaku-za would enjoy financial stability at least in the short run. The company also restored its prewar team of three leaders once Kishida Kunio, who had been purged by the Occupation, was available again. So, like the other two main *shingeki* companies, Bungaku-za too sent out signals that strongly suggested continuity with its prewar activities, although the reestablishment of the company had not been an issue. Like Haiyū-za it was also concerned to bring on young actors, directors and playwrights and to that end reorganised its small-scale experimental work, some of which was focused on French drama, into a vigorous programme of what were called '*atelier*' (the French word was used) productions.

However, *shingeki* history during the immediate postwar years was not only the history of these large companies. Other smaller groupings of enthusiastic theatre people mounted a variety of productions during this period, thus laying the foundations of what became the norm during the 1950s – high-profile productions by the three main companies and a myriad of smaller groups, some only semi-professional, contributing to a lively modern theatre culture. One in particular stands out for its distinctive contribution to postwar Japanese theatre and this was Budō no Kai (Grapes Society). This group was formed in 1947 around the actress Yamamoto Yasue (1902–1993), the name being both a symbol of Greek tragedy as the fountainhead of world drama, and something to which their radio audiences of children could relate.[1] Soon the group moved on from radio plays to live theatre and in January 1950 they performed a new play by Kinoshita Junji (1914–) entitled *Yūzuru (Twilight Crane)*.

Yūzuru became a phenomenon in Japanese theatre, one of the most frequently performed plays in the postwar period. Kinoshita had spent his war years reading Japanese folktales collected by the famous ethnographer Yanagita Kunio and drafting plays based on them.[2] *Yūzuru* was the third to be performed by Budō no Kai and its remarkable success was a major factor in setting off a boom in folk art and craft of all kinds. It has a simple plot: a poor farmer lives an idyllic existence with a devoted wife, whom he had originally won through selfless kindness, but loses her because his greed for money, fostered by grasping friends, takes control of him. His wife, in fact a crane in human disguise (hence the title), returns to the world of birds at the end of the play. *Yūzuru* is a play that can be understood at several levels: it has a message about greed for children and there have usually been children in its audiences; it comments on how an individual's values can be radically changed by external factors; it can be read as a political allegory. However audiences have interpreted *Yūzuru*, its appeal has continued over more than half a century, perhaps suggesting that Kinoshita's rather pessimistic view of human nature is shared or at least understood by a wide cross-section of the population.

OCCUPATION POLICY TOWARDS *SHINGEKI* HARDENS

All in all *shingeki* flourished during the second half of the 1940s. This should have been a source of satisfaction to the Occupation authorities, as so many of the *shingeki* leaders had been harried by the Japanese police for over fifteen years because of their political views. There were, however, aspects of postwar *shingeki* which SCAP officials thought could be improved on. The monopoly of *shingeki* activity by theatre groups or companies was regarded with suspicion. In general what was perceived as the Japanese group ethic was unacceptable to SCAP, and there was an attempt to encourage in *shingeki* the American model, based on the single production for which a company was specially assembled. The United States was thought to be a suitable model in other ways, notably for its dramatic literature. In 1946 and 1947, while *shingeki* was acquiring a reputation for its productions of plays in translation, not a single American play was seen by its audiences.

In 1948, as American policy towards Japan was beginning to change because of the Cold War, officials of the Civil Information and Education Section of SCAP summoned *shingeki* leaders to the headquarters of NHK, the state broadcasting corporation, and required them to listen to a reading of a Japanese translation of Thornton Wilder's *The Skin of Our Teeth* with the hope of encouraging them to perform it Although *Our Town* had been performed in the 1920s and some of Wilder's preoccupations were familiar to *shingeki* people, *The Skin of Our Teeth* seems to have alienated them. Shinkyō Gekidan performed *The Skin of our Teeth* in September 1948, but the production was a failure. Maybe its application of the principles of everyday middle-class life to a coming Ice Age seemed rather remote to *shingeki* audiences, or perhaps they resented the circumstances in which the play had been brought to their notice. (Burkman 1984: 193)

SCAP's attempts to impose a producer system on *shingeki* were not without success initially. With their encouragement a number of different directors staged a series of productions under the name of Jikken Gekijō (Experimental Theatre). The seven plays performed were mainly foreign, by no means all American but at least including a play by Tennessee Williams and an adaptation of a Steinbeck novel. This way of organising stage productions was, however, unfamiliar to everyone concerned and involved personnel problems new to directors in *shingeki* companies. Opinions on the overall success or failure of Jikken Gekijō differ, but as an organisation it collapsed after the October 1950 production.

Under the Occupation all *shingeki* had the freedom to develop for a short time, but SCAP's attitude towards the more leftwing groups changed as the Cold War intensified and especially after the start of the Korean War in June 1950. The so-called Red Purge, a government policy of restrictions on radical left political activity, affected Shinkyō Gekidan badly, as that was the *shingeki* company most identified with the Japan Communist Party. It also killed off an extensive network of amateur *shingeki* groups based in workplaces.

KABUKI IRREPRESSIBLE

In a neat contrast to this trend, Occupation policy towards *kabuki* was harsh at the beginning and gradually softened. In September 1945 SCAP found '*kabuki*-like theatre', which portrayed vendettas or was premised on 'feudalistic loyalty', not acceptable in the modern world. (Nagayama 1995: 106) Shōchiku was therefore in something of a quandary in planning its November programme and it made what in retrospect seems a surprising decision. It included from the classical repertory just about the most 'feudal' scene that can be imagined. The title of the scene is *Terakoya* and in it a warrior, motivated by intense loyalty towards his lord, identifies the severed head of his own son as that of an enemy's son whom he has been charged with hunting down. In conformity with regulations then in force Shōchiku supplied the Civil Information and Education Section of SCAP with English summaries of each of the proposed items on the November programme and it seems permission was granted. (Nagayama 1995: 106) The run started on 5 November and all seemed to be going well, but, apparently as a result of a tip-off, on 14 November the head of drama at the CIE watched the performance and on the 15th an order came for this item of the programme to be discontinued.[3] From this time on plot summaries in English were not sufficient for the censor; a translation of the full text had to be provided for each programme item.

According to Nagayama Takeomi, later to head Shōchiku, the officials of the Civil Information and Education Section were not high-handed in their treatment of *kabuki* and subsequent events seemed to show that they were amenable to arguments based on the long and rich tradition of the genre. Early in December 1945 a group of experts organised by Shōchiku drew up lists of *kabuki* plays that they considered either acceptable or unacceptable according to the SCAP guidelines. This list was then scrutinised at a meeting between these experts and Civil Information and Education Section officials and a few changes were made, mostly from the unacceptable to the acceptable list. Some of these changes are instructive in understanding SCAP's approach to *kabuki*, which was already evolving. Revenge as a plot subject was forbidden and it was not surprising that *Kanadehon Chūshingura* remained firmly banned. Some types of revenge could be countenanced, however, and several revenge plays were transferred between the lists. In one a peasant girl takes vengeance on a *samurai*, and this was tolerated both because the perpetrator was a woman and because the attack was on a member of a privileged class. (Nagayama 1995: 109) Similarly the most celebrated ghost play in the classical *kabuki* repertory, *Yotsuya Kaidan* was allowed because, although it was technically connected to the *Chūshingura* story, it portrayed a wronged woman visiting retribution on an evil *samurai*.[4] While these reasons may seem simplistic, all the plays permitted were based in a similar feudal morality and it is just possible that some members of the audiences may have reflected on why these were permitted while others were not.[5]

One way for *kabuki* to please the censors was to perform original plays that conformed to CIE guidelines. Funahashi Seiichi (1904–1976), later to become the playwright to whom Shōchiku looked for certain commercial success, obliged with a play entitled *Takiguchi Nyūdō no Koi* (*Priest Takiguchi's Love*), which delighted the head of the CIE when it was performed in 1946. The female lead was played not by an *onnagata* but by *shimpa*'s Mizutani Yaeko. This otherwise unexceptional play included a scene in which Mizutani and the male lead Ichikawa Ennosuke II kiss, and this caused a sensation. SCAP seems to have regarded kissing as useful to democratisation and therefore encouraged the stage and film kiss. *Kabuki* and Funahashi exploited the commercial potential of this new eroticism in several subsequent plays, giving rise to the term *keikō* (tendency) *kabuki*. The *keikō eiga* (tendency films) of the early 1930s had taken advantage of a commercial opportunity to incorporate socially progressive content taken over from proletarian drama. It may not be entirely flippant to suggest that the new 'tendency' did something similar.

Audiences flocked to *kabuki* productions in 1946 and 1947. Inflation and exorbitant entertainment taxes meant that, officially at least, Shōchiku took little financial comfort from its success, but at least the durability of the genre seemed to be beyond question. By the spring of 1947 the censors allowed a performance of the very scene that had provoked the banning measures less than two years before, and in November *Kanadehon Chūshingura* itself was permitted. Tickets for the whole month's run of the latter were sold out on the day that advance booking began. Not only that, but the empress and empress dowager had a special performance of certain scenes organised for them at the theatre – the first time that members of the imperial family had visited a theatre to watch *kabuki*. Clearly SCAP's attitude had changed, and this had been largely because of the efforts of a young major in the US Army named Faubion Bowers (1917–1999), who had acquired a love of *kabuki* while in Japan just before the Pacific War. (Nagayama 1995: 111) Bowers is affectionately known in *kabuki* circles as 'the man who saved *kabuki*', and the story of his arrival in Japan in the first party of American occupation soldiers is part of Japanese theatre legend. Bowers cut through a dangerously tense atmosphere by asking some Japanese reporters in Japanese: 'Is Uzaemon still alive?' (Okamoto 2001: 14)

Thus, *kabuki* after a short period of intense anxiety about its future in the first months after the defeat quickly regained its prewar position in Japanese theatre. Gradually, theatres were being rebuilt: the Kokusai Gekijō towards the end of 1947, the Shinbashi Enbujō, an important *shimpa* and *kabuki* theatre in central Tokyo, in March 1948, and then in September 1949 work started on the reconstruction of *kabuki*'s Tokyo home, the Kabuki-za. Shōchiku was anxious to bring on some of the younger actors and to that end organised a number of naming ceremonies (*shūmei*) in 1947. Name-taking performances, in which an actor is granted a stage name more senior than the one he currently uses, were always a way of indicating that *kabuki* was moving on and that there might well be stars in the next generation as artistically talented as those who were attracting audiences in the present one. In the first half of 1949 *kabuki* briefly faced a more traditional type of crisis, as the successive deaths of three leading actors led to dire prognostications of collapse in the media (as in 1904). However, there were some good actors coming through – the naming ceremonies had not been empty shows by any means – and mainstream *kabuki* entered the 1950s with some confidence.

Kabuki was able to withstand the shock of early Occupation prohibitions because, even if its 'feudal' period pieces were banned, it was able to fall back on the other two staples of its repertory, the dance pieces and the domestic dramas. So although some actors who specialised in warrior heroes found their favourite roles denied to them, those whose forte was either dancing or non-violent roles kept the tradition of *kabuki* alive. Shinkokugeki, however, owed its fame still to its spectacular swordfight sequences, which it had emphasised in its repertory during the war years, and these were now banned. After the war ended in defeat for Japan, Hyōdō Takeo, who had singlehandedly managed Shinkokugeki for all but two years of its existence, took personal responsibility for its collaboration during the war and resigned. Leadership of the company devolved onto some of the younger actors and they took the opportunity to redirect some of Shinkokugeki's activity towards contemporary plays. In this they were greatly aided by the playwright Hōjō Hideji. His play *Ōshō* (*Chess Master*), written for them in 1947, confirmed this trend and established the popularity of plays set in the present day. The devotion of the eponymous chess master's wife as he struggles tirelessly to become a master was not a particularly new subject, but Hōjō had managed to imbue it with the emotional sincerity for which he was known and audiences reacted positively.

ZENSHIN-ZA JOINS THE JAPAN COMMUNIST PARTY

Like Shinkokugeki, Zenshin-za had not fared badly during the war, as its performances of period plays from the classical *kabuki* repertory had been well-received. The latter were denied to it early in the Occupation, but the company had always been flexible in its acting styles and it was not difficult for it to adjust its primary activity to a different and more acceptable type of play. Notwithstanding its encouragement of the war effort, Zenshin-za quickly projected an image of a company mindful of its left-wing past, to such an extent that Shōchiku, deeply anxious that SCAP policy would take away much of its traditional audience, signed a contract with Zenshin-za in November 1945 for four productions per year. For Shōchiku Zenshin-za performed programmes that combined acceptable *kabuki* plays with modern plays with democratic themes, such as, for example, a drama about Abraham Lincoln by John Drinkwater and a resistance work by the Communist French playwright Jean Richard Bloch. Thus Zenshin-za were positioning themselves neatly both to serve both their current master and to rebuild their ideological integrity.

Zenshin-za was a big company, however, and to survive financially it needed many more performance opportunities than could be provided by Tokyo alone. It restarted regular touring activity and in 1947 began a programme of school visits that earned it much praise at the time. Starting with schools in the Tokyo area, Zenshin-za soon began organising tours that took in large areas of Japan. Often the tour would include factories and other workplaces in the same locality, but the emphasis was on performing to school pupils in their schools. Most of the repertory consisted of plays of Shakespeare, and it was said that perhaps as many as a million people watched their production of *The Merchant of Venice*. (Sakamoto 1953: 169) While audience figures of this size, even composed mainly of school pupils, must have benefited Zenshin-za in financial terms, the company still put much emphasis on education in that clarity and understandability were the priorities in both direction and acting. For this Zenshin-za was awarded the Asahi Cultural Prize in 1948.

In 1949 the whole Zenshin-za company joined the Japan Communist Party. While other individuals in the theatre world had become members of the JCP, relishing the freedom to join a party that had been illegal from its inception until late 1945, for sixty-nine people to join at once as a group was sensational news which attracted much media coverage. The exact motives for this move are unclear: there could have been a financial incentive as the most powerful labour union federation at the time was Communist-backed, but in view of Zenshin-za's patent inability in the past to function openly as the ideologically progressive organisation it claimed to be, maybe the more likely explanation is an idealistic belief that this demonstration of commitment would give the company self-confidence for the future.

Whatever the true motives of this extraordinary action, Zenshin-za soon found that clear identification with the Japan Communist Party brought it into conflict with both Occupation and Japanese Government policy. Just as left-wing *shingeki* companies, especially Shinkyō, were weakened by the consequences of the Red Purge, so Zenshin-za too was barred by many head teachers from performing in their schools. Union sponsored productions were still possible, but increasingly subject to police interference. In these circumstances the atmosphere at Zenshin-za performances seemed to recreate some of the excitement of proletarian drama of the late 1920s. Unfortunately the police tactics against Zenshin-za also recalled aspects of prewar surveillance of left-wing theatre. To take just one example of this, students in the audiences could expect their landladies to be questioned about them.

There was considerable irony in the situation, particularly as Zenshin-za was careful now not to perform plays that had any kind of overt socialist message. Shakespeare and classical *kabuki* plays were their staple offerings during this period, and the police seem to have been worried mainly, as in the 1930s, by the encouragement that potential subversives might take from simply being present at a performance by actors who were committed socialists, even though the play itself might be unequivocally 'feudal'. In the early 1950s the police particularly pursued Nakamura Kan'emon, one of the leaders of the company. During a tour to Hokkaido in 1952, with a production of the *kabuki* classic *Shunkan,* Kan'emon evaded arrest several times by having heavily made-up doubles appear onstage in his place while he escaped through the back of the theatre. The persecution became so intolerable that Kan'emon was eventually forced to flee to China, where he remained until 1955.

SHIMPA DIVERSIFIES

In the immediate postwar years it should have been *shimpa* which developed smoothly on the basis of what had been achieved in the 1930s. To be sure, *shimpa* was subject to the demoralising effects of lack of performance space, like all other genres, in the wake of the bombing, but it had a number of advantages. Like *kabuki* it had a number of accomplished actors who had performed with some regularity throughout the war period. Like *kabuki* it had suffered little interference from the wartime authorities and had on several occasions received marks of approbation from them, but unlike *kabuki* it was not likely to fall foul of the Occupation censors. As we have seen, the latter were particularly sensitive to period plays where a feudal ethos would be combined with martial acts. Tales of lovesick geisha and sensitive men, however 'feudal' the basis of their relationships might be, did not worry the American censors unduly, nor in general would the contemporary plays set outside this world which Shinsei Shimpa had prided itself on incorporating into the genre.

It did not work out like this, however, as the bombing demolished more than just theatres for *shimpa*. The huge Tokyo bomb sites included areas where the geisha houses and other traditional entertainment facilities – restaurants, music teachers, dance teachers, etc – had been concentrated, and no-one expected the old atmosphere to be recreated in these areas when they were rebuilt. They might, as they mainly did, resurrect themselves as entertainment districts, but the unspoken conventions, the ambiguities and the grace of life there, which had been the stuff of *shimpa*, would not survive into a world of harsh economic conditions and rapidly changing social relations. If *shimpa* was not going to become a theatre of nostalgia, it would need new plays and a more contemporary relevance.

All three *shimpa* companies existing at the end of the war were conscious of this and made efforts to develop a new repertory. *Shimpa*'s main audience base, however, was accustomed to watching a style of presentation, centred on the acting, that was highly professional and could be seriously compared with *kabuki*. Plays on contemporary subjects presented in this way looked odd and *shimpa* was not able on its own to effect the changes it thought necessary. It could, however, and did, fall back on the nostalgic option and perform plays from what was regarded as its traditional repertory, such as adaptations of the stories of Izumi Kyōka. In addition, it did have some new actors coming through to prominence and a little later the actresses Mizutani Yoshie (Mizutani Yaeko's daughter,1939–) and Namino Kuriko (1945–).

To maintain its vitality in this time of rapidly changing social conditions *shimpa* also needed the help of those theatre genres which were most sure of their own artistic premises. The self doubt of *shimpa* was not shared by *kabuki*, *shinkokugeki* or *shingeki*, and *shimpa* found co-operation with these other genres profitable in several senses during the first decade after the war. Thus *shingeki* directors such as Murayama Tomoyoshi and Okakura Shirō were invited to direct *shimpa* performances and *shingeki* actors were sometimes to be seen in *shimpa* productions. For example, in June 1951 Hanayagi and Mizutani Yaeko played opposite each other (something that frequently happened in the 1950s although they represented different forms of *shimpa*) in a production of Dumas fils' *La Dame aux Camélias* directed by a *shingeki* director. A third leading part was played by Takizawa Osamu, an actor who had quickly re-established his left-wing *shingeki* career after the end of the Pacific War. This production was sponsored by Shōchiku, who billed it as a 'Grand Co-operative Production of Contemporary Drama' (Gendai Engeki Daigōdō).

From the perspective of the late 1990s, one can view *shimpa*'s co-operation with other genres not only as having helped it survive, but also as confirming its existence as the 'middle-of-the-road' theatre (*chūkan engeki*) that Inoue Masao dreamed of in the mid-1930s. *Kabuki* actors also performed in *shimpa* and some still do. A type of theatre which successfully incorporates representatives of the major classical form of Japanese theatre and actors from the modern tradition that developed in opposition to it, can reasonably claim to have fulfilled a useful function in the history of theatre in modern Japan.

In spite of, or perhaps because of, this dilution – or again perhaps one should say 'diversification' – of its acting profile, *shimpa* maintained regular activity during the 1950s, and as a force in Japanese theatre during the decade it was still spoken of alongside *kabuki* and *shingeki*. This tripartite division of mainstream theatrical activity seemed to suit the theatre-going culture of 1950s Tokyo. There was at least adequate audience support for each of these genres and each succeeded in consolidating their particular style of performance. Economic conditions improved rapidly in the early part of the decade through the procurements boom created by the Korean War, and theatre benefited both from this and the high growth of the later 1950s. Television and films provided competition that put some pressure on the live stage during the decade, but all three genres could later look back at the 1950s as a period of useful development.

SHINGEKI IN THE 1950s

The 1950s saw *shingeki* coalescing into three dominant companies complemented by a small number of groups that did some important work somewhat in the shadow of their larger counterparts. There were also many smaller groups scattered through the inner suburbs of Tokyo. These latter were professional in that their actors regarded acting as their main occupation but amateur in the sense that the paid work that they did to support their drama was more likely to be unconnected with theatre. Thus, in the Tokyo area at least, *shingeki* activity was sufficiently widespread for most people to be aware of it, if only sporadically. This was not the case in the Kansai area or elsewhere in Japan. In the later 1940s there had been quite a vigorous amateur modern drama movement based on workplaces, but much of this had been connected with left-wing unionism and had suffered greatly as a result of the Red Purge of 1950. In the 1950s most *shingeki* performances outside Tokyo were controlled by audience associations, particularly Rōen. Rōen is an abbreviation of a longer name meaning Workers' Theatre Association (Kinrōsha Engeki Kyōkai). The first one had been founded in Osaka in 1949, and others sprang up in all major cities over the next few years. Rōen would take charge of all the business side of a performance, meeting the expenses of the performing company and filling the auditorium (there were no purpose-built theatres) with its own members, who paid a regular membership fee. As the system developed, Rōen became so powerful that even the three main Tokyo *shingeki* companies could sometimes only contemplate a tour if they had the support of Rōen.

At the beginning of the 1950s *shingeki* was still perceived as the type of theatre that introduced the best or newest Western drama to the Japanese stage, and a survey done for the Haiyū-za by an independent organisation over four days during the company's production of Chekhov's *The Cherry Orchard* showed that *shingeki* audiences wanted it that way. Some 58% stated that they preferred Western plays in translation to original Japanese works and listed productions of plays by Ibsen, Beaumarchais and Chekhov as their favourite three since the end of the war. For future productions four of their first five choices were by Western playwrights, headed by Chekhov. (Kurahashi 1966: 220) Perhaps not unconnected with this was the age profile of *shingeki* audiences. A survey over nine days in April of the same year revealed that 68% were in their 20s, with progressively declining percentages under 10% for older age groups.

Many productions by all the three big *shingeki* companies answered to the demand for modern Western drama. Two plays in particular caught the popular mood and also contributed greatly to the reputations of their leading actors. These were Tennessee

Williams' *A Streetcar Named Desire*, performed by Bungaku-za in March 1953, and Arthur Miller's *Death of a Salesmanō*, performed by Mingei in April 1955. Both productions were very successful, *A Streetcar Named Desire* being performed no less than 110 times over the succeeding two years. Both plays had leading characters who lived lives built on lies, and this similarity was picked out by one reviewer of the Williams play. More than any resonances that audiences might have felt with the agonies of self-definition that both leading characters suffer, it was the searing psychological realism and the possibilities that this offered for Japanese drama that gave these mid-fifties productions their landmark status in postwar *shingeki* history. It happened that the actors playing Blanche and Willy Loman, although both were already famous, came into their own with these performances. Blanche and Willy became their new *atariyaku*, the parts that were associated with them and regarded almost as their monopoly from then on. Sugimura Haruko continued playing Blanche well into her seventies and Takizawa Osamu's Willy was remembered decades after he first played the part.

SHINGEKI'S AGE OF REALISM

Realism was a major preoccupation of *shingeki* in the 1950s. At its formation Mingei had announced that its main objective was to establish a theatre of realism. As we have seen, *shingeki* had a weighty history of debate over realism and Mingei was a good example of a group whose view of realism was deeply coloured by Shinkyō productions of plays such as Shimazaki Tōson's *Yoake Mae* in the 1930s. While it could be said that in the nineteenth century European drama had been moving fairly steadily in the direction of a realism whose general parameters were at least recognised by theatre practitioners of the time, Japan's modern theatre had always had to contend with a number of different 'realisms'. In the 1950s *kabuki* and *shimpa* could lay claim to a certain type of 'realism', and within *shingeki* itself the major split between the 'socialist-realism' of Shinkyō and the dialogue-based realism of Kishida Kunio was still being debated. It is likely that Mingei chose *Death of a Salesman* because the experiences of the characters could be interpreted as emblematic of larger social trends; although *A Streetcar Named Desire* is capable of such an interpretation, it is also likely that Bungaku-za would have had other preoccupations when selecting it for production. Acting was also affected, as actors within each of the major companies were well aware of the prevailing aproach to stage representation of reality. Even within a single company there could be differing views of realism that would be discernible in individual productions. Mingei was said to incorporate no less than three such approaches in the mid-1950s. A new factor entered the debate, however, and by the end of the 1950s some consensus on common elements of realism was achieved.

The new factor was the theories and practice of Constantin Stanislavski. Although Stanislavski's work had been known about since the 1920s, it was the publication of the Japanese translation of Part 2 of *An Actor Prepares* in 1954 that concentrated interest in his methods. Prior to this a few directors were known as exponents of his system in Japan, especially Okakura Shirō. Okakura's hallmark in his prewar productions had been a close, almost pernickety, attention to detail and it was natural that he would respond positively to a system that grounded this in inner motivation. Okakura was at the heart of *shingeki* around 1950, as he was a founder member of Mingei and closely associated with Budō no Kai, for whom he had directed *Yūzuru* in 1949. In the early 1950s a number of directors and leaders of small *shingeki* groups were also experimenting with the Stanislavski system. After 1954, however, a veritable Stanislavski boom started and Stanislavski jargon was bandied about almost everywhere in *shingeki* dressing rooms. The *shimpa* actress Mizutani Yaeko is reported to have been seen poring over *An Actor Prepares*. As if to reinforce the relevance of the Stanislavski system beyond representational realism, the Peking opera actor of female roles Mei Langfeng, who visited Japan for the first time in the postwar period in 1956, deeply impressed *shingeki* people. Those who were old enough to remember his performances in Japan in the 1910s detected a distinct change in his style, towards a superb stylised acting technique motivated from within. Kinoshita Junji was later to write that Mei Langfeng was in his opinion the greatest exponent of Stanislavski acting.

There was thus great excitement in the world of *shingeki* when it was announced that the home of Stanislavski acting, the Moscow Art Theatre, would be visiting Japan. The visit took place in December 1958 and to gladden *shingeki* hearts even more the productions performed included *The Cherry Orchard* and Gorki's *Lower Depths*, two plays central to the history of modern theatre in Japan. The official history of Shōchiku commissioned for its 90th anniversary scoffed mildly at how *shingeki* people wept during the performances, but this was a highly emotional experience for the veterans among them. Many of them had been directed by Osanai Kaoru in Chekhov and Gorki during the 1920s and remembered how director and actors scrutinised photographs of moments in Stanislavski productions. (Toita 1961: 262) Nor was the eager anticipation felt only by those who had been involved in the left-wing manifestations of *shingeki* before the Pacific War. Sugimura Haruko remembers feeling like a child looking forward to a festival. (Sugimura and Koyama 1970: 307)

Many of these now middle-aged actors have left accounts which record how the Moscow Art Theatre answered all their expectations. The two *shingeki* journals, *Teatoro* and *Shingeki*, both published extensive assessments of the visit, and almost everything was positive. Much of what was noticed was predictable: references to the outwardly perceivable means by which certain effects were achieved by the actors and the sheer scale of their success in achieving them were prominent in the recorded comments of actors and directors who watched the performances. Beyond this the quality of the acting and the intense feeling of a true ensemble at work were deeply impressive to *shingeki* theatre people. *Shingeki* actors had been performing Chekhov for more than thirty years; why could they not achieve anything comparable, especially as Chekhov was regarded as virtually a Japanese playwright? (Sugimura and Koyama 1970: 310)

Thus, the visit of the Moscow Art Theatre was greeted with great joy by the *shingeki* world, but the joy was not unalloyed. Many felt they had been reminded of how far *shingeki* had to go before it could achieve anything comparable, and this created a renewed determination to establish a stage realism appropriate to Japanese theatre. The most keenly felt need, however, was for more new plays written by Japanese playwrights. The Moscow Art Theatre had shown what could be achieved by concentrating on productions of plays written by playwrights in tune with the company's ideals. Somehow a similar phenomenon had to be created in Japan and the journal *Shingeki* urged actors, directors and writers to begin urgent discussions on the subject.

POSTWAR *SHINGEKI* PLAYWRIGHTS

Overawed by the presence in Japan of the company they had worshipped from afar for so long, some commentators seemed to have forgotten that *shingeki* playwriting since the war had achieved some notable successes itself. Many *shingeki* groups had playwrights attached to them and working closely with them. Often in the past a playwright had headed a *shingeki* group, for which he had written and directed his own plays. In the postwar period Murayama Tomoyoshi was fulfilling these functions for the Shinkyō company. Perhaps the most successful partnership of playwright and company in the 1950s was that of Tanaka Chikao (1905–) and Haiyū-za. Tanaka had started his playwriting career in the 1930s with a play entitled *Ofukuro* (*Mother*), which had shown him to be skilled at realistic dialogue in a situation of highly charged family relationships. He had written for the journal *Gekisaku*, thus aligning himself with the apolitical wing of *shingeki*, and it was therefore not surprising that at the end of the war he was associated with Bungaku-za. He came into his own when he joined the directors' group in Haiyū-za in 1951. From then on he directed often for

Haiyū-za, including the many plays that he wrote for the company. Many of his postwar works were designated, in his own words, as 'misogynistic plays', in which he worked out his confrontation with the problem of the existence of a Christian god through women driven by unnatural desires and fears. *Kyōiku (Education)*, performed by Haiyū-za in 1954, provoked much comment through its determined pursuit of these themes. (Rimer 1976)

1950s' *shingeki* playwriting is also notable for the involvement of novelists in writing for the stage. This had been a feature of Taishō *shingeki* in the 1910s, but at that time active engagement with the theatre had been rare. In the 1950s and 1960s established novelists saw the possibilities offered by stage performance, and several of them were closely associated with *shingeki* companies. Mishima Yukio (1925–1970) was well known as a novelist by the mid-1950s, having the successes of *Confessions of a Mask*, *Thirst for Love* and *Forbidden Colours* behind him. From 1950 the fascination with Japanese classical literature which had coloured many of his early works of fiction found dramatic expression in his modern adaptations of *nō* plays. These did not find much favour with *shingeki* groups at this time, but other more conventional plays attracted the attention of the major *shingeki* companies and Mishima was performed by both Haiyū-za and Bungaku-za from 1953 onwards. He was primarily associated probably for political reasons with Bungaku-za and it was later a politically explicit play of his which precipitated a split in Bungaku-za in 1963. His most popular play has been *Rokumeikanō*, premiered by Bungaku-za in 1956. Rather conventional in plot and structure this work might seem more suitable to performance under the auspices of a large commercial theatre, and since the 1950s it has mainly been seen in that milieu. It is a play of colourful intrigue set in the mid-Meiji period involving the aristocrats and other members of the élite who attended Western-style grand functions at the Rokumeikan, a Western-style building intended for the entertainment of foreign guests.[6]

Several of the 1950s plays that stand out in *shingeki* history have either as a major theme or as a *leitmotiv* the atomic bombing of Hiroshima and Nagasaki. It needed a few years for playwrights to come to terms with this unprecedented event of the recent past, but when they did, they offered various solutions to the problem of how to represent it or its legacy on the stage. Hotta Kiyomi (1922–), schooled in the workplace drama movement that had been stifled by the Red Purge, burst onto the *shingeki* scene in 1957 with a realist play entitled *Shima (Island)* whose teacher hero, devoting his life to encouraging the growth of a non-violent culture, sees his personal life ruined by delayed onset radiation sickness.[7] Another realist dramatist, Koyama Yūshi (1906–1982), in a play (*Futari dake no Butōkai, A Dance Party for Two*, 1956) which focused on the involved emotional relationships between a group of people none of whom can be called the leading character, had one of them commit suicide partly because of anxiety at the thought of developing radiation sickness. In many of Koyama's plays Hiroshima appears, unforgotten, in the background to the plot. Tanaka Chikao's play *Maria no Kubi* (*The Head of Mary*, 1959) portrayed a group of Nagasaki Christian survivors trying to steal, and identify with and be saved by, the pieces of a statue of Mary shattered in the atomic blast.[8] This latter play is determinedly non-realist in method and may, as Goodman suggests, presage the confrontation with cataclysmic events of Japanese history by the various anti-realist currents of the 1960s.

For a decade in which rapid urbanisation was taking place it is notable that many plays are set in the country. Kinoshita Junji's *Yūzuru* was only the first of a series of *minwageki* (folktale plays) that this playwright produced in the 1950s, all of them exposing some human foibles or worse. *Yūzuru* had questioned urban values with its strongly implied criticism of the capital, and Katō Michio's (1918–1953) *Nayotake* (its main female character), performed twice in the 1950s (in 1951 by *kabuki* and 1955 by *shingeki*) did this too. Both plays also had a young female character (Tsū in *Yūzuru* and Nayotake in *Nayotake*) from a non-human realm who was bitterly disappointed in the human beings she encountered. *Nayotake* had many resonances of Jean Giraudoux's *Ondine* which was performed by a *shingeki* company in 1958. More optimistic about human nature was Mayama Miho's (1922–) *Dorokabura* (*Muddy Turnip*, 1951) whose leading character has the same transparent goodness of Tsū and Nayotake but succeeds in reforming those who mean her harm. This latter play has the distinction of being the most performed play in modern Japanese theatre history, having passed its ten thousandth performance in the early 1990s.

THEATRE BUILDINGS IN TOKYO

The achievements of Japanese *shingeki* playwriting for the first fifteen years after the end of the Pacific War were considerable. There was much more variety than has been suggested here and this complemented the mainstream realistic current which, whatever its political background, was moving towards a credible expression of emotional conflict on the stage. Playwrights worked in very unfavourable conditions. From November 1946 Tokyo *shingeki* companies had enjoyed access to the theatre which the Mitsukoshi Department store had incorporated into its new building. In the autumn of 1952 the Mitsukoshi management decided that they could no longer keep the theatre open in the evenings. This had little effect on the traditional performing arts for which the Mitsukoshi Theatre was also used, but it was a serious blow for *shingeki,* whose working and student audiences could only be sure to be free for playgoing in the evenings. After the loss of the Mitsukoshi Theatre even the big three *shingeki* companies could only expect to mount productions in a variety of halls in Tokyo and other major cities, which had not been constructed with modern theatre performance in mind. The large commercial theatres were prohibitively expensive to hire and Mingei was not alone in 1953 in making a huge loss at one of them. All the big three *shingeki* companies made plans to overcome this situation, but only Haiyū-za felt confident enough to plan the construction of a new theatre. Its main actors were noticeably absent from its productions in 1953, because they were undertaking film and radio work in order to raise money for this theatre. They were successful, and in April 1954 the 401-seat Haiyū-za Theatre (official English name: 'Actors' Theatre') held its opening performance of Aristophanes' pacifist *Lysistrata*. This was an event to be celebrated by the whole *shingeki* movement and representatives from Bungaku-za and Mingei helped entertain the guests at this first performance.

Kabuki too regained the use of a purpose-built acting space at the beginning of the decade. The Kabuki-za, badly bombed in the closing stages of the war, was reopened in January 1951. The glittering gala productions that marked this opening were designed not only to show to the *kabuki*-going public that after the deaths of several leading actors in the recent past a new generation was ready to take their places but also to demonstrate the advanced technical capabilities of the new theatre. The Kabuki-za quickly resumed its place as Shōchiku's flagship theatre in Tokyo.

As a commercial venture the Kabuki-za was very successful and the way it was marketed changed the character of *kabuki*. Before the end of 1951 this theatre had become one of Tokyo's tourist attractions. The management was quick to provide appropriate facilities for groups of visitors who could take in a visit to the Kabuki-za while on a short stay in Tokyo. Many Japanese from outside Tokyo were thus given to understand that this theatre and the actors who appeared in it were representing traditional culture in one of its highest manifestations. Foreign residents in Tokyo and foreign tourists were often to be seen there, and the rising interest of Western scholars served to increase its aura of cultural authority.

Establishment approval of *kabuki* was marked in the 1950s, but unlike what happened in the Meiji period this was not accompanied by requirements that *kabuki* change. In November 1953 the emperor and empress attended a performance at the Kabuki-za. This was the first time that they had watched *kabuki* together and was in stark contrast to the imperial performance of 1887 when actors had been told where they might have the honour of performing. This glittering charity performance on behalf of the

Japanese Red Cross (of which the empress was patron) was attended by other members of the imperial family, vice-President Nixon, the British ambassador and many other notables. A further, and singular, mark of establishment approval was given to *kabuki* when Ōtani Takejirō, who has often been credited with ensuring the survival of *kabuki* during its most difficult times, was awarded the Cultural Prize in 1955 and he commemorated this event the next year by founding a research facility for *kabuki* called the Ōtani Library. Foreign dignitaries were frequently to be seen at the Kabuki-za and it was here rather than in the more modest *nō* theatres or at *shingeki* performances that diplomatic and business entertainment took place.

NEW DEPARTURES FOR *KABUKI* IN THE 1950s

The commercialism that went with the success of the Kabuki-za did not please everyone. Shōchiku, and especially Ōtani, have been variously praised for defending *kabuki* or critised for adjusting it to take fullest advantage of the commercial opportunities offered. Some streamlining did take place in the postwar period and the pattern that developed was of groups of actors who habitually acted together. As almost all *kabuki* actors were under contract to Shōchiku, the company was in the enviable position of having numerous possibilities for assembling casts that met exactly a play's needs, but it was commercially more certain to set up a star actor as the nominal leader of a company and for that company to become known as the principal exponent of one type of play. Thus the Ennosuke Company was known for its performances of *shin-kabuki* plays and the Kichiemon Company for classic plays that had been adapted from the puppet theatre. Some bewailed the cost this entailed in artistic terms, as actors narrowed the range of their performances to fit in with the stereotypes that the system had created. (Kawatake and Shimomura 1959: 22–3)

Particularly critical of this trend was Takechi Tetsuji (1912–1988), who has the historical distinction of having a type of *kabuki* named after him. 'Takechi *Kabuki*' was a phenomenon of the early 1950s and refers to a series of productions of *kabuki* plays directed by him. Born the son of a wealthy businessman, Takechi had been a theatre journalist in the 1930s, but his trenchant criticism of the way *kabuki* was organised even then earned him the disapproval of the *kabuki* establishment. His chance to make an impact came in the early postwar period when he began directing *kabuki* productions in the Kansai area. By the early 1950s he was directing productions regularly for Shōchiku and up to the last Takechi *Kabuki* in August 1953 he had taken charge of twenty-five productions. He was known for his respect for text and unwillingness to centre his productions round star actors.

The new plays that were written for *kabuki* in this period take on a new character, so much so that the term 'new *kabuki*' had to be redefined. Before the war *shin-kabuki* plays had mainly indicated works written for *kabuki* by playwrights who were associated with the theatre in some way and were therefore utilising and in some cases adjusting known conventions to bring their art to life. By contrast the plays most mentioned by theatre historians as having a significant impact in the 1950s were written by novelists. Starting without experience of writing for *kabuki*, they instinctively adapted their style to suit the new medium for which they were writing. Whereas playwrights such as Mayama Seika and Okamoto Kidō had hoped to persuade *kabuki* afficionados that *kabuki* could be developed, postwar writers for *kabuki* such as Funahashi Seiichi and Osaragi Jirō (1897–1973) were educating Kabuki-za audiences to what *kabuki* was.

Both these novelists had singular successes in the early 1950s. Funahashi was responsible for a stage adaptation of the tenth-century classic prose work *Genji Monogatari* (*The Tale of Genji*) which opened at the beginning of March 1951. His lyrical, episodic adaptation of this great romance of ancient Japan brought young people into the theatre and set off something of a Genji boom. *The Tale of Genji* was a new subject for *kabuki*, as it revolved around the loves of the members of the imperial family and had consequently been banned from the stage in the 1930s. This and the dreamlike qualities imparted to it by Funahashi, after a decade totally devoid of dreams, made it compelling theatre to a new generation of theatregoers.

The actor Ichikawa Ebizō IX (1909–1965) commissioned Osaragi Jirō to write a play on the sixteenth-century warlord, Oda Nobunaga. As one of the three unifiers of Japan who had helped the country out of a century of civil war, Nobunaga had invariably been painted as a villain in the group of pre-modern *kabuki* plays that treat his life. In the modern era he has received more balanced treatment and this began with Osanai Kaoru's 1913 play about Nobunaga's utilisation of Christianity for political purposes (first performed by Shinkokugeki). Osaragi's Nobunaga is a young man who is impatient with empty ritual and hates shams. He causes suffering as a result of actions on his part that accord with his convictions, but he suffers himself because he is misunderstood by the world. Like Funahashi's play this too touched a chord in its audiences, who were aware that Ebizō, who played Nobunaga, also felt himself isolated from those around him. (Kawashima 1971: 200)

SHIMPA, SHINKOKUGEKI AND COMEDY IN THEIR NEW ENVIRONMENTS

Many of the elements that made up *kabuki*'s success in the 1950s were mirrored by *shimpa*, which maintained its popularity during this time. The various companies performed a judicious mix of plays to appeal to nostalgia in their traditional audiences and to the different concerns of the younger generation. For example, *shimpa* fostered a sense of continuity in their fans' minds by staging *kabuki*-like self-introductions of new actors or of actors who assumed a new name. The most spectacular example of this was the debut in August 1955 of Mizutani Yaeko's daughter, who announced her stage name of Mizutani Yoshie (she was later to become Mizutani Yaeko in her turn). This took the form of a bilingual production in which the Japanese actors spoke in Japanese and the Western actors in English, to the bemusement of the audiences. In performance terms *shimpa* also played upon the advantage that it held over *kabuki* in using actresses as well as *onnagata*. Its most famous *onnagata*, Hanayagi Shōtarō, and its most famous actress, Mizutani Yaeko, would be presented together in ways that suggested they were rivals not only in acting but also in physical beauty. The ambiguities evident in this 'rivalry' were deliberately emphasised in a production of 1959 where, although they both played elderly female parts in a play, at the start of the programme they appeared on stage to greet their fans dressed as if they were bride and bridegroom.

Shinkokugeki, like *shimpa*, presented a dual face to its fans during this period. Having been forced by SCAP policies to abandon much of its traditional reliance on stage sword fights, it had developed the part of its repertory which emphasised help for the weak through the actions of freebooter figures from the Edo period. Once the Occupation ended, sword fight dramas (*kengeki*) were reincorporated regularly into the *shinkokugeki* repertory and revivals of such plays from the prewar repertory were often placed second in a programme, thus giving them considerable prominence. The popularity of *kengeki* in the 1950s, coming so soon after its heyday during the war, has prompted speculation on a possible relationship between the two. It has been suggested that audiences watched these plays in the 1950s with different eyes and regarded them somewhat as Japanese versions of the very popular American Westerns, as expressions of a romantic fight for justice. (Kawashima 1971: 210) There was indeed an excitement here to which audiences could respond and, given the parallel popularity of women's *kengeki* at the end of the decade, this may have been the primary attraction. On the other hand, the principal motivation for characters' actions – the tension between obligation and private emotional inclination – was in these plays linked to violence in a way that it was not in *shimpa* or even in *kabuki*, where the violence was made to seem remote through extreme stylisation.

Comedy was another genre that had to operate in a much changed environment after the war. While Iizawa Tadasu had been forced to use great care in writing his satirical comedies during wartime, he and fellow comedy playwrights could satirise human nature as much as they wished during and after the Occupation. The varied extremes in lifestyle which the political and social situation encouraged in the first decade after the end of the war provided much material for playwrights like Iizawa and Fukuda Tsuneari (1912–). Fukuda's 1950 *Kitī Taifū* (*Typhoon Kitty*) cast a satirical eye at a group of expatriates in China who continue chattering inconsequentially and without suggesting that anything serious binds them together while two of their number die. Both Iizawa and Fukuda were performed by mainstream *shingeki* groups, but comedy flourished elsewhere in the entertainment world as it had before the war. The focus now was more on individuals rather than institutions with which the individuals were connected, and few were surprised when the Moulin Rouge closed its doors in spring 1951. Furukawa Roppa is reported to have commented not long afterwards that now performers like Toni Tani (1917–1987) had appeared the end was in sight for performers like himself. (Nakahara 1972: 75) Toni Tani was essentially a compère, but the shows he compèred were popular not because of the turns in them but because of Toni himself. He had a number of outrageous traits, one of the most enduring being a verbally sadistic attitude towards his audiences. Vaudeville and its compères were very popular during the 1950s, but the tradition of comic plays, usually short, was not lost. Shōchiku set up a company called Shōchiku Shin-kigeki (Shōchiku New Comedy) in 1948. Based in Osaka this company performed programmes of playlets that were very popular. The company's brief was to bring on young comedy actors and by the mid-1950s one had emerged who was soon to dominate comedy acting in Japan. This was Fujiyama Kanbi (1929–1990), whose deadpan face managed on stage to conceal deep emotions and high moral principles. Although Shōchiku Shin-kigeki is primarily associated with Kansai theatre, the Shinbashi Enbujō, which was one of the most successful Tokyo theatres in the mid-1950s, often featured programmes of comedy by this company, and Tokyo audiences joined their Kansai counterparts in their affection for Fujiyama Kanbi.

It is difficult not to end each chapter in this book with comments on the vitality of Japanese theatre during the period under consideration and this would particularly apply to the first fifteen postwar years. It became a commonplace in the 1970s to refer to the Tokyo theatre scene as the most varied in the world, but the 1950s also showed how seriously Japanese theatregoers took their theatre. Partisan though much of their support might have been, overall this amounted to a metropolitan theatre culture that might have been the envy of Broadway and the West End – had they known about it – in its involvement of a wide range of age groups and social classes. By early 1960 there was a general sense of satisfaction that firm foundations for the development of theatre henceforth had been laid. The term 'postwar *kabuki*' (*sengo kabuki*), which came into currency at the time, indicated that the achievements of the great prewar stars had been assimilated and their inheritors were ready to move on. *Shingeki* too felt secure in the artistic direction it had followed and faced the future with confidence. In the event this confidence was misplaced, as a singular political success in the summer of this year unleashed forces within the *shingeki* movement that were to challenge its cherished assumptions. The next decade would see *shingeki* ousted as the leader of modern theatre in Japan.

7

One Tradition Promoted, One Challenged and One Created

1960

1960 has been perceived as a pivotal year for both *kabuki* and *shingeki*. In the decade that followed *kabuki* achieved successes of many kinds. The same can be said for *shingeki*, which built on the laborious process of reestablishment carried out in the 1950s and in many of its productions showed the maturity that rightly belonged to it in terms of chronology and effort. At the beginning of 1960 the leaders of *shingeki* and *kabuki* might well have – and probably did – looked forward to a decade in which the respective roles assigned to them in the Japanese theatre world would be developed and even broadened. *Kabuki* flourished as a theatre art for those who wanted their emotions stirred in a particular, familiar way, as a venue for corporate and VIP entertainment and as a showcase theatre to present to the world. *Shingeki*, by contrast, served as a showcase for the Western world's best drama for the benefit of its younger audiences and proved to them that Japanese playwrights could write in a similar idiom. While *kabuki* broadened its role by looking outwards to the world, some within *shingeki*, which had artistically always looked outward, decided that its role as a theatre for the contemporary age could only be executed successfully outside the *shingeki* framework.

KABUKI FOR THE ÉLITE

While the crown prince and princess never watched *shingeki* in the 1960s, even though it was often performing the plays that the social élite of London and New York were enjoying in the West End and on Broadway, they made several visits to the Kabuki-za to watch *kabuki*. Such was the acceptance of the Kabuki-za as a place to which it was proper for members of the imperial family to go for entertainment that it received the singular endorsement of the imperial house in September 1960 when the crown prince and princess attended a gala programme of classical *kabuki* to celebrated the tenth anniversary of the theatre's reconstruction after the war. While visits of this kind could be regarded as largely ceremonial, their next visit to the theatre in October 1962 was to see a new play that had, against expectations, become a great popular success within its one month run. The imperial couple saw it towards the end of the month and this suggests that they had chosen to see something in which they were interested. This was indeed an unusual production; the director was a member of a *shingeki* company (Mingei) and the script was the work of a well-known film scenario writer. (Shochiku 1985: 163) Theatre-going to *kabuki* by members of the imperial family in connection with their work for charity continued. By the end of 1963 the official history of Shōchiku was able for the first time to refer to the 'numerous' occasions on which members of the imperial family were visiting the Kabuki-za. (Shochiku 1985:166)

It was, however, the easy acceptance of the Kabuki-za both by the Japanese government and by the various diplomatic missions in Tokyo as an appropriate place to display the Japanese cultural heritage to foreign dignitaries that marked the complete absorption of *kabuki* into the establishment. With growth rates in GNP that were attracting the attention of Western economists and with the imminence of the Tokyo Olympics (1964) it was perhaps not surprising that state visits to Japan by European heads of state and monarchs should increase in frequency. In December 1963 King Frederick IX of Denmark and in January 1964 the king and queen of Belgium visited Japan and trips to the Kabuki-za in the company of the crown prince and princess were arranged for them. *Kabuki* was now accustomed to royalty and other visiting celebrities; actors were becoming accustomed to receiving such visitors in their dressing rooms; the managers were fast acquiring experience in greeting the great and the famous in the spacious foyer. The Kabuki-za had now achieved all the reforms initiated by Morita Kan'ya at the Shintomi-za and endorsed by the Meiji government through the Drama Reform Movement. Audiences sat quietly in comfortable seats. Instead of the frequent and loud shouts of approval directed at certain actors that had in the past come from all parts of the house, now the only general noises emanating from the auditorium were occasional muted buzzes of conversation and a little polite clapping. The *kakegoe* cries to the actors now mainly came from the galleries where specialists in *kakegoe*, sometimes let in through the backstage area by the actors they supported, could find vacant seats. Still in the 1960s there was some eating of food even in the stalls, but patrons were daily exhorted through the loudspeaker system to refrain from this practice that had once been an inseparable part of theatre-going. Actors, officially despised a century before, now met kings.

Kabuki carried all before it abroad too. Ōtani Takejirō had for many years been expressing publicly his desire to take *kabuki* to the West. Its only other foreign tour, in 1928, had been surrounded by controversy, although the enthusiasm of the Moscow audiences and prominent theatre people on that occasion had already indicated that *kabuki* was a theatre genre in which other theatre cultures would take interest. Before the end of 1965 *kabuki* had undertaken three ambitious tours abroad and had been greeted rapturously by all its foreign audiences. It could of course count on core support from the local expatriate Japanese populations, and in some cities visited this was substantial, but it was clear from many of the press reviews that Western theatre was ready to accept the premises on which *kabuki* was based. In June 1960 the touring company played to packed houses in New York, Los Angeles and San Francisco and a year later in June 1961 a company numbering seventy-one persons received a similarly rapturous welcome on a tour to Moscow and Leningrad. Four years later, in October 1965, *kabuki* made a similarly triumphal tour of Europe, with much encouragement from André Malraux, then French Minister of Culture, and delighted audiences in Paris, Berlin and Lisbon.

During the Tokyo Olympics of October 1964 *kabuki* fulfilled its international role with aplomb. It lined up its star actors in a programme of its most frequently performed and spectacular classics. Those athletes or spectators who were able to visit the Kabuki-za for the morning/afternoon programme were treated to Onoe Shōroku II (1913–1989) in the lead part in *Terakoya*, in which the actor portrays a series of conflicting emotions through his bodily and facial movements while he knows his young son is being sacrificed offstage, all the while dissembling his grief before the other characters on stage. Nakamura Utaemon VI, the leading *onnagata* of the day, danced *Musume Dōjōji* also in this programme. One of the most beautiful and striking dance-dramas in the classical *kabuki* repertory, *Musume Dōjōji* taxes the skills of the most experienced *onnagata* who must portray comely and alluring feminine beauty and the frustrated rage of an evil, murderous serpent in a single scene. Apart from the consummate technique and expressive skills, which with these plays could have been appreciated by anyone, the complicated motivations behind the characters' actions needed to be explained to the foreign audience members and Shōchiku made a special effort to provide such an explanation. Plot summaries were available in English already as the English-language Kabuki-za programme predates the Olympics. In addition, however, a short introduction to each play in English was broadcast through the theatre before the curtain went up. (Shochiku 1985: 167) During the actual period of the Olympics (from the 8th to the 16th) Shōchiku scheduled an extra show specifically targeted at foreign visitors to Tokyo from 9.30 until midnight each evening.

A NEW DANJŪRŌ

This internationalist aspect of *kabuki*'s activities in the early 1960s was not allowed to hinder its regular work for its local audiences. In particular these years saw two spectacular name-taking (*shūmei*) performances that generated much interest. The first, in 1962, involved the name Danjūrō. There had been no Danjūrō on the *kabuki* stage since the great Ichikawa Danjūrō IX, who had died in 1903. There was now a candidate in the person of Ichikawa Ebizō IX, who had been adopted into the main Ichikawa house (which disposed of the name Danjūrō) in 1939. His fans had already thought in the 1950s that he deserved the Danjūrō name, but he had always refused out of deference towards and respect for his adoptive father, Ichikawa Sanshō who, it seemed, was not in line for the name. When Sanshō died in 1956, Ebizō bestowed the name Danjūrō X on him posthumously, thus leaving the way clear for him to take it on later. Finally in 1962 he acquiesced in the many calls for a Danjūrō *shūmei*. The house-name (*yagō*) for the main Ichikawa family is Naritaya, because the Narita Fudō shrine near the present international airport is the patron shrine of the family and Ebizō led a widely publicised procession of his fans to Narita Fudō in February. (Shochiku 1985: 163) In April he took the name Danjūrō XI and the glittering programme that month was a commercial and artistic success.

SHINGEKI AND *ANPO*

The early 1960s were, therefore, a triumphal period for *kabuki*; they could have been so for *shingeki* too, in that the Moscow Art Theatre performances had reaffirmed the value of the artistic goals it was seeking. Some parts of the *shingeki* world pursued the establishment of a valid realism with renewed vigour, even challenging the Moscow Art Theatre on its own ground. Both Haiyū-za, by choosing to perform *The Cherry Orchard* in January 1960, and Mingei with *The Lower Depths* in March attempted build on what had been achieved in the past with these plays and to use the experience of having seen Russian realist plays performed by Russians to surmount the doubts that many Japanese theatre people entertained concerning the stage realism that had developed thus far. From the perspective of the first four years of the 1960s, *shingeki*, at least as represented by the three big *shingeki* companies, showed a stability and financial security that gave it a somewhat misplaced confidence. These three companies appeared not to be aware that many aspects of this artistic and institutional stability were already indicating to some within the movement that what was being pursued was unworthy of the chase.

In part this was due to a strengthening of the links between *shingeki* and the world of politics in 1960. Initially this centred around the nationwide anxiety at the proposed renewal of the US–Japan Security Treat signed originally in 1951. There was enough feeling among *shingeki* people for them to found an organisation to represent their views while negotiations between the two governments were proceeding. This happened in September 1959 and leading members of all three big *shingeki* companies attended. The revised treaty – though not revised enough in Japan's favour in the opinion of many – was signed in Washington in January 1960 and then had to be ratified by the Diet in Tokyo. An extraordinary mobilisation of opposition took place during the first half of this year, with almost daily demonstrations taking place around the Diet compound. On 17 May thirty-four *shingeki* groups jointly issued a signed statement opposing the treaty and nine days later forty-eight groups formed an anti-Anpo (as the treaty was called in an abbreviation highly effective as slogan language) organisation. By this time the Japanese conservative government had forced the ratification through, but the intensity of the demonstrations only increased as they were now focused on preventing President Eisenhower's planned visit to Japan, and in the climactic Anpo riots of 15 June, which are remembered for the death of a Tokyo University student, more than thirty *shingeki* demonstrators were injured.

The Anpo struggle saw both failure (the security system based on Anpo did come into being) and success (Eisenhower's visit was cancelled) and led to great internal debate in the *shingeki* world over what kind of, or how much political commitment (if any), was appropriate for *shingeki* groups and individuals. The question of whether *shingeki* should be politically committed at all was solved by a tour to China in September and October that year (1960). Five groups, representing a wide spectrum of political views, cooperated in this tour, which was *shingeki*'s first venture abroad, well behind *kabuki*, *nō* and *bunraku*. The effort required to organise the programme of performances for this tour and the degree of cooperation achieved between the five groups suggested, not least to their hosts, that this was *shingeki* on show to the outside world for the first time as a distinct genre. Hence the heroes' welcome that the tour members received as veterans of the Anpo struggle did much to reinforce the idea of *shingeki* as a whole comprising an opposition force in Japanese politics. The inclusion of Bungaku-za, hitherto not active politically in any way, both in Anpo and in the

China tour, seemed designed to complete this stereotypical image of *shingeki*. While being associated with opposition politics was nothing new to most *shingeki* practitioners, with hindsight we can see that the identification reinforced here – at Anpo and in China – was with an old style of politics and a longstanding political system that was soon to be rejected by youth in Japan.

Ideologically Mingei seemed to be the company most disposed to perpetuating this image in the two years after Anpo. In 1961 it performed Kubo Sakae's *Kazanbaichi* complete, Part 1 in August and Part 2 in September.[1] Again the sheer scale of the achievement sent a strong message to the *shingeki* world that this method – the socialist realist method – of portraying the world and all its problems was still relevant. During these same few years Kinoshita Junji enjoyed considerable success with two plays that portrayed intellectuals trying to maintain their integrity in the face of a hostile and powerful establishment, in *Ottō to Yobareru Nihonjin* (*A Japanese Called Otto*, 1962) during the 1930s and in *Fuyu no Jidai* (*Winter Season*, 1964) during the 1910s. While these plays can now be seen as part of Kinoshita's developing dramaturgy, they told the students who saw them at the time that old battles were still being fought.

Haiyū-za's exploration of Western and Japanese classics during these years meant that, as far as repertory was concerned, it appeared less prone to look back on recent Japanese political and theatre history. The exceptions to this were perhaps its high-profile productions of Brecht in 1960, 1962 and 1966. While the anti-war message of *Mother Courage and her Children* (1966) would always have been in the postwar period something to which no-one in Japan could take exception, the linking of personal morality to social conditioning in *The Good Person of Setzuan* (1960) and the lampooning of the bourgeoisie in *The Threepenny Opera* (1962) were easily identified as issues of the past. Theatrically, however, these productions of Brecht were important in showing to *shingeki* actors that non-realistic theatre could be modern. The naturalness with which such actors seemed to slip into the epic style and express the alienation-effect at least of the periodic disengagement of actor and character was noticed by Westerners who watched these productions. (Arnott 1969: 228) This type of acting has roots in traditional Japanese theatre, in which Brecht was interested, and Haiyū-za's Brecht may well have shown the way to a new generation of directors – the 'angura' generation – eager to eschew realism and incorporate music into their shows.

MUSICALS

Music in theatre was a topical issue in the early 1960s and *The Threepenny Opera* was judged a production in which the possibilities of incorporating music had been successfully exploited. The release of the film version of *West Side Story* set off something of a boom in musicals in Japan, which was encouraged greatly by a live production sung and acted by the Broadway cast in 1964. Most productions with Japanese casts were translations of Broadway musicals, and Tōhō promoted these actively in 1963 and 1964. However, Japan already had an incipient musical genre of its own in the work of Izumi Taku (1930–1992), who composed two musicals for Rōon (the equivalent of Rōen for music) in 1960 and became well-known thereafter. Izumi contributed actively to the debate on the significance of the Broadway musical to Japanese theatre, rejecting criticism of his own work as not being in the American idiom. One may speculate that the scrutiny of *kabuki* in this debate as a possible base for the development of a specifically Japanese musical may have distantly presaged the rise of Ennosuke III's 'Super Kabuki' in the 1980s.

SHINGEKI IN THE 1960s

The general picture painted of *shingeki* in the first half of the 1960s, however, is of a genre increasingly concerned with stability. The frequent revivals in the repertory of many *shingeki* companies served the purpose of achieving some measure of financial stability. The increasing importance of Rōen as a buyer of theatre seats is also noticeable during this period and from time to time commentators writing in the two main *shingeki* magazines expressed fears that Rōen's need to fill the theatres they had booked was contributing to the conservative nature of *shingeki* production schedules. This particularly affected the big three companies who needed full houses to sustain their numerous actors and technicians; even at the 1965 rate of ¥350 per seat for the company at Rōen-sponsored performances (out of the ¥800-¥1000 that Rōen charged its own members) a few nights at 100% capacity could make a lot of difference.

There are, however, some spectacular exceptions to the widely perceived image of *shingeki* as middle-aged theatre, becoming a little sedate in its organisation and unadventurous in its repertory policy. Some startling new plays were written and performed which added substantially to what had already been achieved by the genre. Combined with revivals of Western classics which attained high professional standards, these new plays augured well for *shingeki*'s future development. During these few years, however, media attention was concentrated on the organisational upheavals of Bungaku-za, the epitome of continuity and confident artistic principles within the *shingeki* world.

Bungaku-za's troubles in 1963 on the one hand exemplify the generational problems that were soon to afflict the whole *shingeki* movement and on the other illustrate what would now be taken for granted – that there was no such thing as apolitical theatre. According to Sugimura Haruko, Bungaku-za's leading actress in the postwar period, discontent within the company started in 1960 when it became known that during the *shingeki* China tour some adjustments had been made to the text of *Onna no Isshō*, Bungaku-za's flagship play, to accommodate objections by the Chinese hosts. (Sugimura and Koyama 1970: 321-3) By early 1962 rumours of trouble within the company were circulating and it soon became clear that all was not well, as company rules were being changed time and time again. During 1962 a number of decisions on repertory were made by time-honoured means, which included discussions involving the whole company but also reinforced a perception among the younger members that seniority was over-respected. Finally in the middle of the New Year's production of a play by Marcel Aymé twenty-nine young members, together with two veteran actors, announced that they were leaving Bungaku-za to form their own company. This was the Gekidan Kumo (Cloud) and it was led by the playwright Fukuda Tsuneari. Sugimura expressed her utter shock and amazement at the time and bitterly compared this (in her eyes) self-indulgent defection to the ideologically and emotionally charged split of the Tsukiji Little Theatre after the death of Osanai Kaoru. (Sugimura 1963: 302)

A further blow came to Bungaku-za in June of this year (1963) with the death of Kubota Mantarō, a founder member and central figure throughout the company's existence. As if this was not enough, the only surviving member of the group of three that had founded the company, Iwata Toyoo, announced his resignation and became an adviser to Kumo. Clearly something was troubling members of the company at all levels. Into the gap in senior leadership created by this death and this defection stepped Mishima Yukio, whose play *Rokumeikan* had been triumphantly revived on tour by Bungaku-za towards the end of 1959. Mishima had written new plays for the company in 1960 and 1961 and one of his modern *nō* plays had been performed on tour in 1962. In May 1963 he worked up a translation of Victorien Sardou's play *Tosca* and this production (June) is described in the Bungaku-za official history as the first step in the realisation of the 'Mishima New Conception' for Bungaku-za. (Kitami 1963: 128) This 'new conception' consisted of three parts: 1. Productions of new works by contemporary playwrights, 2. Contemporary productions of *kabuki* plays, 3. Reappraisal of the Western theatrical tradition. Perhaps reassured that Bungaku-za was in safe hands and certainly encouraged by the success of *Tosca* to think that the company's fortunes were reviving, Sugimura joined a small group of theatre people on an extended theatre-going tour of the USSR, Eastern European Communist countries, Western Europe and finally

China. On her return in the middle of November she was immediately involved in further upheavals within the company, this time over a play by Mishima entitled *Yorokobi no Koto* (*The Joyful Koto*).

Mishima had apparently undertaken to write a play suitable for the 1964 New Year production. Bungaku-za had established a convention of performing something light – often a comedy – at this time, but Mishima wrote an uncompromisingly realist play, that was referred to as an 'anti-communist drama' (*hankyōgeki*) and had strong resonances of a train-derailing incident in 1949 which was attributed to communist activity. During 1963 the judgement by which several of the suspects had been found guilty and executed was overturned. According to Ii Shirō, who was the decision-maker in Sugimura Haruko's absence, Mishima seemed to be obsessed with the possible presence of communists in Bungaku-za at the time, and when Ii decided that the production would have to be postponed, Mishima and several others left the company. (Kitami 1963: 125)

Ideological problems of another kind would afflict the other two big *shingeki* companies within a few years, but Mishima's contribution to Bungaku-za and *shingeki* in general through his playwriting should not be forgotten. Kinoshita Junji has been described as the Arthur Miller of Japan; had his politics been very different, Mishima might also have been compared to Miller in that he was capable of creating immensely powerful dramatic situations. In *Tōka no Kiku* (*Chrysanthemum on the Tenth Day*), written for Bungaku-za and performed in 1962, the leading character Kiku saves her old master from rebels and in the process is humiliated in front of her son who is one of those rebels. A *kiku* (chrysanthemum) is something that is discarded on the tenth day because the Chrysanthemum Festival (Chōyō) takes place on 9 September, and Kiku in the play, loyal though she was, is duly discarded. As *Tōka no Kiku* is set against the background of the revolt of 26 February 1936, when young officers stormed ministers' homes, it is a highly political play, but maybe its sheer dramatic qualities prevented problems such as *Yorokobi no Koto* occasioned later. Mishima in much of his playwriting transferred from his fiction his uninhibited and keenly targeted use of language and his unwillingness to leave alone any subject that he regarded as dramatic.

These qualities are apparent in *Sado Kōshaku Fujin* (*Madame de Sade*), which he wrote for his post-Bungaku-za company, NLT (New Literary Theatre) in 1965. The rhetoric of the play was noted in Japan as one of its strongest characteristics. Right at the beginning one of the six female characters (no males) objects to not naming things as what they are. We never see Sade himself; he is entirely created for us by Mishima using the medium of the womens'speeches. As the six women (Sade's wife, her mother, her younger sister, two friends and the housekeeper) – the patient wife with the romantic image of her now imprisoned husband, her mother and her anxiety about the family name, the younger sister who has had an affair with Sade, the friend who is pure but admits later, after becoming a nun, that she was fascinated by accounts of Sade's adventures, the friend who delights in such adventures and describes them in the play, the sullenly revolutionary housekeeper – conjure up their own pictures of Sade, we are forced to imagine a highly complex personality, as Mishima intended. Few plays in modern Japan are so animated by their language.

Potentially de-stabilising activity was not confined to the art-first end of the *shingeki* spectrum at this time. Another playwright who attracted much attention in the early 1960s was Fukuda Yoshiyuki (1931–). Unlike Mishima he was committed to that part of the *shingeki* movement which was anti-establishment and left-wing, but like Mishima he grew impatient with the ideology of those he was working with. He was a founder member, in 1960, of a new company, Seinen Geijutsu Gekijō (usually abbreviated to Seigei; Youth Arts Theatre), whose acting members were graduates of the acting school run by Mingei. There was some dissatisfaction among young actors being trained both by Mingei and Haiyū-za, because there were simply not enough vacancies in those groups for the graduates of their schools. In the case of Seigei the dissatisfaction was compounded by an ideological difference, which soon became apparent during the Anpo demonstrations. Seigei was unable to accept the guiding discipline of the demonstrations, provided primarily by the Japan Communist Party and generally accepted by the *shingeki* movement, and preferred to align itself with anti-JCP student groups. (Goodman 1988: 36–7)

Fukuda's playwriting career began in a conventional left-wing way. His first play was in the idiom of the socialist-realist plays that he, like Kinoshita, came to reject. *Nagai Bohyō no Retsu* (*Long Rows of Gravestones*, 1958) concerned the Kawai Eijirō Incident of 1938, in which a liberal professor had had some of his books banned – an event that had made a deep impression on Kinoshita as a student. In 1959 this play was specially commended by the Kishida Drama Prize committee. By Seigei's opening programme in October 1960, however, Fukuda had moved on to experiments with other dramatic methods. Alongside the two rather conventional *shingeki* plays that were the other items on this programme Fukuda introduced a part-*sprechtchör*, part real, part discussion-based, avowedly Brechtian account of the actors' involvement in the Anpo struggles which he entitled *Kiroku Number 1* (*Record No 1*). His next play was virtually a musical and was criticised as lightweight, although the political commitment was still there: *Sanada Fūunroku* (*Sanada's Chance of Greatness*, 1962) had been specially commissioned by Rōen to celebrate the fortieth anniversary of its founding and Fukuda was thus in effect being adopted by the *shingeki* establishment that he opposed. His major achievement at this time, however, was a play performed by Seigei in 1964 that has an established place in *shingeki* history.

Hakamadare wa Doko da (*Where is Hakamadare?*; trans *Find Hakamadare*) brought together several strands of Fukuda's developing playwriting technique.[2] It was his first play to find general and enthusiastic acceptance among the drama critics of the time. Fukuda had little patience with reviewers in general, but even he was surprised at the ferocity of the attacks on *Sanada Fūunroku*. (Fukuda 1995: 8591) A modernised version of Kawakami Otojirō's *Oppekepe* followed and was thought to be lightweight. With *Hakamadare wa Doko da* Fukuda was getting his anti-left-establishment message across through an innovative and tense drama. Based on multiple and varied sources, from medieval Japanese legends to a modern Chinese short story and a Marxist *manga* (comic book), it charts the naive but deeply committed quest of some poor villagers for the hero who will bring justice to the world, only to discover that he (Hakamadare) needs to set up a secret police to do it. They kill him and become Hakamadare themselves. The play was performed by Seigei under the direction of the radical *nō* actor Kanze Hideo, who had been a founder member of the company. To the dismay of the conservative *nō* establishment Kanze Hideo, scion of the most famous *nō* family, was associated with much modern experimental drama from this time on, and this production of *Hakamadare wa Doko da* bore signs of his *nō* background. According to Fukuda, Kanze Hideo was always unwilling to use *nō* or *kyōgen* techniques in modern theatre, but he prevailed upon him this time and the play included a dream interlude which the stage directions require to 'parody the structure and staging of classical *nō* drama'. (Fukuda 1995: 93) The powerful theme and the rich and inventive dramaturgy made this a memorable production.[3]

In this way *shingeki* across the political spectrum, in spite of its quest for stability, was enlivened by plays that were uninhibited before the environment in which they would be performed. The same could not be said for *shimpa*, which lost much ground during the decade and was reduced to three or four one-month programmes per year. It was top-heavy with established stars and the commercial pressures to retain the two-performances-per day system were blamed for instances of serious illness amongst its older actors. Mizutani Yaeko, on whom the company depended heavily at this time, was forced by illness to leave a production after it had opened in June 1962 and she was not fit to act again until the end of the year. At the beginning of 1965 *shimpa*'s leading *onnagata*, Hanayagi Shōtarō, died of a heart attack and the next month Mizutani again had to leave a production. In an autobiographical book published in 1971 Mizutani refers to the mounting criticism of *shimpa* for not having enough new acting talent working its way up the company. (Mizutani 1971: 242) The target audience was clear: people with families and households (and given the hours of performance, this would mainly have referred to women); the type of theatre aimed at was less specific and harder to achieve. Mizutani termed it *taishū-gendai-geki*, popular contemporary drama, and it was its links to the contemporary world that were most suspect. While *shimpa* had achieved much in just surviving social change since the end of the war, it was now finding great difficulty retaining even its chosen conservative audiences. As of 2001, however, *shimpa* performances were still continuing, albeit on a limited scale.

Shinkokugeki did not fare so well, going out of existence in 1987, just after its 70th anniversary production. Zenshin-za kept going in spite of serious internal problems in the 1960s caused by the Sino–Soviet split, a fundamental ideological and political confrontation between the world's two largest Communist powers.

All three companies were now performing in Tokyo for only a few months per year, and this raises the question of how much prominence their activities should warrant in a brief history of modern Japanese theatre. Although all three could claim to have stimulated discussion on the future course of Japanese theatre in their time and one could argue that both *shimpa* and *shinkokugeki* could be considered genres in their own right, by the 1960s their productions were individual events in a rich theatrical offering that probably gave the Tokyo public more choice than any other theatregoers in the world. Unlike the Haiyū-za Theatre, which only had *shingeki* productions, the spaces in which these companies played were also used for various other types of commercial theatre, for example comedy in the case of the Shinbashi Enbujō, the theatre that *shimpa* considered its home. In 1966 the Teikoku Gekijō was rebuilt and this became a focus for big-budget productions, such as a highly popular adaptation of *Gone with the Wind* in November of that year. (Arnott 1969: 238–40) Thus Tokyo had its equivalent of Broadway in New York and the West End in London, where in most cases plays were commercial ventures and used time-honoured methods to attract audiences: star actors, comfortable surroundings, expensive publicity, and scenery on which it was clear that a lot of money had been spent. It differed from its Western counterparts as a theatrical city in also supporting traditional genres of theatre – *nō* and *kabuki* – that had remained relatively unchanged for centuries.

SHINGEKI'S MALCONTENTS

Tokyo could also be proud of *shingeki*, which always referred to itself as non-commercial theatre. The sheer size of the *shingeki* movement in the early 1960s was remarkable. More than a hundred companies were operating, staffed by fiercely proud actors who sacrified the possibilitiy of making a stable living in order to be able to act. The enthusiasm of these groups was infectious and it could be felt through the whole range of *shingeki*, from the big three companies to the smallest, struggling, suburban troupe.

Shingeki defined in this way was an extensive cultural enterprise that was pyramidal in shape. At the top were the three big *shingeki* companies – Bungaku-za, Haiyū-za and Mingei – and the organisation that provided many of their audiences: Rōen. In the early 1960s there were several *shingeki* companies that came close to the big three in terms of members and activity – such as Seinen-za, Bunka-za, Shinseisaku-za. By far the greatest number of *shingeki* groups, however, were locally based and had a financially precarious existence. Their members subsidised their acting by part-time jobs, not, like the stars of the big three, in television and films, but by driving cement-mixer lorries, working in bars etc. If a comparison is made with British metropolitan theatre at the time, a similar structure can be seen, from weekly repertory companies through monthly repertory companies to the dominating West End. The West End, however, with its system of recruiting casts through auditions for individual productions, allowed every repertory actor in the country to hope that one day s/he might act on a West End stage. For better or for worse, the *shingeki* world at the top was virtually a closed one, because actors did not come and go and vacancies for new members were very limited. Most *shingeki* actors were sacrificing much to have the opportunity to operate in an artistic environment perceived by them as very different from that of the commercial theatre, where there were plenty of parts to be acted. Their aspirations were, however, blocked.

In defence of the big *shingeki* companies it must be acknowledged that they had all been aware of the necessity to provide opportunities for younger actors to develop their skills. Already in 1949 Bungaku-za had established its Atelier and it used this structure to perform plays that might otherwise not have been viable commercially and to give its younger actors the chance to play large parts. Later, in the latter half of the 1950s, a number of satellite groups emerged around Haiyū-za, particularly the Haiyū-za Shōgekijō (Haiyū-za Little Theatre). The use of the word '*shōgekijō*' ('little theatre') is significant in echoing the name of the company – Tsukiji Shōgekijō – that pioneered *shingeki*. In the 1920s '*shōgekijō*' indicated protest against the size and scale of commercial theatre, principally *kabuki*. In the early 1960s *shingeki* magazines commented frequently on the enthusiasm and artistic achievements of these smaller-scale groups (*Sanada Fūunroku* had been a joint production by four such groups) and by 1965 were noting the great increase in *shōgekijō* activity. By now the designation was increasingly taking on an anti-*shingeki* colouring.

NEW THEATRES

The opening of two new small-scale theatre spaces in 1963 and 1964 greatly encouraged *shōgekijō* activity. While the Haiyū-za Theatre was itself small and had always been available for *shōgekijō* productions, use of it inevitably associated the production with the company that owned it. The two new theatres had no connections with any of the big three *shingeki* companies. Both were situated in the Shinjuku area of Tokyo, thus prompting the suggestion that Shinjuku was becoming the equivalent of Off Broadway, a phenomenon that was exciting interest in Japan. In June 1963 an avant garde cinema called the Art Theatre Shinjuku Bunka began allowing its small auditorium to be used for live theatre after film screenings – so this meant that shows started at about 9.30 in the evening. Then in April 1964 the Kinokuniya Hall opened; this was a small proscenium theatre space in a multistorey bookshop. From the first, Art Theatre Shinjuku Bunka was associated with forces hostile to large-scale *shingeki*, as its first production was mounted by one of the groups that had been formed by the first Bungaku-za split. The Art Theatre went out of existence in 1974, but the Kinokuniya Hall was still flourishing in 2001. Between them in the mid-1960s they gave to smaller groups a sense of independence that enabled them to follow their own lines of development.

It may be worth mentioning that large-scale theatre productions also acquired new venues during the mid-1960s. In October 1963 a 1300-plus seat theatre opened across from Hibiya Park in the very centre of Tokyo. This was the Nissei Gekijō, so named from the life insurance company (Nihon Seimei – the first syllable of each word was used) in whose grand new building it was situated. The president of the company had been deeply affected as a child by a performance of Maeterlinck's *L'Oiseau Bleu* (*Blue Bird*) by *shimpa* in 1920 and had retained a love of theatre and opera throughout his life. (Ōzasa 1999: 143) Nissei Gekijō had long been his dream and with this theatre he realised it in a spectacular way. Superbly equipped, the Nissei oozed luxury with its large, soft seats, its pink carpeting and its oyster-shell decorated ceiling. Apart from shows organised by its own production company, the theatre was available to *shingeki* companies. Haiyū-za performed a notable *Hamlet* (with Nakadai Tatsuya, best known in the West as a film actor, in the title role) there in 1964 (June). A controversial production of *Richard III* with Nakamura Kanzaburō, a *kabuki* actor noted for his playing of evil roles, as Richard, also took place in the same year (March). The Nissei production company itself sponsored a production of Mishima Yukio's *Yorokobi no Koto*, the play that had caused the second Bungaku-za split. Over the years the Nissei has continued to host diverse theatrical and operatic shows by both Japanese and foreign companies.

The Nissei Gekijō injected an element of variety into mid-1960s Japanese theatre and is significant for providing neutral ground where *shingeki* and commercial theatre could meet. The two other new theatres of the time, the Teikoku Gekijō (Imperial Theatre, opened September 1966) and the Kokuritsu Gekijō (National Theatre, opened in November of the same year), did this occasionally, but in general they were more focused in the type of theatre they wished to provide. The Imperial Theatre was not strictly new, as the prewar building had survived the bombing, but from 1955 it had been used as a cinema. Now in 1966 it was rebuilt (like the Nissei inside an office block) and became a mainline commercial theatre featuring big-budget shows such as the very successful adaptation of *Gone with the Wind* performed in November of 1966. The National Theatre, by contrast, was dedicated to the preservation of Japan's traditional performing arts, principally *kabuki*, *bunraku* and dance. It bought in *kabuki* actors from Shōchiku for productions that in many cases presented whole *kabuki* plays to their audiences in place of the succession of excerpts that was the norm in Shōchiku controlled theatres. The National Theatre was not suitable for *nō* and in 1983 the Kokuritsu Gekijō Nōgakudō (National Nō Theatre) was built. While *bunraku* performances could be and were often held in the National Theatre in Tokyo, the puppet theatre acquired its own national base in the area of Japan where the genre had developed and flourished: the Kokuritsu Bunraku Gekijō (National Bunraku Theatre), designed by the internationally famous architect Kurokawa Kishō, was constructed in Osaka also in 1983.

ANGURA – THE *SHINGEKI* UNDERGROUND

Thus, performance spaces were greatly on the increase at this time, but the provision of lavish theatres built with state or big business money only exacerbated the sense of alienation that young *shingeki* actors felt towards large-scale theatre organised rationally and commercially. Partly, but by no means entirely, from within the universities politically radical playwrights and directors emerged to confront mainstream *shingeki* more comprehensively than the existing *shōgekijō* groups. What these pioneers created has been described by various terms by Japanese commentators. The theatre that settled into an anti-realistic mode during the last two decades of the twentieth century has generally been called '*shōgekijō*'. In the 1960s, however, both this term and another – '*angura*' – were current. In general, although there are many exceptions to this, the more radical side of little-theatre activity was referred to as '*angura*'.

Angura is a contraction of the phonetic equivalent of the English word 'underground'. Most Japanese *angura* was not 'underground' in the literal sense (although some was) or politically underground (in that freedom of speech was guaranteed by the constitution). Its basic meaning indicated a radical alternative theatre and I will use it here to refer to historically significant anti-*shingeki* drama of the late 1960s and early 1970s.

Radicalism in the arts was not confined to staged drama. Parallel to and supportive of *angura* theatre were developments in various cognate art forms. For a while the word '*angura*' seemed as ubiquitous as '*kairyō*' (reform) had been in the 1880s. 1968 saw booms in '*angura*' records and '*angura*' films. Across the Western world frustration with intransigent political systems and helplessness before the intensification of the Vietnam War were incensing young people and it was natural that some of this would be expressed in artistic ways. Of particular relevance to the *angura* theatre movement in Japan were dance and poster design.

BUTŌ

During the early part of the decade a dancer named Hijikata Tatsumi (1928–1986) had developed a form of modern dance which he termed *ankoku butō*. The two words mean 'darkness' and 'dance' respectively and both are significant in the context of 1960s radical arts. Hijikata used '*butō*', which emphasises the planting of the feet on the ground, to differentiate his dancing from both classical and modern forms of Japanese dance, which are both referred to as '*buyō*', a word in which both elements indicate dancing. The 'darkness' was also in contrast to the brightness associated with much previous dance in Japan. Hijikata's dance gave prominence to the darker side of human nature; it was never fast and joyous, but slow, deliberate and often sinister. No taboos were honoured. The human body was central – not in its capacity for athletic movement but in its capacity to express through agonisingly slow transformations the deepest human propensity for eroticism and violence.

POSTERS

In concert with Hijikata's work in *butō* (which has become the generic term for this type of dance) an artist named Yokoo Tadanori (1936–) developed a poster style, again iconoclastic and uninhibited, that established him as Japan's leading exponent of pop art. Utilising images from popular culture of the nineteenth and early twentieth centuries and juxtaposing them in non-combinatory collages, Yokoo presented the same kind of challenge to Japan's modern art movement as Hijikata was doing to modern dance. There was plenty of light in Yokoo's posters for *butō*, but an underlying metaphorical darkness can usually be sensed. Yokoo designed many posters for *angura* theatre groups and he helped positively to reinforce their strongly felt need to delve below the realism of *shingeki*, once regarded as progressive but now so despised by them. (Goodman and Clarke, 1998)

THE LEADERS OF *ANGURA*

Angura presented a very confused picture at the end of the 1960s, but with hindsight a few groups and personalities can be seen as significant in the development of this type of theatre. In most cases their theatrical activity has lasted into the twenty-first century. They differed greatly in such things as performance modes, attitude to playscript as text, utilisation of performance space, etc, but they held two tenets in common: they were united in their opposition to *shingeki* and its hard-won realism, and they shared with *butō* and Yokoo's posters an insistence on investigating and exposing the latent darker side of human nature. While theatre buildings for all main genres of theatre had become progressively more comfortable over the past century and as audiences for *kabuki* and *shingeki* alike came to expect to be cherished as patrons, *angura* set out to shock and disturb. Watching late 1960s *angura* was rarely a comfortable experience in any sense. This attitude was typified by Kara Jūrō (1940–) who has bluntly stated: 'what I want to do is to make them laugh and then just when they're laughing pull the carpet out from under their feet. I want to make them go pale. I want to force them into terrifying situations.'[4]

Kara had close connections with *butō* in that one of his actors from the early sixties became a leading *butō* dancer.[5] He also had posters designed for him by Yokoo. From the beginning Kara was in no doubt that drama had to act upon its audience and the first production of the group he formed in 1962 was of Jean Paul Sartre's *La Putain Respectueuse* (*The Respectable Prostitute*, 1946), where the irony is so obvious that an audience would be hard put to it to avoid confronting its own prejudices. Kara had written his graduation thesis on Sartre at Meiji University in Tokyo and he gave his group the name Jōkyō Gekijō (Situation Theatre), another reference to Sartre whose idea of a 'theatre of situations' Kara knew well. Somewhat ironically Kara was in good *shingeki* company in thinking Sartre offered ideas relevant to modern Japanese theatre; both Bungaku-za and Mingei had been enthusiastic about performing his plays, and Kinoshita Junji quoted him frequently.

Kara was later to reject the West and he stands out among the *angura* playwrights/directors discussed here for avoiding tours to Europe and North America, preferring instead to take his troupe to countries such as South Korea and Bangladesh. He is comprehensively a theatre man and his talents extend over most aspects of theatre performance. Perhaps for this reason his opposition to *shingeki* is expressed partly through a reexamination of Japan's own theatre history. Styling his actors 'riverbed beggars' (*kawara kojiki*), as that was how respectable society regarded *kabuki* actors in the premodern period, Kara had references to *kabuki* in much of his directing work. He often used a version of the *kabuki hanamichi* walkway. He believed true theatre to be actor-centred and built the major part of his drama theory on that belief. In his plays he rejected any sense of real time.

Kara's opposition to normalising institutions meant that in many cases his references were not to the highly institutionalised urbanised *kabuki* that developed towards the end of the Edo period but to the smaller troupes who were denied access to the main *kabuki* theatres and wandered the countryside performing in whatever temporary acting spaces they could. Kara was sufficiently well known by the late 1960s to be acceptable to commercially conscious theatre managers, but he still preferred to have his plays performed in makeshift locations. The first, in 1966, was in the ruins of a building that had no roof or walls, from which the police and local authorities tried to evict him, thus leading him to dub the spectators who braved all this 'the real cream of theatregoers'. Various other outdoor locations subsequently became venues for performances by the Situation Theatre until in the summer of 1967 the red tent that became the company's trademark was pitched for the first time – in the grounds of a Shinto shrine in the Shinjuku area of Tokyo. The red tent was subsequently taken all over Japan and it became a potent symbol of opposition to drama in respectable theatres. The hundred or so spectators in the cramped interior, where they might be stepped on by actors, suffered the dust of summer and the cold of winter. The atmosphere, however, was electric and Kara's Situation Theatre is generally credited with bringing a vibrancy and immediacy back to the stage/front-of-house relationship.

Kara's actors, and, it must be said, Kara's texts were crucial to the creation of this atmosphere. His designation of actors as 'privileged physical beings' (*tokken-teki nikutai*) indicated how important the person and personality of the actor were before s/he uttered a line from the stage. Within them a force had to exist that would work on conventional views of reality with the object of exploding them. In the process something new would be created. Conceivably this could have been done, as Kara's avowed forbears had done it, by the actors adlibbing around agreed themes, but after the first production of Situation Theatre it became the practice for Kara to provide play texts that embodied exactly what he wanted to achieve on stage. The language was therefore designed to be unbridled. It obeyed no conventions, mixing scatological slang with difficult vocabulary, jumbling metaphors and injecting comic puns where comedy seemed inappropriate. Making sense of all this was reportedly beyond most of the spectators, but the dark intensity of their experience seems to be generally acknowledged. (Ōzasa 1980: 21) Kara's concern was not that his plots should be followed and understood, for he deliberately fashioned them to be fragmented, but, given the ambience he had created and given his known anti-establishment and anti-authority views, his audiences were expected at least to pick up his references to his own political, social and ideological *bêtes-noires*.

Like Situation Theatre the Waseda Shōgekijō (Waseda Little Theatre), also active in the mid-1960s, was dominated by one strong personality: Suzuki Tadashi (1939–) This was a common pattern for all the *angura* groups that survived for a decade or more. In the case of these two groups this phenomenon takes what may be called an extreme form, for at a later stage their names were changed to include the name of the leader. Situation Theatre became Kara-gumi (Kara Troupe) in 1989 and Waseda Shōgekijō changed to SCOT. While Kara later rejected the West and concentrated the touring activities of his group elsewhere, Suzuki Tadashi became such an international figure with his connections in the United States and Europe that he gave his company a name that is an English-sounding acronym of a full English name: Suzuki Company Of Toga.

In 1961 Suzuki and Betsuyaku Minoru (1937–), both recent graduates of Waseda University, founded a group which they called Jiyū Butai (Free Stage). This partnership of director and playwright lasted until 1969 and gave a stamp to Jiyū Butai and its successor group Waseda Shōgekijō that Suzuki felt progressively less comfortable with. Suzuki is known, like Kara, for his emphasis on the centrality of the actor and especially the actor's body, but during this early phase of his career his fortunes were bound up with a disciplined playwright, Betsuyaku, who wrote scripts where every word counted. Betsuyaku was later to characterise the differences between them as opposite conceptions of what was universal: to Suzuki it was the movement of the body; to Betsuyaku the more locally based a play was, the more likely it was to attain universality and he was concerned in his plays to express the 'hushed murmurings of members of small communities'.[6] Although these two strong personalities went their separate ways after 1969, before that their collaboration was very fruitful and it resulted in two events that were important in the theatre history of the period. The first was Jiyū Butai's production of Betsuyaku's *Zō* (*Elephant*) in 1962, 'the play that launched the postmodern theatre movement', and the second was the award of the prestigious Kishida Prize for Drama in 1968. (Goodman 1986: 191) Betsuyaku was the first of his generation to be recognised in this way.

Betsuyaku was born in Manchuria and has linguistically felt something of an outsider in Japan, in that, although he is a native Japanese speaker, he is excluded from the all-important unspoken aspects of interpersonal communication in Japan.[7] His plays are written in a language that frequently follows the logic of only what is spoken rather than that of the whole situation. This is one of the dramaturgical techniques used by European Absurd Drama playwrights and may explain why Betsuyaku in English translation seems quite accessible to Westerners. Behind his relatively simple language lies an intense involvement in the Anpo movement of 1960, which resulted in him leaving Waseda University before finishing his course. Nothing is quite as simple as it seems in Betsuyaku's work.

The 'elephant' of the title *Zō* may be any one of a number of overwhelming realities, such as the atomic bombing of Hiroshima and Nagasaki or, to Betsuyaku and his fellow demonstrators, the state apparatus against which the Anpo struggle was directed. The ostensible subject of the play is the bombing of Hiroshima, but audiences were invited to view this event quite differently from those of the 1950s plays that treated the same subject through realistic depiction of the consequences for individuals. There are two individual survivors in *Zō* and there is a thread of consistency to their diametrically opposed methods of confronting their experiences. Whether one conforms to the post-experience reality, as one of the two tries to do, or whether one attempts to escape this reality to force others to remember the experience, the result, after a long, painful and momentarily violent process, is oblivion. (Tsuno 1970b: 60–70)

In March 1966 Suzuki, Betsuyaku and an actor named Ono Seki, who had played one of the two protagonists in *Zō*, reorganised Jiyū Butai and renamed it Waseda Shōgekijō, which quickly became one of the leading *angura* companies of the late 1960s. Much of the considerable attention that Waseda Shōgekijō received in the media came from the combination of Suzuki's powerful direction, Betsuyaku's provoking dramas and Ono's intense acting. Its regular venue, however, contributed to its reputation, as the group performed in a room above a café in the vicinity of Waseda University, thus rejecting conventional performance spaces. It was there that it performed Betsuyaku's *Matchi-uri no Shōjo* (*The Little Match Girl*) in November 1966, one of two plays cited by the Kishida Drama Prize committee when awarding the prize to Betsuyaku in 1967. In common with most *angura* playwrights, Betsuyaku here rejects the linear time that is a quintessential element of the realistic drama that they were rejecting. *The Little Match Girl* establishes a time zone in which several vertical axes of memory are operating: that of Hans Christian Andersen's tale, remembered by the audience from childhood, and at least two versions of memories linking the characters' lives. (Rolf and Gillespie 1992: 16–17) Again, dominating all this is an overwhelming reality – this time it may be the imperial institution – alternately accepting and rejecting those appealing to it but ultimately unchanging in its ritualised existence.

Betsuyaku continued to write plays after he and Suzuki parted company and he was no longer the principal playwright of Waseda Shōgekijō. He is unusual among his generation in being able to establish himself as a playwright who is not beholden to any one company or group. While the more normal close relationship between playwright and company can be enriching for both parties, Betsuyaku has shown that an independent playwright can also thrive in Japan. Suzuki, on the other hand, did not have to face this particular challenge. His position as leader of Waseda Shōgekijō was secure and, now he was free of the creative presence that was pulling in a different direction from himself, he had the actors and other staff with whom to develop his own form of theatre.

Like Kara Jūrō and like other directors at the time, Suzuki was convinced of the centrality of the actor in theatre, and he had an actress in Waseda Shōgekijō whose stage presence was something quite exceptional. Shiraishi Kayoko (1941–) had joined the company in 1967 and two years later Suzuki built a whole programme around her. He entitled it *Gekiteki naru Mono o Megutte I*, which has been variously translated into English as *On the Dramatic Passions I*, *On the Dramatic I*, *In Search of the Dramatic I*, etc. As the title indicates, Suzuki was seeking to explore the roots of what was dramatic, and he chose to do this through one actor who acted in a series of scenes from previous classics. Shiraishi's vocal range and riveting powers of expression astonished her audiences, but it was the second of these collage programmes, in 1970, that brought her to national attention as the foremost actress in contemporary drama. The collage consisted of ten scenes taken from two *kabuki* plays by the nineteenth-century decadent playwright, Tsuruya Nanboku IV, a *shimpa* classic and a dramatisation of a story by Izumi Kyōka. All centred on a woman who had been grievously wronged. Shiraishi expressed the uncontained feelings of these women – feelings of rage, disbelief, sorrow, vengeance – with a tortured depth of emotion that engaged the whole being of members of the audience in a way not known before.

Shiraishi was compared with Okuni, the legendary founder of *kabuki*, thus suggesting a link, no doubt welcome to Suzuki, with Japanese theatre before its seventeenth-century institutionalisation. Suzuki at this time was developing his own theory of actor training and he was consciously looking back beyond the time when theatre in Japan began divesting itself of its religious function of mediating between the gods and man. From the earliest origins of theatre in

Japan foot stamping has been an important part of ritualised performances and Suzuki built up a theory of acting, which claimed that the whole body of the actor could be trained to produce emotional and spiritual powers of expression through contact with the earth.[9] By putting his actors through extremely rigorous training of the lower part of the body, Suzuki developed a highly disciplined company capable of communication with their audiences at an intense level. What became known as the Suzuki Method led to workshops abroad, mainly in the United States.

As Suzuki looked more and more to early forms of Japanese classical theatre, he became convinced that urbanisation might have been responsible for Japanese theatre losing its past intensely dramatic nature and he took his company, at least for the summer months, to a village called Toga high in mountains near Toyama City. Here from 1976, away from the distractions and irrelevances of city life, the company lived together, trained together and developed new productions under Suzuki's direction. Waseda Shōgekijō fans showed themselves very willing to make the eight-hour train and bus journey from Tokyo to Toga and the Toga Festival, founded in 1982, consistently attracted capacity audiences. Increasingly the complex of traditional farmhouses and, later, Isozaki Arata buildings became an international theatre centre, with companies and individual actors from Europe and the United States participating in both the training programme and Toga Festival productions. Suzuki turned progressively to Greek tragedy and Shakespeare for his repertory. Apart from providing him with what he considered valid drama for his actors, often set by him in a new context (for example, *King Lear* in an old-people's home), knowledge of these classics among the various nationalities that made up the audiences at Toga enabled him to pioneer a remarkable series of bilingual productions, where Japanese and English-speaking actors acted together delivering their lines in their own language.

Within a few days of the opening production of Waseda Shōgekijō in 1966 the only group which could claim to be literally *angura* or 'underground' also commenced activities. This was Jiyū Gekijō (Free Theatre) and it performed in a basement room in the Shibuya area of Tokyo. It was led not by university graduates like Situation Theatre and Waseda Shōgekijō but by young people whose ambition for careers as actors had led them to the Haiyū Yōseijo, Haiyū-za's acting school. They were therefore similar to the actors in a number of little-theatre groups active at the time, but the vehemence of their anti-*shingeki* stand singles them out from these counterparts. When Jiyū Gekijō merged with a university-based group in 1969, their combined resources allowed them to launch a 'concerted, systematic, and highly self-conscious attack on the orthodox paradigm of Japanese modern theatre'. (Kullman and

Young 1986: 115) Like Situation Theatre before it this company freed itself institutionally from *shingeki* and Rōen in 1970 by adopting a tent as its performance space. The company now called itself Black Tent Theatre 68/71 (Kuro/Kokushoku Tento Roku-hachi Nana-ichi) and toured regularly with the black tent each spring and autumn. Its tent was considerably larger than that used by Kara's company and could accommodate about eight hundred people. (Kullman and Young 1986: 115)

Jiyū Gekijō performed plays by a number of contemporary playwrights, but it was particularly associated with the work of Satō (usually referred to in English as Satoh) Makoto (1943–), who also directed many of its productions. Satō's plays around 1967-9 aptly caught the mood of the times. Students throughout the world were experiencing mounting frustration over the course of the Vietnam War and this was a strong contributory factor in the student revolt in Paris in May 1968, which sparked off student protests against the establishment everywhere, often targeted at the universities themselves. The Japanese student protests of 1968 and 1969 were especially bitter and succeeded in closing down some universities temporarily. While all *angura* groups were part of a youth protest against an orthodoxy that included communism (which had of course represented rebellion to many of the middle-aged professors now attacked), the claustrophobic performances of Jiyū Gekijō in its stifling basement room communicated the deeply felt anger and frustration to their enthusiastic audiences.

In 1969 Satō directed his own *Nezumi Kozō Jirōkichi* (*Young Jirōkichi, the Rat*) in this basement room. The production was an extraordinary combination of wild, noisy acting and dense text. The play itself was a *tour de force* of multi-layered signifiers that mystified many of the audience but as a text was awarded the Kishida Drama Prize in 1969. With initial references to popular folklore about a nineteenth-century good-hearted bandit who always robbed the rich at the hour of the Rat (midnight) and a previous *kabuki* dramatisation of his story, the play sees the hopes of its five rat-figures eternally destroyed by the persistence of the status quo. It is the imperial system and the establishment supporting it that emerge triumphant in this play. This was powerful theatre but even at close quarters too much to take in at one sitting. Like much great drama *Nezumi Kozō Jirōkichi* sent its audiences away from the performance conscious of having had their senses and emotions fully engaged but also expecting to be able later to find much more in it. (Tsuno 1970a)

In the productions of Satō and Kara text was quite important albeit sometimes overshadowed by performance modes that did not foreground it. Ōta Shōgo (1939–), by contrast, preferred to base his drama not on the 20% of the time when human beings were giving utterance but on the 80% when they were not and were maybe having thoughts that were not to be communicated to the outside world. His plays had minimal dialogue, and in the case of *Mizu no Eki* (*The Water Station*, 1981) none at all. The action was extremely slow, on the assumption that things normally missed would be revealed. (Senda 1995: 126) New concepts of the use of (apparently empty) space on the stage were also opened up by the interminable time it seemed to take characters to move towards or away from each other, and Ōta acknowledged his debt to *nō* performance. (Brandon 1997: 161) Ōta admits no debt to *butō* dance but has himself assumed some significance in the simultaneity with which the new dance and his form of theatre developed. Watching *butō* and an Ōta play can be a similarly draining experience as the outcome that the audience expects from the agonisingly slow movements of the actors is either denied it or subverted in an unforeseen way.

Yet another approach to the creation of modern theatre can be seen in the work of Terayama Shūji (1936–1983) during these years.[11] The group he formed at the beginning of 1967 was given the name Engeki Jikkenshitsu Tenjō Sajiki (Drama Laboratory, Gallery Seats) and this indicated his concerns to find new ways to challenge realism and link effectively to the audience. Terayama's theatre was probably the most rebellious and theatrically iconoclastic of all the *angura* groups considered so far. Apart from powerful anti-establishment and personal themes in his plays, in performance every aspect of *shingeki* convention was derided and rejected in favour of some alternative. The right of the audience to see a whole play after having bought a ticket, the right of the audience to watch a performance rather than being involved in it, even the expectation of an audience that drama would be brought to them rather than they having to go in search of it – over the course of the next decade all this and much more was challenged by Terayama and Tenjō Sajiki. Terayama confronted his spectators, sometimes at very close quarters, with untrained actors drawn from the margins of society, intending, as he put it, 'to reinstate fairground freaks – just by being in the theatre your breast will leap and your heart palpitate – you'll be shocked – at giants, attractive dollies, dwarfs, bizarre and curious performers of all kinds'. (Ōzasa 1980: 24) By the 1970s Terayama had moved out onto the streets and *Knock*, performed in 1975, required its spectators to appear at various locations over a period of about thirty hours. Senda Akihiko, at the time modern drama critic of the *Asahi Newspaper*, did not find the events themselves very theatrical. 'What seemed theatrical to me were, instead, the puzzle-filled maps, which turned the familiar streets into ciphers. . . . In those moments, this theatricality seemed to allow the city to transform itself into something peculiar and strange'. (Senda 1997: 60)

CHANGE

The close of the 1960s brings to an end the century of theatre in modern Japan with which this book is concerned. From the first glimmerings of a changed attitude to theatre on the part of the government in the years after the Meiji Restoration in 1868 to the extraordinary diversity of Japanese theatre in 1970 the century witnessed the spectacular results of the prodigious amount of energy and resources that theatre people had put into their art over this hundred year period. There was of course much activity that has had to be neglected in an introductory work such as this.

During this hundred years Japanese theatre went through two changes that affected its subsequent development profoundly. The first was the challenge to *kabuki* that began with the Drama Reform Society and culminated in the Tsukiji Little Theatre in 1924. This produced *shingeki*. *Shingeki* had many detractors in the last decades of the twentieth century as realism in theatre came to be questioned, but in its time its attack on *kabuki* also included a different approach to overall artistic control of productions (something taken for granted by the leaders of most *angura* groups) and the establishment of freer access to the profession for those wanting to make their life in theatre. Whatever the inspiration for their work, the *shingeki* pioneers started a process of widening participation in theatre, which brought about the development of university amateur dramatics that was so important to the theatre of the 1960s. Theatre was an open, rather than a closed, world after the advent of *shingeki*.

The second great change undergone by modern Japanese theatre was the challenge to *shingeki* in the 1960s, described in this chapter. *Shingeki* was in one sense doomed from the outset because it started out in a world of international politics that was polarised between two main ideologies each demonising the other. To many intellectuals and creative artists in the West at the time it was the capitalist system that had made the first World War possible and they eagerly embraced the initial hopes for an alternative system that the Bolshevik revolution in Russia seemed to offer. Some Japanese intellectuals too were searching for remedies to the ills of their own society, which they thought had been caused by over-rapid industrialisation, and socialism seemed to offer the answer. There were some benefits to *shingeki* in the dominance of proletarian drama at a crucial formative stage of its existence, but the course of Japan's history over the next decade and a half made it inevitable that this period would always loom large in *shingeki*'s post World War II development. While the association of much of the *shingeki* movement with left-wing socialism and communism made it possible for 1960s anti-communist youth to accuse parts of it of Stalinism in the 1960s, there had been a genuine attempt on the part of many *shingeki* practitioners to go beyond the 1930s-type socialist realism for which it was condemned in the 1960s. Like much Western theatre at the time, the spectrum of *shingeki* productions included realistic plays alongside others that used quite different strategies of stage presentation.

This is not to belittle in any way the achievement of the 1960s. Whether the ideological attacks on *shingeki* were fair or not, the theatrical impetus given to the work of those young theatre people who believed they were amply justified, gave Japan (and the world) an exciting type of theatre that in many ways changed the quality of the theatrical experience. The vehemence with which *angura* playwrights, directors, actors and designers rejected all *shingeki* led to a fundamental reappraisal of the art form called theatre and we have therefore much to thank that anger for.

CONTINUITY

If change twice brought about major revisions of assumptions about the nature of theatre in Japan during the century under review here, the strong historical tendency to preserve art forms in Japan has meant that continuity has enabled us to view simultaneously both the theatre genres that have been rejected and those that have done the rejecting. We have also observed some genres which have been content to adapt rather than challenge. Although by the early twenty-first century one of the genres mentioned here had disappeared, the result of change and continuity in Japanese theatre between the 1860s and the 1960s is the availability of a wide range of theatrical experience at any one time.

Every genre mentioned in the last two chapters continued into the 1970s and beyond. The rhetoric of the *angura* movement suggested that there was no future for *shingeki*. The word *shingeki* itself fell into disuse in the 1990s, but the genre continued and continues. *Shingeki* was by no means quiet in the 1960s, as the full repertories of the three main companies and scores more smaller ones show well. In addition a few individuals linked but not beholden to the three big companies were in the 1960s developing new ideas that found fruition in the 1970s.

Celebrated productions by the big three *shingeki* companies are not hard to find in the last three decades of the twentieth century. *Shingeki* became the counterpart of the serious segment of Western metropolitan theatre cultures. Its productions were often performed in large theatres, which dramatically increased in number in Tokyo during the 1980s. The development of new media meant that *shingeki* shows often included well-known media personalities who were members of the company concerned. Established classics and new writing have, as always, formed the backbone of *shingeki* repertories. *Shingeki* moved a step closer to the commercial theatre, but that may be its natural place. The *avant garde*/progressive role that *shingeki* once played has long been taken over by the *angura* pioneers and their successors.

A production by Bungaku-za in 1970 may illustrate the way *shingeki* was tending at the time. This was a commercially very successful, award winning production of a play by a popular novelist who had previously been known as a playwright for the commercial theatre. *Hanaoka Seishū no Tsuma* (*The Wife of Hanaoka Seishū*) was an adaptation by Ariyoshi Sawako (1931–1984) of her own novel of the same title. The play was one of many studies of women by Ariyoshi and depicted the struggle of a wife and mother for the affection and esteem of a mid-nineteenth century medical researcher trying to develop an anaesthetic for breast cancer operations. Sugimura Haruko, known – as were several other members of the cast – throughout Japan for her film and television work, played the mother. The fans of Bungaku-za would have attended performances of this play anyway; they would have known Bungaku-za and Sugimura Haruko from previous productions, to which many of them would have been going regularly. In addition the production of *Hanaoka Seishū no Tsuma* attracted spectators who knew of Ariyoshi through her best-selling novels or productions by the commercial theatre of plays she had been commissioned to write.

The young Bungaku-za director, Kimura Kōichi (1931–), is an example of an individual who stayed within the general *shingeki* ambience but moved away from the big company with which he was associated. He had joined Bungaku-za in 1955 and by the mid-1960s was one of the company's leading directors. He directed an acclaimed production of Tennessee Williams' *A Streetcar Named Desire* with Sugimura Haruko as the lead in 1964. His strong social conscience and a conviction that theatre should address issues affecting the society of the day made the sixties a stimulating and inspiring time for him, but he preferred to work inside the existing *shingeki* framework. In 1967 Kimura met Arnold Wesker in England. Wesker expressed a desire to visit Japan and on his return Kimura and some friends started planning to invite him. After several meetings early in 1968 it was decided to combine a production of his trilogy with discussions of theatre's role in society, which he would lead. In the July issue of *Teatoro*, as it happened the 300th anniversary issue, an appeal for support was launched above the signatures of theatre personalities from a wide range of companies. It was announced that Wesker would be coming to Japan in October that year, that there would be a production of the trilogy and that the themes for the discussion meeting with Wesker would be 'What does theatre mean for our age?' and 'What does the age mean for our theatre?' The organisation gave itself the name Wesker 68.

Wesker spoke on the problems of communication in a fragmenting society and in the discussion session after his talk aroused strong feelings in his audience. Some shouted nonsense at his insistence that the theatre that educates towards social change should be artistic; others accused Wesker 68 of organising the event in an attempt to gain hegemony over contemporary theatre. Kimura had, maybe unwittingly, started something that confirmed for many within and outside *shingeki* that theatre needed commitment to social or political ends. His career blossomed after this. In the 1970s he directed several plays by Inoue Hisashi (1934–), a playwright with whom he had had a long association. Kimura found Inoue's comedies with their eclectic use of elements from traditional theatre an appropriate vehicle for his participatory approach to direction. Inoue's occasionally mordant but always incisive wit matched well with Kimura's belief in theatre's duty to confront important issues through both tears and laughter. Kimura's productions of *Yabuhara Kengyō* (*The Great Doctor Yabuhara*, 1973), a bitterly funny comment on triumph over adversity leading to abuse of power, and *Keshō* (*Make-up*, 1982), performed by Chijin-kai, which Kimura founded to give expression to his ideas on theatre, gave both him and Inoue international reputations.

Abe Kōbō (1924–1993) also moved from an auspicious start in *shingeki* as a playwright to founding in 1971 a company, the Abe Studio, in which as a director he would be more free to develop his ideas. Abe, a celebrated novelist, became a playwright by accident but seemed fired by the experience to explore more the levels of reality that had occupied his attention in some of his novel writing. Between 1955 and 1971 Senda Koreya directed nine plays of Abe's for Haiyū-za. Thus Abe had a close and long-standing connection with one of the three big *shingeki* companies, but he became convinced that he personally could only accept productions of his own plays (the *shingeki* world had certainly accepted them) if the actors had been trained in such a way that their minds and bodies could convey the dreams/nightmares which Abe considered the core of reality for human beings. The Abe method involved the Studio actors in long hours of physical and psychological exercises in quest of a state which would enable them to navigate the dangers of confusing self as person, self as actor and self in role. (Shields 1996) Abe's plays are varied but in the main use Absurdist techniques to challenge accepted notions of reality.

Kinoshita Junji similarly had maintained close connections with Mingei of the big *shingeki* companies but had in addition worked through smaller groups dedicated to his own plays. The last of these was called the Yamamoto Yasue no Kai (Yamamoto Yasue Society, founded in 1965) and was novel in conception in that it only ever had one member – the actress Yamamoto Yasue, around whom casts were assembled for productions of Kinoshita plays, mainly *Yūzuru*. Although the author of several realist plays – notably *Ottō to Yobareru Nihonjin* (*A Japanese called Otto*) performed by Mingei in 1962 – Kinoshita had constantly been troubled by what he perceived as the central problem of *shingeki* realism: the inadequacy of modern Japanese as a stage language. At the end of 1967 the Yamamoto Yasue Society sponsored the foundation of a study group which would search for the dramatic qualities in the Japanese language that Kinoshita was convinced were there. This was given the name Kotoba no Benkyō-kai (Society for the Study of Language) and at a meeting in May 1968 the members of the society found themselves unexpectedly moved by a reading aloud of portions of the thirteenth-century classic *Heike Monogatari* (*The Tale of the Heike*).

The society members perceived a natural rhythm in the text and after further experiments with choral readings from the same work Kinoshita began to fashion a play around an event – a sea battle of 1185 – and a character – Tomomori, commander of the losing side – that themselves met other of Kinoshita's criteria for drama. Tomomori in particular is a quintessential Kinoshita hero overtaken, despite himself, by historical events and possessed of an enigmatic attitude towards fate. He takes his own life after a line of (in Japanese) great linguistic simplicity: 'My eyes have witnessed all I have to see' (*Mirubeki hodo no koto wa mitsu*). The rest of this monumental play, whose title presages its cosmic dimensions – *Shigosen no Matsuri* (*Requiem on the Great Meridian*, 1978) – moves linguistically in and out of the *Heike* text, as direct quotations give way to group-chanted narrative, which in turn becomes dialogue as characters step out of the group(s). With this play Kinoshita succeeded in transcending genre to the extent that no actor's training would exclude him/her from playing in it. The cast of each production of *Shigosen no Matsuri* has included actors trained in *nō*, *kyōgen*, *kabuki* and *shingeki*. Although for Kinoshita and many commentators *Shigosen no Matsuri* offered something new to modern Japanese theatre, it is unlikely that it will be copied on a wide scale, but on its own it stands as a signal achievement. (Kinoshita 2000)

Meanwhile *Yūzuru*, Kinoshita's folktale drama from the late 1940s, is still being performed at the beginning of the twenty-first century. With Yamamoto Yasue in the leading part of Tsū performances passed the 1000 mark in 1984. The appeal of this play has been extraordinary and it has continued to draw spectators of all ages throughout Japan. Yamamoto Yasue's interpretation of her role as an outsider trying to bring warmth, love and common sense into an ultimately corrupt human adult world has played a major part in this popular success. Since her death in 1993 the part has been taken over by a *kabuki* actor of female roles, Bandō

Tamasaburō V (1950–). Tamasaburō became enormously popular from the late 1960s onwards and he brought many young female fans into *kabuki* theatres. He is an actor of great range. Apart from celebrated performances in many *kabuki* and *shimpa* classics, he has played in Shakespeare (Lady Macbeth) and Mishima Yukio (Madame de Sade). Tsū in *Yūzuru* was a particular challenge to him, as he was following Japan's most famous *shingeki* actress in a part written for and created by her. He has brought to the part a sense of formal beauty that seems to have ensured its continuing success.

Ahead of *Yūzuru* in the league table of most performed plays in modern Japanese theatre is Mayama Miho's *Dorokabura (Muddy Turnip)*. This play has been performed over five decades by a company that represents another variation in the standard *shingeki* pattern. Shinseisaku-za (New Production Company) was founded in 1950 by *shingeki* actors and its early repertory included typical *shingeki* playwrights such as Chekhov. Throughout its history, however, the emphasis has always been on bringing theatre to people who might not otherwise have an opportunity to see it. This coupled with a policy of not allowing members to accept contracts in film or television has meant that this very successful company, which lives communally in a complex of buildings including a theatre, rehearsal rooms and accommodation just outside Tokyo, does not have the glamorous image of some primarily metropolitan companies. In the 1950s Shinseisaku-za turned away from *shingeki* realism and its repertory developed in three ways. Mayama Miho (1922–) created for the company compilations of dramatic sketches, folk dances and songs from Japan, Okinawa, China, Poland and many other countries, which were given the title *Shinseisaku-za Festival*. From the early 1970s the company toured regularly with productions of plays written for *kabuki* by Mayama Seika, Mayama Miho's father. The acting style, therefore, in these latter has had to be adjusted to take account of the genre for which Mayama had written them. Thirdly the company performs Mayama Miho's own plays, principally *Dorokabura*.

Another company that rejected early postwar *shingeki* realism and forged a distinctive future for itself was Gekidan Shiki (Four Seasons Company). Organised as a small group of ten under the leadership of Asari Keita (1933–) in 1953, it signalled its opposition to the expression of inner psychological realism by focusing on modern French drama, notably the plays of Jean Giraudoux and Jean Anouilh. Later, it broadened its repertory to include classics of world drama, including plays by Shakespeare, Molière and Racine. By the 1960s Shiki was not noticeably different from many other *shingeki* companies, but its fate was changed by the Broadway production of *West Side Story* at the Nissei. Asari was one of the two managers of the Nissei Theatre and he was determined to foster the growth of a culture of musicals in Japan. Asari believed in confronting Western culture head-on and was convinced that a Japanese synthesis would not emerge until the middle of the twenty-first century. In pursuit of that goal Asari was very successful in training his actors to perform Western musicals to as high a standard as in their home cultures. In the process, however, Shiki became big business itself, helped greatly by its productions of Andrew Lloyd Webber musicals. In 2001 its impressive website boasted of 2200 performances per year ranging over musicals, ballet and straight plays. Not surprisingly, Shiki frequently has to defend itself against the charge of over-commercialisation.

Reactions to an early experience with *shingeki* have therefore been of many kinds, and *shingeki* can claim beneficiaries who have adjusted their heritage in a way that they did not believe was possible within the mainstream movement. *Shimpa* can be regarded as a similar adjustment of *kabuki*. *Shingeki*, like *kabuki*, reached a point in its history where it generated feelings of hostility in those who thought it unworthy of its age, and the *angura* little theatre movement was born. At the time of writing there is no sign that this movement itself is going to foment any similar radical reaction. Most of the 1960s *angura* pioneers were still active at the end of the twentieth century and thirty years afterwards their work still seemed to be fresh. To be fair to *shingeki* it too was doing interesting work thirty years after its effective start in the early 1920s. Like *shingeki*, *angura* has stimulated much further work in those who have adjusted its initial methods of opposition to realism. Already in the 1990s commentators were writing of the third generation of the little theatre movement, and any visitor to Tokyo was faced with a bewildering array of young theatrical talent. A description of the second, third, and maybe by now fourth or fifth generations is beyond the scope of this book and I would refer the reader to the extensive studies of the 1970s, 1980s and 1990s by Senda Akihiko, one of whose books, *Nihon Engeki no Kōkai*, is available in English in a translation by J. Thomas Rimer and has the English title *The Voyage of Contemporary Japanese Theatre*. (Senda 1997)

JAPANESE THEATRE IN THE WORLD

It is a measure of Japanese theatre's changed presence in the world that a book like this can be available to a non-Japanese reading public. In contrast to the infrequent tours abroad of traditional theatre from the 1920s to the 1960s, the last three decades of the twentieth century saw Japanese theatres of all types travelling to many parts of the world outside Japan. In most capital cities with a thriving theatrical culture a theatregoer will have been able to watch *nō*, *kabuki* and some form of modern theatre. The Japan

Foundation has been instrumental in encouraging theatre companies to consider foreign tours a natural part of their activities and has helped many to realise their plans to travel abroad. It should not be thought, however, that this has always been in the context of a specially promoted programme of things Japanese. Drama has of course benefited greatly from large-scale Japan festivals in various countries, but arts festivals, such as the annual Edinburgh Festival, also regularly include Japanese theatre groups. Beyond this companies have toured abroad outside such specially created frameworks and individual theatre people have increasingly worked abroad with foreign actors.

Ninagawa Yukio (1935-), for example, has several times brought companies to the Edinburgh Festival from Japan; productions of his have also been invited independently to the Royal National Theatre in London (his company was in 1987 the first foreign company to perform at this theatre). Foreign audiences have watched his Japanese actors perform Shakespeare and plays by Japanese playwrights. He has also worked as a director in Britain, directing English-speaking actors in a translation of a Japanese play and in Shakespeare's *King Lear* at the Shakespeare Memorial Theatre in Stratford-upon-Avon. Taking his Japanese production of *Medea* to Greece was one of the great triumphs of his career as an international director.

Ninagawa's career is interesting in that he is also someone who changed course after a promising start. His shift looks greater than that of anyone mentioned here because he went from *angura* to the commercial theatre, but in terms of Japanese theatre history this was not as radical as it appears. The pragmatism of prewar commercial theatre in Japan has been noted in Chapter 4 and it made sound commercial sense for Tōhō to recognise Ninagawa's potential for injecting new life into their productions and invite him to direct *Romeo and Juliet* for them in 1973. When he accepted, it was certainly a great shock to the members of the company he had founded, who were used to performing plays by the young, radical playwright Shimizu Kunio (1936-). The company was clearly identified with the new left, to the extent that several members were said to have had links with radical student organisations, and Shimizu's plays, referred to as *tōsō-geki* (struggle dramas), reinforced that image. Ninagawa, however, saw the possibilities afforded by the availability of much increased resources and, without compromising his artistic principles, moved on to the grandiose yet subtle, flamboyant yet thought-provoking productions of Shakespeare that have brought him his international reputation.

THE ULTIMATE CONTINUITY THAT HAS EMBRACED CHANGE?

Looking back over a century of modern theatre at the end of the 1960s one was even then surprised at the staying power of the various new genres that had developed during the period. *Kabuki*, already venerable in 1868, continued; *shingeki*, in early middle-age by the 1960s, continued; *shimpa* and *shinkokugeki*, decidely middle-aged, continued; comedy and popular drama continued. By 1970 the new genre of *angura* or little theatre had joined this formidable array and one suspected this was going to survive too. It did, and at the beginning of the twenty-first century the range of theatre available to Tokyo theatre-goers is even more astonishing than it had been thirty years before. There has only been one clear casualty. A few months after commemorating the 50th anniversary of Sawada Shōjirō's death with an impressive programme in the Shinbashi Enbujō Shinkokugeki filed for bankruptcy. It revived briefly in 1987 to celebrate its own 70th anniversary, but then almost immediately went out of existence. Of the others, *shimpa* has a low level of activity compared with what it once was, but it successfully celebrated its centenary in 1987 and its leading actors and actresses, including Mizutani Yaeko's daughter (who took the name herself in 1995) have a considerable following of fans. Popular theatre has had only one suitable venue in Tokyo since 1975, but it has developed a new audience in the many health centres patronised by Japan's ageing population. (Powell 1991)

In this story the staying power of *kabuki* must excite admiration. The genre has had many detractors and some powerful enemies; it has been subject from time to time both to interference and to control by powerful institutions; there has also been periodic speculation that its end was nigh. Belying all this, *kabuki*'s activity during the last three decades has been at an unprecedented level.

For its productions of the classics it has been fortunate to have at its disposal the acting ability of superb artists such as the *onnagata* Nakamura Utaemon VI. Many productions during the period have been memorable. Initiatives like that of Nakamura Senjaku II (later Ganjirō III, 1931–), who in 1982 instituted his Chikamatsu-za with the intention of producing one Chikamatsu play per year, have emphasised to *kabuki* fans the importance of the classics to their theatre. In 1983 Tamasaburō and Kataoka Takao (now Nizaimon XIV, 1944–) caused something of a sensation when they acted together in the classic play *Sukeroku*. In 1986 the National Theatre celebrated its 10th anniversary by performing all eleven plays of the *kabuki* version of *Kanadehon Chūshingura* with the late Kataoka Nizaemon XIII (1903–1993) in the leading part. The plays of *shin-kabuki* have not been neglected and the Kabuki-za has seen two 'complete' runs of Mayama Seika's 1930s ten-play version (directed by Mayama Miho). Many new plays by living playwrights have also been premiered.

During this time *kabuki* has also been able to embrace experiment. Ichikawa Ennosuke has tried, with the enthusiastic collaboration of his fellow actors and disciples, to recover the essential features of pre-Meiji *kabuki*. His 'Za Kabuki' ('Za' is the romanised form of a Japanese pronunciation of 'the') revived plays from the early nineteenth century, emphasising the stage business (*keren*) that was popular at the time. Almost all of Ennosuke's Za Kabuki productions featured him flying out from the stage over the auditorium in the finale, and he made skilful use of other devices, such as quick changes of costume or entrances that followed almost immediately on an exit from a completely different part of the stage. This brought younger audiences into the theatres where Ennosuke was playing. Ennosuke is a versatile player of most types of *kabuki* role, both male and female, and such audiences would also find themselves watching his performances of more established *kabuki* classics. Another innovation by Ennosuke was his 'Super Kabuki', of which still the most famous production was of *Yamato Takeru* in 1986. Again in the cause of popularising *kabuki*, which historically had always been sensitive to changes in popular taste, he performed this new play (by Umehara Takeshi, 1925–) about a fourth-century hero (Yamato Takeru) with speeded-up traditional *kabuki* acting performed to a pre-recorded modern soundtrack. Ennosuke is a tireless innovator very conscious of his duty in society as an artist and, while many have criticised Super Kabuki, it is acknowledged that this has shown once again how flexible *kabuki* can be.

Kabuki in Tokyo moved out from the Kabuki-za/National Theatre axis with the opening of the Sunshine Theatre (Sanshain Gekijō) in 1978 away to the north-west in Ikebukuro and the inauguration of 'Asakusa Kabuki' in 1980 in a new theatre (Asakusa Kōkaidō) situated in modern Tokyo's most famous popular entertainment district. *Kabuki* also became quite familiar through overseas tours during the last third of the twentieth century, and foreign audiences, especially in Europe and the United States, began to stop seeing it as something exotic but without relevance to their own concerns. As theatre in the West has moved, if in some cultures only spasmodically, towards foregrounding the actor's body, the expressive possibilities of *kabuki* acting have been recognised widely outside Japan.

It may seem strange to end a book on theatre in modern Japan with comments on *kabuki* acting, but the range of acting environments chosen by *kabuki* actors in the last three decades is remarkable. While maintaining their *kabuki* careers, which meant continuing to learn and display traditional acting skills, *kabuki* actors have appeared in Shakespeare, modern Japanese and Western plays, musicals, films and television. Many *kabuki* actors have therefore demonstrated their ability both to convey emotion from a distance in a large theatre and to be emotionally credible to spectators sitting close to a television screen.

All three of what one may term the major genres of theatre in modern Japan – *kabuki*, *shingeki* and *shōgekijō* – have great achievements to their credit. All three have won through in spite of various forms of opposition: *kabuki* against sustained attacks on its artistic basis through much of the Meiji period and against Occupation disapproval of its perceived ideological underpinning; *shingeki* against the authorities and the police throughout the first two decades of its existence, with a demoralising cuff from the Occupation when it thought its troubles were over, and then against the artistic onslaught from the *shōgekijō* movement; and *shōgekijō*, which has had the easiest time, against suspicious authorities. Both *shingeki* and *shōgekijō* early in their development entertained severe doubts about the political structures of the society in which they were operating and this inevitably coloured the essential nature of their theatre.

Kabuki was only briefly forced to consider what sort of message its plays were sending out to its audiences when after the Pacific War it searched its entire repertory for feudalism-free plays to perform. It saw its primary purpose as the regular performance of classics by actors thoroughly trained physically to cope with them but also able to add something to what their predecessors had achieved. Its capacity to absorb and internalise limited but sometimes significant change within its existing artistic and institutional framework has been constantly in evidence since the 1870s and the result today is a sophisticated form of theatre admired throughout the world.

Many of the changes that have broadened *kabuki* over the last one hundred and thirty years have been initiated by actors – Danjūrō's *katsureki-geki*, Sadanji's *shin-kabuki*, Ennosuke's Super Kabuki, to name only the most prominent examples – and, as always, it is on its actors that *kabuki* depends. Unlike the actors of *shingeki* or *shōgekijō*, *kabuki* actors have been and still are trained rigorously from an early age. They are also placed regularly on the stage from an early age. The decision to become a *shingeki* or *shōgekijō* actor is something that has usually come in early adulthood, and these actors therefore miss out on more than a decade of apprenticeship. Again, *kabuki* actors practically live in the theatre building once they are appearing in regular programmes. Arriving around ten in the morning, they rarely leave before nine-thirty in the evening. The financial framework and the production norms of *shingeki* and *shōgekijō* do not allow that. The *kabuki* actor, therefore, has a feeling of complete familarity as he moves round his acting environment; he is confident in his body and in the bodies of those with whom he is acting. Paradoxically the long and arduous acquisition of this confidence has rarely stifled creativity. Throughout the modern period individuals have used their artistic confidence as a base on which to build something a little different. In the last thirty years the possibilities of doing this have greatly increased and *kabuki* actors have taken full advantage of them. All major genres of theatre in modern Japan have shown the capacity to change, but it is *kabuki* that has so far most clearly championed the centrality of the actor in maintaining continuity.

Notes

INTRODUCTION

1. See below p. 190.
2. For an introduction to *kyōgen* in English and a selection of translations, see Kenny 1989.
3. Principally plays by Kinoshita Junji.
4. Technically '*bunraku*' refers to a theatre which revived and reestablished puppet theatre in the mid-nineteenth century and so the word should not be italicised as if it were the Japanese word for a theatre genre. However, the genre is now almost ubiquitously referred to as *bunraku* and I have adopted that convention here.
5. The names of the three were: Takeda Izumo II (1691–1756), Miyoshi Shōroku (1696–1772) and Namiki Senryū (1695–1751).
6. Samuel Leiter has recently collected together a number of articles on the history and performance of *kabuki*. See Leiter 2002.
7. *Kanjinchō* is categorised in several different ways but is particularly famous for its *aragoto* elements.
8. The play is translated into French: Tsuruya 1979.
9. For description and analysis of the elements of performance in productions of classic plays spanning the premodern and modern periods, see Leiter 1979.

CHAPTER 1

1. The principal sources used for general information on theatre in the Meiji period are: Akiba 1971, Akiba 1975, Ihara 1975, and Ōzasa 1985.
2. See above, pp. xxiii-xxvi.
3. See above, p. xxvii.
4. For *hanamichi* see above, p. xxvii.
5. He is also referred to as Suematsu Kenchō.
6. For a study of Kawakami Sadayakko, see Kano 2001.
7. Izumi Kyōka's plays are the subject of a new study by M. Cody Poulton: Poulton 2001

8. For contemporary debates on the theory of humour, see Wells 1997.
9. The company's original name was Matsutake Gōmei-sha ('*shō*' is an alternative reading for '*matsu*' and '*chiku*' for '*take*').

CHAPTER 2

1. This was called the Ekifū-kai.
2. *Shinkyoku Urashima*.
3. Shingeki Fukyū Kōgyō.
4. Cast lists for Jiyū Gekijō productions may be found in Tanaka 1964: 914.
5. *Jōjōji Monogatari*.
6. While it is sometimes difficult to separate company from genre, italics will be used here when the emphasis is on the style of production.
7. The play was *Onnaoya*.

CHAPTER 3

1. For a detailed account in English of Takarazuka early history, see Robertson 1998.
2. Much of the description of the Tsukiji Shōgekijō here is based on Powell 1975.
3. For a full translation of this manifesto see Powell 1975: 757.
4. See above, Chapter 2, p. 52.
5. The proletarian theatre movement has been extensively treated in Tschudin 1989. (See also Powell 1971.)
6. The title of the magazine was *Tanemaku Hito*. See Tschudin 1979.
7. This was *Byakuya*, published in *Chūō Kōron* in 1934. See Shea 1964: 357.

CHAPTER 4

1. See above, Chapter 3, p. 79.
2. See above, Introduction, pp. xxix-xxx.
3. See above, Chapter 2, pp. 40-41.
4. This was *Kazanbaichi*. See below, pp. 109-110.
5. The title in Japanese was *Shingeki no Kiki*.
6. The term used was *shingeki daidō danketsu*.
7. This was the Bijutsu-za. See Toita 1956: 226.
8. J Thomas Rimer, in the first monograph on *shingeki* by a Western scholar, made an extensive study of this playwright in Rimer 1974.
9. This novel is available in English translation by Ann Waswo (Nagatsuka 1989).
10. *Kazanbaichi* is available in translation by David Goodman with a substantial Introduction (Kubo 1986).

CHAPTER 5

1. For a study in English of government control of writers in wartime Japan, see Shillony 1981.
2. This is not to say that *kabuki* escaped interference. For example, the ending of the play *Naozamurai* had to be altered because to wartime censors it was unthinkable for a fugitive to escape from the police who were closing in on him. (Okamoto 2001: 23)

3. For an account in English of wartime touring *kabuki*, see Okamoto 2001: 17-29.

CHAPTER 6

1. The name also resonated with *shingeki* history, as the Tsukiji Shōgekijō had adopted a bunch of grapes as its logo in the 1920s. Yamamoto Yasue was the Tsukiji Shōgekijō's first actress.
2. His family name is often Romanised Yanagida.
3. For an extended account of this incident see Okamoto 2001: 524.
4. The main plot of this chilling play concerns a disloyal samurai, Iemon, whose wife, Oiwa, is horribly disfigured as a result of drinking poison. She dies a violent death and susequently torments her husband as a ghost. See Keene 1976: 468–9 and 569–70.
5. Technically censorship was in the hands of two departments in SCAP: the CIE and the Civil Censorship Detachment, whose responsibilities overlapped somewhat. See Okamoto 2001: 90–1.
6. For a summary of the plot of this play see Ortolani 1963: 171-2.
7. This play is translated in Goodman 1986.
8. Also translated in Goodman 1986.

CHAPTER 7

1. See above p. 109.
2. The play is translated in Goodman 1988. For translations of drama from this period see Takaya 1979 and Rolf and Gillespie 1992.
3. His brother, Kanze Hisao (1925-1978), was later associated with the experimental work of Suzuki Tadashi, who looked to *nō* and its predecessors in the formulation of his style of actor training. See below, p ??
4. Interview with author and Ned Chaillet of the BBC in August 1991.
5. This was Maro Akiji.
6. Interview with author and Ned Chaillet of the BBC in August 1991.
7. Interview with author and Ned Chaillet of the BBC in August 1991.
8. For extended assessments of this play in English see Goodman 1986, which includes a translation, and Tsuno 1970b. The Tsuno articles appeared in a short-lived but important journal entitled *Concerned Theatre Japan*, edited by David Goodman.
9. Suzuki's basic statement of theory is available in English in Suzuki 1986.
10. Translated as *Nezumi Kozō: the Rat* in *Concerned Theatre Japan* I. 1 (Spring 1970) For an extended analysis of this play, see Tsuno 1970a.
11. For work on Terayama Shūji in English see Rolf and Gillespie 1992 and Sorgenfrei 1992. The most comprehensive piece of research on Terayama is unpublished: Sorgenfrei 1978.

Bibliography

Adachi, B. C. (1985) *Backstage at Bunraku: a behind-the-scenes look at Japan's traditional puppet theatre*, Tokyo and New York: John Weatherhill.
Akiba Tarō (1975) *Tōto Meiji Engeki-shi*, Tokyo: Hō Shuppan.
—— (1971) *Nihon Shingeki-shi*, 2 vols, Tokyo: Risō-sha.
Arnott, P. D. (1969) *The Theatres of Japan*, London: Macmillan.
Brandon, J. R., Malm, W. P., and Shively, D. H. eds (1978) *Studies in Kabuki*, Honolulu: University of Hawai'i Press
Brandon, J. R. ed (1982) *Chūshingura, studies in Kabuki and the Puppet Theatre*, Honolulu: University of Hawai'i Press.
—— (1997) *Nō and Kyōgen in the Contemporary World*, Honolulu: University of Hawai'i Press.
Burkman, T. W. ed (1984) *The Occupation of Japan: Arts and Culture*, Norfolk, Virginia: The General Douglas MacArthur Foundation.
Dunn, C. J., and Torigoe Bunzō (1969) *The Actors' Analects*, New York: Columbia University Press.
Engeki Hakubutsukan (Waseda Daigaku Tsubouchi Hakase Kinen Engeki Hakubutsukan) (1962) *Engeki Hyakka Daijiten*, 6 vols, Tokyo: Heibon-sha.
Ernst, Earle (1974) *The Kabuki Theatre*, Honolulu: Hawai'i University Press.
Fujimura Tsukuru ed (1950–1) *Nihon Bungaku Daijiten*, Tokyo: Shinchō-sha.
Fukuda Yoshiyuki (1995) *Dorama no Mukō no Sora*, Tokyo: Yomiuri Shinbun-sha.
Gerstle, C. A. (1986) *Circles of Fantasy, convention in the plays of Chikamatsu*, Cambridge, Mass: Harvard University Press.
Goodman, David trans (1986) *After Apocalypse: four Japanese plays of Hiroshima and Nagasaki*, New York: Columbia University Press.

—— (1988) *Japanese Drama and Culture in the 1960s, the return of the gods*, New York: Sharpe.
—— and Clarke, J. V. (1998) *Concerned Theatre Japan: the Graphic Art of Japanese Theatre 1960 to 1980*.
Gunji Masakatsu (1990) 'Kabuki and its social background', in Nakane and Oishi eds, *Tokugawa Japan*, Tokyo: University of Tokyo Press.
Hare, T. B. (1986) *Zeami's Style: the Noh Plays of Zeami Motokiyo*, Palo Alto: Stanford University Press.
Hijikata Yoshi (1947) *Nasu no Yobanashi*, Tokyo: Kappa Shobō.
Ibaraki Tadashi (Ken) (1956) *Shōwa no Shingeki*, Tokyo: Awaji Shobō.
Ihara Toshirō (1975) *Meiji Engeki-shi*, Tokyo: Hō Shuppan.
Iizuka Tomoichirō (1941) *Kokumin Engeki to Nōson Engeki*, Tokyo: Shimizu Shobō.
Imai Seiichi (1971) *Taishō Demokurashī*, Tokyo: Chūō Kōron-sha.
Inoue Masao (1946) *Bakesokoneta Tanuki*, Tokyo: Ubun-sha, 1946.
Ishizawa Shūji (1964) *Shingeki no Tanjō*, Tokyo: Kinokuniya Shinsho.
Izumi Taku (1964) 'Doko ni aru n darō – Nihon no mujikaru?' *Teatoro* no 251.
Kano Ayako (2001) *Acting Like a Woman in Modern Japan: theater, gender, and nationalism*, New York: Palgrave, 2001
Kawashima Junpei (1961) *Nihon Engeki Hyakunen no Ayumi*, Tokyo: Hyōron-sha.
Kawatake Shigetoshi (1959) *Nihon Engeki Zenshi*, Tokyo: Iwanami Shoten.
Kawatake Shigetoshi and Kubota Mantarō (for Japanese National Commission for UNESCO) (1963) *Theatre in Japan*, Tokyo: Ministry of Education.
Kawatake Shigetoshi and Shimomura Masao (1959) *Gendai Engeki Kōza*, vol. 6, *Nihon no engeki*, Tokyo: Mikasa Shobō.
Kawazoe Kunimoto (1953) *Shimamura Hōgetsu*, Tokyo: Waseda Daigaku Shuppan-bu.
Keene, Donald (1976) *World Within Walls, Japanese literature of the pre-modern era 1600–1867*, London: Secker and Warburg.
—— (1984) *Dawn to the West, Japanese literature of the modern era, poetry, drama, criticism*, New York: Henry Holt and Company.
—— (1990) *Nō and Bunraku*, New York: Columbia University Press.
Kenny, Don trans and ed (1989) *The Kyōgen Book, an anthology of Japanese classical comedies*, Tokyo: Japan Times.
Kinoshita Junji (2000), Powell, Brian, and Daniel, Jason, trans and ed, *Requiem on the Great Meridian and Selected Essays*, Tokyo: Nan'undō.
Kitami Haruichi ed (1963) *Bungaku-za Zashi*, Tokyo: Bungaku-za.

Kominz, Laurence (1997) *The Stars who Created Kabuki: their lives, loves and legacy*, New York: Kodansha International.
Komiya Toyotaka ed (1969) *Japanese Music and Drama in the Meiji Era*, Tokyo: Tōyō Bunko.
Kornicki, P. F. (1982) *The Reform of Fiction in Meiji Japan*, Oxford: Ithaca Press.
Kubo Sakae (1986), Goodman, D. G., trans and ed, *Land of Volcanic Ash*, Cornell: Cornell University Press.
Kullman, C. H., and Young, W. C. (1986) *Theatre Companies of the World*, New York: Greenwood Press.
Kurahashi Seiichirō (1966) *Shingeki Nendaiki, sengo-hen*, Tokyo: Hakusui-sha.
Leiter, S. L. (1979) *The Art of Kabuki: famous plays in performance*, Berkeley: California University Press.
—— ed, (2002) *A Kabuki Reader, history and performance*, New Yorke: M. E. Sharpe.
Lindenberger, H. S. (1975) *Historical Drama, the Relation of Literature and Reality*, Chicago: Chicago University Press.
Maruyama Sadao Ikō-shū Kankō Iinkai ed (1970), *Maruyama Sadao, yakusha no isshō*, Tokyo: Rupo Shuppan.
Matsumoto Shinko (1974) *Meiji Zenki Engekiron-shi*, Tokyo: Engeki Shuppan-sha.
—— (1980) *Meiji Engekiron-shi*, Tokyo: Engeki Shuppan-sha.
Miyake Shūtarō (1943) *Engeki Gojūnen-shi*, Tokyo: Masu Shobō.
Miyoshi Jūrō (1980) *Shingeki wa doko e itta ka*, Tokyo: Shirakawa Shoin.
Mizushina Haruki (1954) *Osanai Kaoru to Tsukiji Shōgekijō*, Tokyo: Hato Shobō.
Mizutani Yaeko (1971) *Sugikoshikata*, Tokyo: Nichigei Shuppan.
Morris, Ivan (1976) *The Nobility of Failure, tragic heroes in the history of Japan*, New York: Meridian.
Nagatsuka Takashi (1989), Waswo, Ann, trans and ed *The Soil*, London: Routledge.
Nagayama Takeomi (1995) *Kabuki Gojūnen, watakushi no rirekisho*, Tokyo: Nihon Keizai Shinbun-sha.
Nakahara Yumihiko (1972) *Nihon no Kigekijin*, Tokyo: Shōbun-sha.
Nishiyama Matsunosuke (1997) *Edo Culture: daily life and diversions in urban Japan, 1600–1868*, Honolulu: University of Hawai'i Press.
Okakura Shirō and Kinoshita Junji eds (1960) *Yamamoto Yasue Butai Shashinshū, shiryō-hen*, Tokyo: Mirai-sha.
Okamoto Shirō (2001), Leiter, S. L. trans and ed, *The Man who Saved Kabuki, Faubion Bowers and theatre censorship in occupied Japan*, Honolulu: University of Hawai'i Press.
O'Neill, P. G. (1958) *Early Nō Drama*, London: Lund Humphries.
Ortolani, Benito (1963) 'Shingeki: the Maturing New Drama of

Japan', in Roggendorf, Joseph, ed, *Studies in Japanese Culture*, Tokyo: Sophia University Press.

—— (1990) *The Japanese Theatre, from shamanistic ritual to contemporary pluralism*, Leiden: Brill.

Ōyama Isao (1969–73) *Kindai Nihon Gikyoku-shi*, 4 vols, Tokyo: Kindai Nihon Gikyoku-shi Kankō-kai.

Ozaki Hirotsugu (Kōji) (1956) *Shingeki no Ashiato*, Tokyo: Tōkyō Sōgen-sha.

Ozaki Hirotsugu and Ibaraki Tadashi (Ken) (1961) *Hijikata Yoshi*, Tokyo: Chikuma Shobō.

Ōzasa Yoshio (1980) *Dōjidai Engeki to Gekisakka-tachi*, Tokyo: Gekishobō.

—— (1985) *Nihon Gendai Engeki-shi, Meiji Taishō-hen*, Tokyo: Hakusui-sha.

—— (1994) *Nihon Gendai Engeki-shi, Shōwa senchū-hen II*, Tokyo: Hakusui-sha.

—— (1995) *Nihon Gendai Engeki-shi, Shōwa senchū-hen III*, Tokyo: Hakusui-sha.

—— (1999) *Gekijo ga enjita Geki*, Tokyo: Kyōiku Shuppan.

Parker, H. S. E. (2002) *Progressive Traditions: An Illustrated Study of Plot Repetition in Traditional Japanese Theatre*, Leiden: Brill.

Poulton, M. Cody (2001) *Spirits of Another Sort, the plays of Izumi Kyōka*, Ann Arbor: University of Michigan Press.

Powell, Brian (1971) *Left-wing Theatre in Japan, its Development and Activity to 1934*, DPhil thesis, Oxford University.

—— (1975a) 'Japan's first modern theatre: the Tsukiji Shōgekijō and its company,1924–6', *Monumenta Nipponica* XXX. 1.

—— (1975b) 'Matsui Sumako, actress and woman', in Beasley ed, *Modern Japan, aspects of history, literature and society*, London: Allen and Unwin.

—— (1990) *Kabuki in Modern Japan, Mayama Seika and his plays*, Basingstoke: Macmillan.

—— (1991) '*Taishō engeki* and the dwindling masses', *Japan Forum*, III.1.

—— (2002) 'Communist Kabuki: a Contradiction in Terms?' Leiter, S. L., ed, *A Kabuki Reader, history and performance*, New Yorke: M. E. Sharpe.

Rimer, J. T. andYamazaki Masakazu trans and ed (1984) *On the Art of the Nō Drama, the major treatises of Zeami*, Princeton: Princeton University Press.

Rimer, J. Thomas (1974) *Toward a Modern Japanese Theatre, Kishida Kunio*, Princeton: Princeton University Press.

—— (1976) 'Four plays by Tanaka Chikao', *Monumenta Nipponica*, XXXI. 1.

Robertson, Jennifer (1998) *Takarazuka, sexual politics and popular culture in modern Japan*, Berkeley: University of California Press.

Rolf, R. T., and Gillespie, J. K. (1992) *Alternative Japanese Drama*,

ten plays, Honolulu: University of Hawai'i Press.
Rubin, Jay (1984) *Injurious to Public Morals, writers and the Meiji state*, Seattle and London: University of Washington Press.
Saeki Shōichi and Kano Masanao eds (1981) *Nihonjin no Jiden*, vol. 20, *Ichikawa Chūsha, Nakamura Ganjirō, Ichikawa Sadanji*, Tokyo: Heibon-sha.
Sakamoto Tokumatsu (1953) *Zenshin-za*, Tokyo: Ōdo-sha.
Sawamura Sadako (1969) *Kai no Uta, ikite kita michi*, Tokyo: Kōdan-sha.
Senda Akihiko (1995) *Nihon no Gendai Engeki*, Tokyo: Iwanami Shinsho.
—— (1997) Rimer, J. T. trans, *The Voyage of Contemporary Japanese Theatre*, Honolulu: University of Hawai'i Press.
Senda Koreya (1980) *Senda Koreya Engekiron-shū*, vol 1, Tokyo: Mirai-sha.
Shea, G. T. (1964) *Leftwing Literature in Japan*, Tokyo: Hōsei University Press.
Shields, Nancy (1996) *Fake Fish: the theatre of Kōbō Abe*, New York: Weatherhill.
Shillony, Ben-ami (1981) *Politics and Culture in Wartime Japan*, Oxford: Oxford University Press.
Shinkokugeki ed (1967) *Shinkokugeki Gojūnen*, Tokyo: Nakabayashi Shuppan.
Shively, D. H. (1991) *The Love Suicide at Amijima: a study of a Japanese domestic tragedy by Chikamatsu Monzaemon*, Ann Arbor: Michigan University Press.
Shōchiku ed (1985) *Shōchiku Kyūjūnen-shi*, Tokyo: Shōchiku.
Sorgenfrei, Carol F. (1978) *Shūji Terayama: avant garde dramatist of Japan*, PhD, University of California, Santa Barbara.
—— (1992) 'Showdown at Culture Gap, Images of the West in the Plays of Shūji Terayama', *Modern Drama* XXXV. 1.
Sugai Yukio (1973) *Shingeki no Rekishi*, Tokyo: Shinnihon Shinsho.
Sugimura Haruko and Koyama Yūshi (1970) *Joyū no Isshō*, Tokyo: Hakusui-sha.
Sugimura Haruko (1963) 'Tsukiji ga Watashi o Sodateta', *Bungei Shunjū* XLI. 4.
Susukida Kenji (1960) *Anten, waga engeki jiden*, Tokyo: Tōhō Shoin.
Suzuki Tadashi (1986), Rimer, J.T. trans, *The Way of Acting*, New York: Theatre Communications Group.
Takaya, T. T. trans and ed (1979) *Modern Japanese Drama, an anthology*, New York: Columbia University Press
Tamura Akiko and Koyama Yūshi (1962) *Hitori no Joyū no Ayunda Michi*, Tokyo: Hakusui-sha.
Tanabe Akio (1994) *Hōjō Hideji, shijō no tatsujin*, Osaka: Henshū Kōbō Noa.
Tanaka Eizō (1964) *Meiji Taishō Shingeki-shi Shiryō*, Tokyo: Engeki

Shuppan-sha.
Toita Yasuji (Kōji) (1956) *Engeki Gojūnen*, Tokyo: Jiji Tsūshin-sha.
—— (1961) *Taidan Nihon Shingeki-shi*, Tokyo: Seiabō.
—— (1963) *Joyū no Ai to Shi*, Tokyo: Kawade Shobō Shinsha.
Tōno Eijirō (1964) *Watakushi no Haiyū Shūgyō*, Tokyo: Mirai-sha.
Tschudin, Jean-Jacques (1979) *Tanemakuhito, la première revue de littérature prolétarienne Japonaise*, Paris: L'Asiathèque.
—— (1989) *La Ligue du Théâtre Prolétarien Japonais*, Paris: L'Harmattan.
—— (1995) *Le Kabuki devant la Modernité 1870–1930*, Lausanne: L'Age de l'Homme.
Tsuno Kaitarō (1970a) 'Of Baths, Brothels, and Hell', *Concerned Theatre Japan* I. 1.
—— (1970b) 'Preface to *The Elephant*', *Concerned Theatre Japan* I. 3.
Tsuruya Nanboku (1979), Sigee, Jeanne trans, *Les spectres de Yotsuya*, Paris: L'Asiatheque.
Wells, Marguerite (1997) *Japanese Humour*, Basingstoke: Macmillan.
Yoshimi Toshiya (1995) The Evolution of Mass Events in Prewar Japan, in Umesao, Kumakura and Powell eds, *Japanese Civilization in the Modern World*, XI amusement, Senri Ethnological Studies no 40.

Index

Notes
References to the two major genres of theatre in modern Japan, *kabuki* and *shingeki*, are not listed here, as each appears on almost every page (from chapter 2 in the case of *shingeki*). *Kabuki*'s main characteristics as a genre are described in the Introduction and *shingeki* is defined on page 30.
Play titles are listed separately with the playwright's name in brackets.
The suffix *-za* can mean either 'company/group' or 'theatre'; when it means the latter, this has been indicated in brackets.

Abe Kōbō, 199
actor training, 63, 140-141, 183
Actors' Theatre, see Haiyū-za
Aiyoku (Mushanokōji Saneatsu), 72, 73, 74
Akita Ujaku, 50, 67
Akutagawa Ryūnosuke, 44
Andreiev, Leonid, 35, 63
angura, 167, 176-185, 186-188, 192, 193, 194
Anpo, 165-167, 171, 181
Aoyama Sugisaku, 64, 139
aragoto, xxix-xxx
Ariyoshi Sawako, 188
Art Theatre Shinjuku Bunka, 175
Asakusa, 39, 46, 55, 71, 74, 84, 104
Asari Keita, 191-192
audiences, 66, 103, 105, 107, 108, 112, 124

ballet, 38-39
Bandō Tamasaburō V, 190-191, 194
benshi, 45
Betsuyaku Minoru, 180-182
Bōryokudanki (Murayama Tomoyoshi), 80-81

Bowers, Faubion, 145
Brecht, Bertolt, 167-168
Buddhism, xxviii, 44
Budō no Kai, 141-142, 152
Bungaku-za, 101, 106, 110-112, 114-115, 116, 128-131, 133, 137, 138, 139, 140, 141, 151, 153, 154, 156, 166, 168-170, 174, 178, 188
Bungei Kyōkai, 23, 25, 27-29, 30, 31, 32-33, 35, 37, 38, 49-50, 62
Bunka-za, 174
bunraku (puppet theatre), xvii, xxi-xxv, xxvii, xxviii, xxix, xxx, xxxiii, 2, 118, 123
butō, 177, 185

censorship, 29, 70,m 72, 74, 75, 81, 84, 96-97, 110, 112-113, 114, 115-117, 118, 129, 131, 132, 133, 136, 143-145, 147, 148
Chekhov, Anton, 31, 35, 63, 71, 138, 150, 152, 165
Chichi Kaeru (Kikuchi Kan), 41-42
Chijin-kai, 189
Chikamatsu Monzaemon, xxi, xxxii,

18, 19, 194
Chiroru no Aki (Kishida Kunio), 102
Chōjūrō, see Kawarasaki Chōjūrō
Chōjū-gassen (Iizawa Tadasu), 129
Chūō Gekijō, 82
chūkan engeki, 94-95, 126-127, 149
Chūshingura (see also *Kanadehon Chūshingura*), xxi, xxii-xxiii, xxv-xxvi, 89, 91-92, 136, 144, 194
comedy, 20, 57, 100, 104-106, 116, 129, 160, 194
Craig, Edward Gordon, 33

Danjūrō, see Ichikawa Danjūrō
Dansō (Hisaita Eijirō), 94, 99-100
Doi Shunsho, 26
Dorokabura (Mayama Miho), 155, 191
Drama Reform Society, see Engeki Kairyō-kai

Edo (see also Tokyo), x, xxiv-xxv, xxix, xxxii, xxxiii-xxxiv
Edo-jō Sōzeme (Mayama Seika), 90-91
Eiji-goroshi (Yamamoto Yūzō), 53
En no Gyōja (Tsubouchi Shōyō), 72-73
Engei Gahō (journal), 124
Engeki Kairyō-kai, 9-10, 13, 30, 38
Engeki Shinchō (journal), 61, 65, 77
Enoken, see Enomoto Ken'ichi
Enomoto Ken'ichi, 104-105

films, 39, 45-46, 55, 71, 76, 85-87, 88, 94, 104, 115, 116, 117, 123, 127, 133, 144, 149
Fujimori Seikichi, 71, 74-76, 100
Fujiyama Kanbi, 160
Fukuchi Ōchi, 5-6, 10
Fukuda Tsuneari (or Kōson), 160, 169
Fukuda Yoshiyuki, 171-172
Funahashi Seiichi, 144, 158
Furukawa Roppa, 104-105, 160
Futari dake no Butōkai (Koyama Yūshi), 154-155
Futasuji-michi (Seto Eiichi), 93-94

Geijutsu-za, 31-33, 38, 42, 43, 45, 47, 50

Gekidan Shiki, see Shiki
Gekisakka Kyōkai, 53
Gekisaku (journal), 101, 153
Genroku Chūshingura (Mayama Seika), 91-93, 96, 121
Genroku period, xxvi, xxix
Giseisha (Hisaita Eijirō), 75
Goethe, 19
Gogol, Nikolai, 139
Gorki, Maxim, 35, 63, 100, 139, 152, 165

Haiyū-za, 134, 137, 138, 139, 140-141, 150, 153, 154, 156, 165, 167, 171, 174, 175, 183
Haiyū-za Theatre, 156, 173, 175, 189
Hakamadare wa Doko da (Fukuda Yoshiyuki), 172
hanamichi, xxviii, 7, 16, 74
Hanaoka Seishū no Tsuma (Ariyoshi Sawako), 188
Hanayagi Shōtarō, 93, 94, 95, 96, 125, 149, 159, 172
Haritsuke Mozaemon (Fujimori Seikichi), 74
Hasegawa Shin, 87, 89, 120
Hijikata Tatsumi, 177
Hijikata Yoshi, 59-64, 67-68, 72, 73, 76, 82, 102, 108, 137, 138
Hikōkan, 100
Hirasawa Keishichi, 67, 68
Hisaita Eijirō, 70, 75, 94, 99-100, 107-108, 127
Hōjō Hideji, 119-120, 122, 126, 146
Hokutō no Kaze (Hisaita Eijirō), 107-108
Hongō-za (theatre), 18, 19, 65
Hōraikyoku (Kitamura Tōkoku), 17
Hotta Kiyomi, 154

Ibsen, Henrik, 28, 29, 31, 33, 34, 35, 36, 42, 49, 63, 76, 139, 150
Ichikawa Chūsha VII, 84
Ichikawa Danjūrō: Ichikawa Danjūrō I, xxix; Ichikawa Danjūrō II, xxix; Ichikawa Danjūrō VII, xiii, xix, xxix, xxxiv; Ichikawa Danjūrō IX, xxix, 4, 6, 7, 9, 10, 11, 13, 18, 84, 123; Ichikawa Danjūrō X, 165; Ichikawa Danjūrō XI, 165
Ichikawa Ebizō IX 158, 165

Index

Ichikawa Ennosuke: Ichikawa Ennosuke II, 40, 42-43, 58, 63, 79, 85, 90-91, 96, 122, 136, 144, 157; Ichikawa Ennosuke III, 168, 195
Ichikawa Kodanji IV, xxxiv
Ichikawa Sadanji: Ichikawa Sadanji I, 4, 10, 18, 33; Ichikawa Sadanji II, 27, 33-36, 39-40, 41, 43, 46, 51, 58, 63, 65, 77-78, 84, 85, 89, 90-91, 92
Ichimura Uzaemon XV, 39-40, 84, 122, 145
Ichimura-za (theatre), 39, 86, 87
idō engeki, 132-133
Ii Tairō no Shi (Nakamura Kichizō), 51-52
Ii Yōhō, 15, 18-19, 46, 48, 93-94
Iizawa Tadasu, 129, 160
Iizuka Tomoichirō, 117
Ikeda Daigo, 43
Ima Harube, 106
Imperial Family, 10-11, 156-157, 162-163
Imperial Theatre, see Teikoku Gekijō
Inoue Hisashi, 189
Inoue Masao, 45, 46, 55, 74, 94-95, 96, 108, 120, 126-127, 138-139, 149
Itachi (Mafune Yutaka), 99, 101
Itō Hirobumi, 5-6, 9, 10
Iwakura Mission, 6
Iwata Toyoo, 110-111, 169
Izumi Kyōka, 19, 149, 182, 198
Izumi Taku, 168

Japan Foundation, 192-193
jidai-mono, xxiii-xxiv, 7
Jikken Gekijō, 143
jitsugoto, xxxi
Jiyū Gekijō (1909), 25, 33-37, 40, 49, 62
Jiyū Gekijō (1966), 183-184
Jiyū Butai, 180
Jōhōkyoku, 115-117, 122, 123, 124, 131-132
Jōkyō Gekijō (Situation Theatre), 178-179

kabuki, see Notes above
Kabuki Shinpō (journal), 9, 10

Kabuki-za (theatre), 15, 18, 22, 38, 39, 47, 58, 60, 66, 84, 89, 94, 95, 124, 125, 145, 156, 163, 164, 194
Kaiser, Georg, 59, 63
Kakka (Hōjō Hideji), 120
Kamisori (Nakamura Kichizō), 32, 43-44
Kanadehon Chūshingura, xxi, xxv, xxvi-xxvii xxx, xxxi, 3, 87, 123, 136, 144, 145, 194
Kan'eki (Miyoshi Jūrō), 132
Kanjinchō, xix, xxx, 20, 87, 116
Kan'ami, xviii
Kanaya Koume (Mayama Seika), 49
Kansai (see also Osaka, Kyoto), xi, xxix, xxx, 13, 21, 65, 104, 150, 157
Kan'ya, see Morita Kan'ya
Kanze house, xviii, xix
Kanze Hideo, xix-xx, 172, 200
Kanze Hisao, xix
Kara Jūrō, 178-180, 182
Kara-gumi (formerly Jōkyō Gekijō), 180
Kataoka Nizaemon: Kataoka Nizaemon XIII, 194; Kataoka Nizaemon XIV, 194
Katō Michio, 155
katsureki-geki, 7, 8, 11, 24
Kawaguchi Matsutarō, 94
Kawai Takeo, 18, 46, 48, 49, 93, 96
Kawakami Otojirō, 13, 14-16, 22, 24, 27, 34
Kawakami Sadayakko, 16, 18, 22
Kawarasaki Chōjūrō, 78-79, 86
Kawarasaki Kunitarō V, 86, 121
Kawatake Mokuami, xix, xxxii-xxxiii, xxxiv, 4, 7-8, 88, 92
Kawatake Shigetoshi, 123
Kazanbaichi (Kubo Sakae), 109-110, 112, 167
Keiō University, 61
Keshō (Inoue Hisashi), 189
Kichiemon, see Nakamura Kichiemon
Kikatsu (Nagata Hideo), 44
Kikuchi Kan, 41-42, 53
Kikugorō, see Onoe Kikugorō
Kimura Kōichi, 188-189
Kinokuniya Hall (theatre), 175
Kinoshita Junji, 141-142, 155, 170,

189-191
Kiroku Number 1 (Fukuda Yoshiyuki), 171
Kishida Kunio, 101, 102, 103, 110-111, 115, 128, 141, 151
Kitamura Rokurō, 19, 48, 93, 96, 125-126
Kitamura Tōkoku, 17
Kitī Taifū (Fukuda Tsuneari), 160
Knock (Terayama Shūji), 185
Kobayashi Ichizō, 56-57, 65, 85
Kobayashi Takiji, 79, 82
kōdan, 12
Kodanji, see Ichikawa Kodanji
Kokoro-za, 78-79
Kokusai Gekijō (theatre), 84-85, 95, 145
Konjiki Yasha (adapted from Ozaki Kōyō), 15, 98
Koyama Yūshi, 154-155
Kubo Sakae, 97, 109-110, 137, 167
Kubota Mantarō, 77, 99, 101, 103, 110-111, 169
Kumo (Gekidan Kumo), 169
Kurahara Korehito, 80
Kurata Hyakuzō, 43, 44
kyōgen, xx-xxi, xxviii, 1, 20, 21, 190
Kyōiku (Tanaka Chikao), 154
Kyoto, xi, xxix, xxx, 20, 21, 50, 65, 124, 125, 141

Living Newspaper, 81

Maeterlinck, Maurice, 22, 31, 35, 55, 63, 175
Mafune Yutaka, 99, 100
Makimura Kōkichi, 133
Mama-sensei to sono Otto (Kishida Kunio), 102
Maria no Kubi (Tanaka Chikao), 155
Maruyama Sadao, 133
Masago-za (theatre), 18, 22
Matchi-uri no Shōjo (Betsuayaku Minoru), 181-182
matsubame-mono, xviii
Matsui Shōyō, 34
Matsui Sumako, 28, 29-30, 31-32, 35, 45, 49, 50
Matsumoto Kōshirō VII, 116, 122
Mayama Miho, 155, 191, 194
Mayama Seika, 47-49, 56, 88, 89-93, 95, 121, 122, 127, 158, 191, 194
Meiji-za (theatre), 18, 22, 34, 35, 124, 125
Meyerhold, Vsevolod, 59-60, 77
michiyuki, xxiii
'middle-of-the-road theatre,' see *chūkan engeki*
Miller, Arthur, 137, 151
Mingei, 140, 151-152, 156, 163, 165, 167, 171, 174, 178, 189, 190
Mishima Yukio, 154, 169-171, 175, 191
Mitsukoshi (including Mitsukoshi Gekijō), 38, 57, 155-156
Miyake Shūtarō, 119, 123
Miyoshi Jūrō, 95, 132
Mizu no Eki (Ōta Shōgo), 185
Mizutani Yaeko, 55, 56, 93, 96, 126, 144, 149, 152, 172-173, 194
Mizutani Yoshie (later Mizutani Yaeko), 149, 159, 194
mobile theatre, see *idō engeki*
Mokuami, see Kawatake Mokuami
Molière, 20, 100, 118, 191
mono, xxiii
Mori Ōgai, 16, 17, 26, 33, 36, 96
Morimoto Kaoru, 129-131, 139
Morita Kan'ya: Morita Kan'ya XII, 4, 6, 9, 10, 11; Morita Kan'ya XIII, 40, 42-43, 44
Morita-za (theatre; see also Shintomi-za), 4-5
Moscow Art Theatre, 59, 63, 138, 152-153
Moulin Rouge, 105-106, 160
Murayama Tomoyoshi, 65, 78, 80, 82, 83, 94-95, 97, 99, 113, 126, 127, 137, 138-139, 149, 153
Mushanokōji Saneatsu, 43, 44, 71, 72, 73, 74
musicals, 85, 167-168

Nagai Bohyō no Retsu (Fukuda Yoshiyuki), 171
Nagata Hideo, 42, 44
Nagatsuka Takashi, 109
Nagayama Takeomi, 144
Nakadai Tatsuya, 175
Nakamura Kan'emon, 86, 147-148
Nakamura Ganjirō III, 194
Nakamura Kanzaburō, 175

Nakamura Kichiemon II, 39, 84, 157
Nakamura Kichizō, 31, 32, 42, 43, 51, 53, 55
Nakamura Utaemon: Nakamura Utaemon IV, xxxv; Nakamura Utaemon V, 39-40, 84; Nakamura Utaemon VI, 164, 194
Nakayama Shinpei, 31
Namino Kuriko, 149
Nanboku, see Tsuruya Nanboku
Nani ga Kanojo o Sō Saseta ka (Fujimori Seikichi), 75-76
National Drama, 117-120, 123, 128
Nayotake (Katō Michio), 155
New *Kabuki*, see *shin-kabuki*
Nezumi Kozō Jirōkichi (Satō Makoto), 184
Nihon Idō Engeki Renmei, 132-133
Nihon Puroretaria Bungei Renmei, see Puroren
Ninagawa Yukio, 193
Ningen Banzai (Mushanokōji Saneatsu), 44
ningyō jōruri, see *bunraku*
Nishiyama Matsunosuke, xxxii
Nissei Gekijō (theatre), 175-176, 191
niwaka, 20
nō, xvii-xxi, xxviii, xxix, xx, xxx, xxxiv, 1, 2-3, 6, 7, 117, 118, 136, 172, 173, 190, 192
noh, see *nō*
Nomura Mansai, xx-xxi
Nomura Mansaku, xx-xxi

Occupation, 135-148, 159
Ōdera Gakkō (Kubota Mantarō), 77
Ofukuro (Tanaka Chikao), 153
Okada Yoshiko, 55-56, 108
Okakura Shirō, 137, 149, 152
Okamoto Kidō, 40-41, 46, 50, 53, 88, 89, 120, 158
Onna no Isshō (Morimoto Kaoru), 129-131, 139, 141, 169
onnagata, xxviii-xxix, xxx, 14, 16, 18, 19, 36, 39, 45, 46, 49, 93, 159, 164, 194
Ono Seki, 181
Onoe Baikō VI, 84
Onoe Kikugorō: Onoe Kikugorō III, xxxv; Onoe Kikugorō V, 4, 7, 9, 10, 13, 18, 123; Onoe Kikugorō VI 39, 42, 44, 58, 84, 89, 122, 123, 125
Onoe Shōroku II, 164
opera, 34, 38-39, 85, 104
Oppekepe, 13
Osaka, xi, xxix, 2, 12, 13, 18, 19, 28, 50, 51, 5256, 57, 65, 85, 116, 124, 150, 160
Osanai Kaoru, xiii, 33-37, 49, 59-65, 69, 71, 76-77, 79, 94, 102, 138, 152, 158
Osaragi Jirō, 158
Ōshō (Hōjō Hideji), 146
Ōta Shōgo, 184-185
Ōtani Takejirō, 40, 48, 52, 53, 65, 77, 89, 92, 95, 123, 157, 164
Ozaki Hirotsugu (or Kōji), 139-140
Ozaki Kōyō, 15, 20, 48
Ōzasa Yoshio, 19, 121

popular drama, see *taishū engeki*
posters, 177-178
proletarian drama, x, 66-72, 74-76, 79-82, 83, 85, 87, 96, 97, 99, 100, 106, 109, 137, 139, 140, 147
PROT, 79, 83
puppet theatre, see *bunraku*
puppets, xxi-xxii
Puroren, 68-69

Racine, 191
realism, xx, 97, 151-153
rensageki, 45-46
Rōdō Gekidan, 67-68
Rōen, 150, 168, 171-172, 174, 184
Rokumeikan (Mishima Yukio), 154, 169
Rolland, Romain, 65, 68
rōnin, xxv-xxvi
Roppa, see Furukawa Roppa
Rosi, Giovanni, 39

Sadanji, see Ichikawa Sadanji
Sado Kōshaku Fujin (Mishima Yukio), 170-171, 191
Sakai Toshihiko, 57-58
Sakura-tai, 133
samurai, xxiii, xxiv, xxvi, 1, 2
Sanada Fūunroku (Fukuda Yoshiyuki), 171-172
Sartre, Jean Paul, 178

Sasaki Takamaru, 68, 69, 126
Satō Makoto, 184
Sawada Shōjirō, x, 32, 49-52, 66, 87, 89, 122, 194
Sawa-shi no Futari Musume (Kishida Kunio), 102
Sawashō, see Sawada Shōjirō
Sayoku Gekijō, 76, 80, 81, 82, 98
SCOT (formerly Waseda Shōgekijō), 180
Seigei (Seinen Geijutsu Gekijō) 171-172
Seika, see Mayama Seika
Seinen-za, 174
Senda Akihiko, 185
Senda Koreya, 70, 81, 100, 134, 139, 140, 189, 192
Senku-za, 68, 69
Seto Eiichi, 93-94
sewa-mono, xxiii-xxiv, 7, 15
Shakespeare, xx, xxiv, 16, 20, 27, 28, 30, 33, 47, 50, 63, 72, 118, 147, 175, 183, 191, 193, 195
shamisen, xxi, xxii
Shigosen no Matsuri (Kinoshita Junji), 190
Shiki, 191-192
Shima (Hotta Kiyomi), 154
Shimamura Hōgetsu, 25, 29, 30-32, 33
Shimazaki Tōson, 33, 98
Shimbashi Enbujō, see Shinbashi Enbujō
Shimizu Kunio, 193
shimpa, xi, xiii, 11-16, 18-19, 20, 21, 22, 24, 29, 30, 33, 34, 37, 44, 45-49, 50, 52, 55, 56, 67, 74, 85, 93, 98, 105, 108, 116, 120, 124, 125-128, 131, 138-139, 144, 145, 148-149, 152, 159, 172-173, 175, 182, 191, 192, 194
Shin Tsukiji Gekidan, 79, 82, 98, 99, 100, 106-110, 112, 113, 127, 133, 138
Shinbashi Enbujō, xiv, 66, 104, 124, 125, 145, 160, 173, 194
shingeki, see Notes above
Shingeki (journal), 153
shin-kabuki, 40, 55, 78, 84, 87-88, 91, 92, 158, 194
shin-kigeki, 20, 105, 160

Shinkokugeki (including the genre), 49-52, 55, 65, 85, 96, 116, 121-122
Shinkyō Gekidan, 98-99, 100, 106-110, 112, 113, 127, 137, 138-139, 140, 142-143, 147, 151, 153
shinpa, see *shimpa*
Shinsei Shimpa, 95-96, 125, 148
Shinseisaku-za, 174, 191
Shintomi-za (theatre), 6-7, 8, 22, 66
Shirai Matsujirō, 51
Shiraishi Kayoko, 182
Shōchiku, 9, 22, 24, 30, 32, 39-40, 46, 47, 49, 50, 60, 74, 78, 79, 84-85, 86, 88, 94, 95, 104, 105, 106, 108, 109, 123, 124, 125-126, 127, 137-138, 143, 144, 145, 146, 149, 152, 156, 160, 164-165
shōgekijō (little theatre [movement]; see also *angura*), 174-175, 176, 196
Shukke to sono Deshi (Kurata Hyakuzō), 44
Shuzenji Monogatari (Okamoto Kidō), 40-41, 42, 88
Shōyō, see Tsubouchi
Soganoya Gorō, 20-21, 57-58, 104, 105
Soganoya Jūrō, 20-21, 57
Sono Imōto (Mushanokōji Saneatsu), 44
Stanislavski, Constantin, 59, 152
Sudermann, Hermann, 28, 29, 53
Sudō Sadanori, 12-14
Suematsu Norizumi (or Kenchō), 10
Sugimoto Ryōkichi, 108
Sugimura Haruko, 111, 129, 130, 133, 151, 152, 169-170, 188
Susukida Kenji, 127
Suzuki Tadashi, 180-181, 182-183, 200

taishū engeki (popular theatre), 87, 194
Taiyō no nai Machi (Tokunaga Sunao), 69
Takada Minoru, 18
Takahashi Yasunari, xx
Takarazuka, 56-57, 65, 85
Takechi Tetsuji, 157

Index

Takizawa Osamu, 137, 149, 151
Tamasaburō, see Bandō
    Tamasaburō
Tamura Akiko, 101, 102, 110-111
Tanaka Chikao, 153-154, 155
Tani, Toni, 160
Tanizaki Jun'ichirō, 42, 96
Tanna Tonneru (Hōjō Hideji), 120, 121
Teatoro (journal), 153, 188
Teikoku Gekijō, 31, 38-39, 53, 55, 57, 58, 65, 66, 71, 76, 79, 116, 122, 126, 173
Tempō, see Tenpō
Tenjō Sajiki, 185
Tenpō Reforms, xxxiii, xxxiv
Terayama Shūji, 185
theatre buildings, xxvii-xxviii, xxxiii, 2, 5, 6, 10, 15, 21, 31, 38-39, 58, 60-61, 65-66, 71, 77, 84-85, 124, 134, 145, 155-157, 175, 178, 195
Tōgei (Tōkyō Geijutsu Gekijō), 137, 138-139, 140
Tōgeki, see Tōkyō Gekijō
Tōgi Tetteki, 26
Tōhō, 86, 88, 104, 106, 108, 111, 122, 137-138, 168, 193
Tōka no Kiku (Mishima Yukio), 170
Tokunaga Sunao, 69
Tokyo, x, 1, 2, 13, 18, 21, 25, 38, 46, 58, 66, 71, 85, 124, 125, 130, 145, 146, 150, 187, 195
Tōkyō Gekijō, 84, 89, 125, 136
Tōkyō Takarazuka Gekijō, 85
Tokyo University (including Tokyo Imperial University), 33, 49, 70, 74
Tomoda Kyōsuke, 101, 102, 110-111
Tolstoy, Lev, 31-32, 45, 50
Tōno Eijirō, 127-128
Toranku Gekijō, 69-70
Trunk Theatre, see Toranku Gekijō
Tsubouchi Shōyō, xiii, 16-18, 20, 23, 25-29, 30, 33, 37, 50, 62, 72-73, 88
Tsukiji Little Theatre, see Tsukiji Shōgekijō
Tsukiji Shōgekijō (theatre enterprise including the company), 58-66, 70, 71-77, 79, 81, 101, 102, 133, 137, 138, 169, 174
Tsukiji Shōgekijō (theatre building), 58, 60-61, 66, 71, 72, 77, 81, 100, 106, 109, 112, 130, 134
Tsukiji-za, 101-103
Tsuruya Danjūrō, 20
Tsuruya Nanboku IV, xxxii-xxxiii, 182

Umehara Takeshi, 195
Umewaka Minoru, xviii
Utaemon, see Nakamura Utaemon
Uzaemon, see Ichimura Uzaemon

wagoto, 29-30
Waley, Arthur, xix
Waseda Shōgekijō, 180, 181-183
Waseda University, 23, 25, 26, 27, 49, 63, 180, 181
Wedekind, Frank, 35, 63, 107
Wesker, Arnold, 188-189
Wilder, Thornton, 142-143
Williams, Tennessee, 143, 150-151, 188

Yabuhara Kengyō (Inoue Hisashi), 189
Yamamoto Yasue, 141, 189, 190
Yamamoto Yasue no Kai, 189-190
Yamamoto Yūzō, 43, 53
Yamato Takeru (Umehara Takeshi), 195
Yeats, William Butler, xix
Yoake-mae (Shimazaki Tōson, adapted by Murayama Tomoyoshi), 98-99
Yoda Gakkai, 15
Yokoo Tadanori, 177-178
Yorokobi no Koto (Mishima Yukio), 170, 175-176
Yotsuya Kaidan, xxxii-xxxiii
Yūraku-za (theatre), 38
Yūzuru (Kinoshita Junji), 141-142, 152, 155, 190

zangiri-mono, 8
Zeami, xviii, xix, xx, xxii
Zenshin-za, 79, 86-88, 91, 96, 114, 117, 121, 122, 146-148, 173
Zō (Betsuyaku Minoru), 180-181